Republican Citizens, Precarious Subjects

Representations of Work in Post-Fordist France

Studies in Modern and Contemporary France   7

Studies in Modern and Contemporary France

Series Editors

Professor Gill Allwood, Nottingham Trent University
Professor Denis M. Provencher, University of Arizona
Professor Martin O'Shaughnessy, Nottingham Trent University

The Studies in Modern and Contemporary France book series is a new collaboration between the Association for the Study of Modern and Contemporary France (ASMCF) and Liverpool University Press (LUP). Submissions are encouraged focusing on French politics, history, society, media and culture. The series will serve as an important focus for all those whose engagement with France is not restricted to the more classically literary, and can be seen as a long-form companion to the Association's journal, *Modern and Contemporary France,* and to *Contemporary French Civilization*, published by Liverpool University Press.

Republican Citizens, Precarious Subjects

Representations of Work in Post-Fordist France

JEREMY F. LANE

Liverpool University Press

First published 2020 by
Liverpool University Press
4 Cambridge Street
Liverpool
L69 7ZU

This paperback edition published 2023

Copyright © 2023 Jeremy F. Lane

The right of Jeremy F. Lane to be identified as the author of this
book has been asserted by him in accordance with the Copyright, Designs
and Patents Act 1988.

All rights reserved. No part of this book may be reproduced, stored in a
retrieval system, or transmitted, in any form or by any means, electronic,
mechanical, photocopying, recording, or otherwise, without the prior written
permission of the publisher.

British Library Cataloguing-in-Publication data
A British Library CIP record is available

ISBN 978-1-78962-214-0 (hardback)
ISBN 978-1-83764-412-4 (paperback)

Typeset by Carnegie Book Production, Lancaster
Printed and bound by CPI Group (UK) Ltd, Croydon CR0 4YY

Contents

Acknowledgements		vii
Introduction		1
Part One: Theoretical Preliminaries		
1	The Crisis of Fordism: Symptoms and Diagnoses	31
2	Modulating Work and Welfare	67
Part Two: Character Types, Trajectories, Uneven Geographies		
3	Modulated Masculinities	103
4	*Femmes Fortes*	139
5	Doomed Youth	175
6	*Sans Papiers*	211
Conclusion		241
Bibliography		255
Index		267

Acknowledgements

The writing of this book was greatly facilitated by the encouragement, advice, and stimulating debate provided by a range of friends and colleagues, most notably Jackie Clarke, Oliver Davis, John Marks, Martin O'Shaughnessy, and Sarah Waters. I am also grateful to the two anonymous reviewers who provided a wealth of helpful suggestions and comments on my manuscript. The research for the project was facilitated by, first, a British Academy (BA)/Leverhulme Small Grant [no.RA2482] and, second, an award from the University of Nottingham's Pro-Vice Chancellor for the Faculty of Arts' Research Fund. I am grateful to both institutions for the essential research assistance these two grants afforded me. Finally, some of the material in Chapters 2 and 4 was first published, in briefer, preliminary form, in the following two articles: Jeremy F. Lane, '"Come, You Spirits … Unsex Me!" Representations of the Female Executive in Recent French Film & Fiction', *Modern & Contemporary France*, vol.23, no.4 (2015), pp.511–28 and Jeremy F. Lane, 'From "Moule" to "Modulation": Logics of Deleuzean "Control" in Recent Reforms to Work and Welfare', in *Work in Crisis*, special no. of *Modern and Contemporary France*, eds. Jeremy F. Lane and Sarah Waters, vol.26, no.3 (2018), pp.245–60, copyright © Association for the Study of Modern & Contemporary France. Excerpts from these articles are reproduced by permission of Informa UK Limited, trading as Taylor & Francis Group, www.tandfonline.com, on behalf of the Association for the Study of Modern & Contemporary France.

Introduction

For a few weeks in the spring/summer of 2016, hundreds of central squares in towns and cities throughout France were occupied by demonstrators protesting against the Socialist government's planned reforms to the French Labour Code, reforms that would erode worker protections and allow employers greater flexibility in the hiring and firing of their staff (Farbiaz 2016). The so-called *Nuit debout* movement represents one in a range of recent such examples of nationwide protests that have had salaried employment – its scarcity or increasingly precarious, flexible and exploitative nature – at their core. Subsequently, the series of rolling strikes in early 2018 against President Macron's plans to reform the terms and conditions of French railway workers would offer another example of such nationwide labour protests. The *gilets jaunes* ('yellow vests') movement that broke out in late 2018 was initially sparked by opposition to an environmental tax on fuel. Nonetheless, its extent and violence reflected much deeper concerns about falling standards of living caused by years of stagnant real wages, combined with the proliferation of insecure, flexible employment.

All of these movements had a series of significant precursors. Among these, we might cite the 2006 protests against the *Contrat première embauche* (first employment contract), a supply-side measure introduced by right-wing Prime Minister Dominique de Villepin that aimed to tackle youth unemployment by reducing the legal protections against redundancy afforded to workers aged under 26. In the face of mass nationwide demonstrations and protests, the government was forced

2 Republican Citizens, Precarious Subjects

to withdraw the measure. In 1995, nationwide protests against the so-called 'Juppé Plan' had proved equally effective, forcing right-wing Prime Minister Alain Juppé to withdraw a package of measures that had threatened the terms and conditions of French public sector workers, eroding established rights to health insurance and pensions. Indeed, the 1995 strike movement is often identified as signalling a revival of labour militancy, political protest, and social critique in France that has continued into the first two decades of the new century (Boltanski and Chiapello 1999:423–500; O'Shaughnessy 2007:1; Waters 2012:88).

At a more local level, since at least 2000 France has seen numerous strikes, workplace occupations, and boss-nappings, typically in protest against factory closures or mass redundancies. Many of these cases have achieved national and even international prominence, serving as further examples of an apparently characteristically French tendency to oppose, by all means available, the erosion of workers' terms and conditions of employment. Graeme Hayes (2012) has identified 32 incidences of boss-napping in France, in which workers held their senior managers hostage, demanding threats of factory closure or redundancies be withdrawn, between early 2008 and late 2011. More recently, in October 2015 the actions of five workers, who ripped the shirts from the backs of two Air France executives in protest at a planned programme of redundancies, received widespread international media coverage. A more tragic and individualised kind of resistance to changes in the nature of salaried employment emerged in France from the late 1990s onwards, in the form of a spate of workplace suicides at major French employers, such as France Télécom, Renault, and Citroën, which sparked a national debate about current management practices and employee burn-out (Dejours and Bègue 2009; Du Roy 2009).

These social and political developments have also been mirrored in the cultural and intellectual fields. A new literary sub-genre, the *roman d'entreprise* (workplace novel), has emerged with, since 2009, its own annual prize. France has thus witnessed a profusion of novelistic depictions of the contemporary workplace. In her critical study of this new sub-genre, Aurore Labadie (2016:10) estimates that there have been 'more than 100 such novels and accounts since 1982, the majority dating from the 2000s'. Michel Houellebecq (1994; 2010), Thierry Beinstingel (2010; 2012), Elisabeth Filhol (2010; 2014), Nathalie Kuperman (2010), Gérard Mordillat (2014; 2017), and Éric

Reinhardt (2011) are just some of the authors to have made significant contributions to this growing corpus.

As well as fictional accounts of the contemporary workplace, there has been a proliferation of personal testimonies and journalistic reportage lamenting the exploitative realities of salaried employment today, sometimes in a satirical, sometimes in a more documentary mode. We might cite here Florence Aubenas's account of low-paid cleaning work in deindustrialised Normandy, *Le Quai de Ouistreham* (2010), Corinne Maier's bestselling satirical account of the realities of contemporary executive labour, *Bonjour paresse* (2004), or Marion Bergeron's dispiriting testimonial of her time working at a French job centre on a temporary contract, *En CDD à Pôle Emploi* (2010), to name but three examples.

In the realm of cinema, meanwhile, a whole range of fictional feature films and feature-length documentaries has sought to portray and lament the current state of workplace relations in France. Laurent Cantet's two workplace films, *Ressources humaines* (1999) and *L'Emploi du temps* (2001), initiated a renewed interest in fictional cinematic depictions of the contemporary workplace. Jean-Marc Moutout's *Violence des échanges en milieu tempéré* (2003) and Robert Guédiguian's *Les Neiges du Kilimandjaro* (2011) have examined industrial restructuring and redundancies. Moutout's *De Bon Matin* (2010), Benoît Delépine and Gustave Kervern's *Near Death Experience* (2014), Louis-Julien Petit's *Carole Matthieu* (2016), and Nicholas Silhol's *Corporate* (2017) have all tackled the sensitive topic of workplace suicides. Meanwhile, documentaries such as Sophie Bruneau and Marc-Antoine Roidil's *Ils ne mouraient pas tous mais tous étaient frappés* (2006), Jean-Michel Carré's *J'ai (très) mal au travail* (2007), or Jean-Robert Viallet's three-episode documentary series *La Mise à mort du travail*, aired on French television in 2009, have denounced the exploitative nature of the contemporary French workplace. Audrey Evrard (2018:311) has identified at least nine feature-length documentary films, released between 2001 and 2004 alone, that focus on factory closures in France. On occasion, such documentaries have fed directly into political protests, as was the case with François Ruffin's *Merci Patron!* (2016), an account of off-shoring, factory closure, and redundancy that was played and widely debated in the town squares occupied by the *Nuit debout* protestors.

These documentary and fictional feature films have often also tapped into developments in the French intellectual field, drawing on

4 *Republican Citizens, Precarious Subjects*

the growing body of theoretical work examining the changing nature of salaried employment in France today. The psychologist of work Christophe Dejours, the political economist Frédéric Lordon, and the sociologist of work Vincent de Gaulejac regularly appear as talking heads in documentaries about work, while acting as behind-the-scenes consultants on fictional feature films. The written output of all three has made a significant contribution to the ongoing public debate about the changing nature of work in contemporary France (Dejours 1998; De Gaulejac 2005; Lordon 2010). As the sociologist of work Danièle Linhart has argued, Dejours's notion of 'workplace suffering', popularised in his bestselling book *Souffrance en France* (1998), has come to occupy a very high profile in the fields of French media, culture, and politics:

> Somewhat provocatively, I would say that one theme that has come to dominate our era is that of workplace suffering. It preoccupies the worlds of art, theatre, and film, as much as it does the media and political institutions. It is becoming ubiquitous. It is often presented as a contemporary phenomenon that casts light onto our society, onto its complexity and the greater fragility of its members. The world of work is of interest to novelists, dramatists, directors of films and documentaries. Over the last fifteen years or so, they have demonstrated a renewed interest in work, which is now associated with violence, with suicide, with murder, with depression and madness. (Linhart 2015:97)

Since about the turn of the twenty-first century, then, work has not only been at the centre of national and local political protest; it has also been a very common subject of novelistic and filmic representation, as well as provoking important new theoretical work in France. Indeed, these political, cultural, and intellectual developments seem to point to the emergence of some kind of crisis in and around work in contemporary France, of a widespread set of anxieties about recent changes to the nature of salaried employment and the possible future evolution of paid work. At the simplest level, this sense of crisis, with its attendant anxieties, could be interpreted as symptomatic of the long-drawn-out crisis of the Fordist regime of capitalist accumulation that had emerged in France in the post-war decades. However, this is a crisis whose effects extend far beyond the limited domain of the workplace since it corresponds to the gradual unpicking of the post-war compromise and hence has implications for French society as a whole.

From Fordism to Post-Fordism

For the economists of the French Regulation School, who first developed this diagnosis, Fordism refers to much more than merely the mass production techniques based on a moving assembly line pioneered by Henry Ford in Detroit. Fordism refers both to a 'regime of accumulation' – the dominant industrial and economic paradigm that secured capital accumulation during the thirty years after 1945 – and its accompanying 'mode of regulation' – the institutional forms that supported and 'piloted' that regime of accumulation. Those institutional forms included collective bargaining and legal protections of terms and conditions of employment, extensive social welfare programmes, and an economically interventionist State channelling investments into strategic industries and operating within a highly regulated global financial system of fixed exchange rates and capital controls. Under Fordism, the dominant industrial paradigm, the primary source of surplus value was indeed mass production of standardised consumer goods on assembly lines operated by low-skilled workers who benefited from relatively stable, well-paid jobs, as well as from the much improved forms of social insurance put in place after the Second World War. As a regime of accumulation, Fordism rested on a virtuous circle of increased productivity based on economies of scale and technological efficiencies, rising profits redistributed to workers through wage increases and welfare benefits, and consequently buoyant consumer demand that itself fed into further profits and further productive investment. As a mode of regulation, Fordism was both peculiarly national and gendered in character: national, on account of the key role played by interventionist States in planning and regulating their own national economies; gendered, because of the centrality of the nuclear family, with the male breadwinner at its head, as the primary unit of consumption (Boyer 2015:59–74).

The global economic downturn of the 1970s, exacerbated by the two oil crises of 1973 and 1979, is widely understood to have signalled the onset of Fordism's long-drawn-out crisis. In the wake of this downturn, the progressive liberalisation of global flows of trade and capital eroded the ability of any single nation state to manage and regulate its own economy. Meanwhile, the economies of the developed nations witnessed the gradual disappearance of stable, low-skilled industrial employment, as manufacturing plants were moved off-shore

6   *Republican Citizens, Precarious Subjects*

in search of lower labour costs and as such economies became ever more tertiarised. High levels of youth unemployment and structural unemployment thus became apparently permanent features of French society from the 1980s onwards and regions or pockets of marked socio-economic deprivation emerged in formerly industrialised regions and areas. Those still in employment found their terms and conditions eroded as trade union power lessened and employers and governments promoted labour market flexibility as the key to regaining profitability and competitiveness in an increasingly globalised market for goods and labour. The French labour market became characterised by the profusion of so-called 'atypical' work contracts – temporary jobs, part-time and agency work, internships, and so on. These tendencies have been exacerbated by the emergence of 'uberised' forms of precarious employment in the web economy. The spectre of the wholesale robotisation of low-skilled work, meanwhile, has contributed to the anxieties generated by such tendencies. All of these developments might be taken as characteristic of a shift to post-Fordism, where that term is understood in its most general sense to refer to the set of unstable economic arrangements that have emerged in the wake of Fordism's crisis.

The increasing precarity and flexibility of contemporary work, the erosion of established terms and conditions of labour, and the prospect of the wholesale disappearance of stable employment are thus topics that have come to dominate the French political, intellectual, and cultural fields over recent decades. The premise of this book is that the intensity of these debates is itself indicative of the extent to which the shift from Fordism to post-Fordism is provoking a profound reordering of French culture, society, and political economy. In her influential study *Fast Cars, Clean Bodies* (1995), Kristin Ross shows how France's transition to Fordism in the immediate post-war decades, accompanied as it was by rapid decolonisation and the adoption of apparently Americanised models of mass consumerism, significantly transformed established ways of life and posed fundamental challenges to received notions of French national identity. In her readings of the feature films, novels, and sociological texts of the 1950s and 1960s she finds extensive evidence of this 'reordering' of French culture in the emergence of a series of new character types, objects, and spaces – housewife-consumers, dynamic young executives, fast cars, the Fordist assembly line – that embodied these rapid social, economic, and cultural shifts (Ross 1995).

Introduction   7

The premise of this book is that, with the crisis of Fordism and the transition to post-Fordism, French culture and society is undergoing a reordering of equivalent dimensions and significance. Thus, in its first, theoretical part, the book will identify more clearly what we understand by the notion of a crisis in Fordism, how this crisis has altered the nature of salaried employment in France, and quite how best to account for these developments. Once our theoretical and interpretative framework has been refined in this way, in the book's second part we will apply it to close readings of a selection of fictional and documentary representations of the contemporary French workplace.[1] The novels, films, and testimonies we study here are an important resource inasmuch as they offer unique insights into the lived realities of contemporary work. Novels, films, even documentaries and testimonies are not, of course, simply reflections of reality; each of these genres necessarily involves a selection and combination of elements in a process of narrativisation or figuration of that reality. As such, they also offer important insights into the cultural or ideological frameworks through which French authors and filmmakers have sought to make sense of the economic and social developments they depict. Closer analysis of our corpus of cultural representations will also help to uncover the extent, nature, and precise implications of these kinds of ideological framing. Rather than attempt an exhaustive survey of this growing body of material, we will focus on certain geographical spaces, character types, and educational and career trajectories that recur throughout this corpus.[2] In this way, we hope to cover a representative sample of such character types and social trajectories that offers important insights into the different ways in which changes in the labour market are understood to have impacted French workers of different social classes, ages, sexes, and ethnicities.

Despite the diversity of our sample of character types, we will argue that they are united in all experiencing increased levels of *precarity*, both as regards their working lives and as regards the ways their changed terms and conditions of employment impact on their broader sense of social identity. Here we follow the sociologist of work, Danièle Linhart, in distinguishing between the *material* or *objective* precarity suffered by those who have either lost their jobs or been forced into insecure forms of employment and the more *subjective* forms of precarity generated by new styles of management imposed even on

8   *Republican Citizens, Precarious Subjects*

those in relatively privileged occupations (Linhart 2015:217). We argue not only that these twin forms of precarity have become increasingly common but also that they pose a fundamental challenge to established notions of French republican citizenship. Indeed, the documentaries, feature films, and novels we study often include laments at the ways in which the contemporary labour market is forcing French citizens to adopt precarious forms of subjectivity that are at odds with established republican ideals, values, and ways of being. In this sense, these narratives raise the possibility that a fault-line has emerged between established notions of French republican citizenship, on the one hand, and the more precarious forms of subjectivity inherent to post-Fordism, on the other.

The French Republican–Corporatist Model

To posit a dichotomy between French republican citizenship and precarious subjectivity in this way is, by definition, to suggest that there is something quite specific to the French experience of post-Fordism. This immediately risks the objection that France is no exception in this regard, that in other developed economies, such as the USA or the UK, for example, the crisis of post-war Fordism has proved just as disruptive, sparking equally intense debates about the effects of flexible employment and socio-economic precarity.[3] While this is undoubtedly true at a general level, it is nonetheless the case that the particular ways in which these disruptions have been experienced and narrativised in France do reflect a range of cultural, political, and institutional factors that are specific to that national setting. Identifying the characteristic forms and peculiar institutional structures of French Fordism will prove vital in understanding the various ways in which the crisis of Fordism has been narrativised in our corpus of recent films, novels, and documentaries.

As a significant number of commentators have noted, one of the specificities of the French Fordist post-war compromise was the manner in which it institutionalised a particularly close interrelationship between salaried employment, rights to social protection, and, through that, access to full republican citizenship. This particularly close interrelationship between employment, social protection, and citizenship was a product of the specifically corporatist nature of the

Introduction   9

French social model (Palier 2005). When at the Liberation, Pierre Laroque, the founding father of French social security, sought to establish the bases of a welfare state, he advocated following the examples set by the American New Deal and the British Beveridge Report (Laroque 2008 [1945]). However, Laroque's ambition to set up a universal, Beveridge-style system was frustrated by the opposition of French employers and sections of the labour movement who argued successfully for the preservation and extension of existing corporatist forms of welfare, based on a patchwork of occupational social insurance schemes, funded by employer and employee contributions. Universalist elements were incorporated into the so-called 'general regime' of social insurance, a fund covering sickness, retirement, and child benefits to which the vast majority of private sector workers continue to belong to this day. Nonetheless, access to these benefits is contingent on a record of accumulated contributions. Unemployment insurance, set up in 1958, follows a similar pattern. However, certain categories of worker – civil servants, police, railway workers, the armed forces, employees of the French electricity and gas suppliers, and others – have retained their own separate social insurance funds for pension and health insurance, the so-called 'special regimes'. Many workers also contribute to 'complementary regimes' that cover supplementary medical costs or, in the case of business executives, pension rights (Palier 2005:65–165).

This complex system of social welfare means that pension, health, and unemployment benefits are covered by a range of often occupationally specific social insurance funds, funded by employer and employee contributions rather than out of general taxation. Although the 'general regime' does embody certain universalist, Beveridgean characteristics, overall the French welfare system is thus closer, on Gosta Esping-Andersen's influential typology, to the 'corporatist-conservative Bismarckian model' than to either the generous universalism of the Scandinavian nations or the minimalist universalism of the UK or US systems (Esping-Andersen 1989).

To characterise the French model of welfare as 'corporatist' is not to employ that term in a pejorative sense. In everyday parlance 'corporatist' has become a synonym for the pursuit by different groups of worker of their own narrow self-interest, an obstinate clinging to particular rights or privileges to the detriment of the general interest. It is important to stress that we are not using the term in that sense.

10   *Republican Citizens, Precarious Subjects*

The philosophy behind French corporatism is anything but narrow or self-interested. On the contrary, the forms of corporatism that emerged in France in the post-war period were rooted in a centre-left, characteristically French republican tradition. As Serge Paugam (2007:2) has argued, the philosophy behind the French social security system was greatly indebted to Émile Durkheim's seminal study of 1893, *De la division du travail social*. Here corporatist structures are seen as the key to ensuring social solidarity, guaranteeing an organic social bond in the face of the corrosive forces of liberalism, urbanisation, and industrialisation by ensuring all workers belong to a corporation that represents their interests. Professional corporations would serve as 'intermediary bodies' between their members and the State or employers, safeguarding their welfare rather than leaving workers to fend for themselves as atomised, liberal individuals. A ramified network of such occupational groups would ensure every individual performed a useful function within society, a function in accordance with their supposedly natural aptitudes as attested to by a rational, meritocratic system of republican education (Durkheim 2007 [1893]). In Durkheim's sociology, as in the post-war welfare system it inspired, corporatism was thus seen as a means of avoiding the atomising tendencies inherent to economic and political liberalism, while integrating particular group interests into a republican pact that would both represent the general interest and secure the social bond. In this way, late nineteenth-century ideas of social solidarity were allied to an older French republican tradition that embodied Rousseauiste ideas concerning the proper role of the State in representing the general will and safeguarding a republican pact between free and equal citizens.

One of the specificities of this kind of corporatism, rooted in the Durkheimian and French republican traditions, is that employment represents much more than just a source of economic income since it also guarantees social and political identity through access to welfare rights. To quote Paugam: 'In reality, employment brings [French workers] more than a salary. It brings them social rights and a position in the hierarchy of statuses derived from the Welfare State and hence a social identity' (quoted in Lavoine and Méda 2008:19–20). In a 2008 survey of salaried employment in all the EU countries, the sociologists of work Lucie Lavoine and Dominique Méda note what they see as a paradox in French attitudes to work. The survey shows that the French are far less likely to declare themselves to be happy or fulfilled in their work but are far more likely than, for example, their British counterparts to agree with the statement 'work is very important in my life'. Seeking to explain this paradox, Lavoine and Méda suggest the following:

> The importance accorded work in each country very often mirrors Esping-Andersen's classifications. In countries with a Beveridge-style tradition in which social rights are not accorded to workers, but directly to citizens, work is less often cited as being 'very important in my life'. In countries with a Bismarckian tradition, where social protection is closely linked to employment, stability of employment takes on, by contrast, a crucial importance since this allows access to social rights. (Lavoine and Méda 2008:34)

In France, then, work is intimately related to social identity. Further, given the French social model's roots in Durkheimian notions of social solidarity, work is also intimately related to each worker's identity as a republican citizen. The series of developments that have rendered work more precarious since the crisis of Fordism have hence not merely threatened French workers' material well-being, they have also challenged their status as full citizens of the Republic. Thus, Eve Caroli and Jérôme Gautié (2009:50–1) note the paradox whereby French workers have higher feelings of job insecurity than the majority of their European counterparts, despite enjoying greater legal protections against redundancy. They conclude that this reflects the fact that, under France's corporatist system of work and welfare, to lose one's job is to risk much more than just a loss of income; it is to risk one's social identity as a full republican citizen as well.

Labour Dualisation, Social Insecurity

The higher feelings of job insecurity among French workers noted by Caroli and Gautié surely also reflect the highly dualised nature of the French welfare system. In recent decades France, in common with all developed economies, has witnessed an increasing dualisation of its labour market, a stark division between a 'core' of often older workers in stable, relatively well-remunerated jobs and a 'periphery' of typically younger workers, forced into more flexible, precarious forms

12   *Republican Citizens, Precarious Subjects*

of employment. This dichotomy is all the more stark in France in that workers in more stable employment, with a so-called CDI (*contrat à durée indéterminée* or permanent contract), enjoy access to much better welfare rights than are available to the periphery of employees, employed as agency workers or on the much less well-protected CDD (*contrat à durée déterminée* or temporary contract). The dualisation of the French labour market is thus exacerbated by an analogous dualisation in the welfare system (Emmenegger, et al. 2012:201–25).

Under the conditions of full employment that prevailed in France until the late 1970s, the system of occupational unemployment insurance was largely able to cover the needs of the relatively small number of unemployed French citizens. However, with the massive rise in unemployment from the 1980s onwards, occupational insurance schemes struggled to cope with the increased demand and, faced with potential bankruptcy, the schemes' managers – French employers and trades unions – called on the government to act. From the early 1980s onwards, successive governments have thus taken measures to reduce the overall level of unemployment benefits and to make their payment ever more dependent on a recipient's history of accumulated contributions. In 1984, the socialist Social Affairs Minister Pierre Bérégovoy brokered a deal with unions and employers to save the occupational schemes by creating a parallel system of less generous benefits, paid out of general taxation. This parallel system would provide benefits to, first, those whose work history meant they had no accumulated contributions to any occupational scheme and, second, to the long-term unemployed, who had exhausted their rights to draw on any scheme to which they had contributed (Palier 2005:220–21).

Health insurance in France is characterised by an analogous dualism. With the rise of long-term unemployment through the 1980s and 1990s, the number of people not covered by an occupational health insurance scheme had risen dramatically. In 1999 the Socialist government responded by setting up a new benefit to be financed out of general taxation, the CMU (*couverture maladie universelle* or universal health coverage), to enable such individuals to access healthcare. Recipients of the CMU have to declare their status to their doctors before receiving treatment. Not only is this stigmatising, since it forces individuals to declare their impoverished status, but there is also significant evidence of healthcare professionals systematically refusing to treat CMU recipients in favour of those with occupational healthcare insurance, since the latter can afford to pay higher charges (Défenseur des droits 2014).

The French welfare system is thus marked by a stark dichotomy. On the one hand, there is a corporatist system that delivers relatively generous benefits to those with histories of stable employment, according to a principle of 'solidarity'. On the other, is a much less generous system financed out of general taxation, the so-called 'social minima' that operate according to a logic of social 'assistance'. As Nicolas Duvoux (2012:87) argues, this dichotomy generates 'inequalities between the different generations and social classes. Those in precarious employment, the unemployed, the economically inactive are doubly penalised: to the absence or instability of their income is added the lack of or decrease in their level of social protection, which remains linked to employment.' It is estimated that fewer than 50 per cent of France's unemployed currently qualify for unemployment insurance, the rest having to rely on much less generous forms of social assistance (Cour des comptes 2013:60). As Duvoux (2012:93) points out, the poorest 10 per cent of the French population receive just 3 per cent of total expenditure on social welfare. It is this that explains why, despite spending well over the EU average on social protection, the French system is less redistributive than is the case for many of its European partners, including the UK, Ireland, and the Nordic countries (Duval 2018:13).

Yann Moulier Boutang (2007:172) argues that it is this kind of dualisation that foments the widespread feelings of 'social insecurity' observable among the general French population today. As he points out, French people are keenly aware that 'the welfare state's safety net lets those lacking the status of salaried employee fall through its excessively wide mesh and that the mechanisms supposed to compensate such failings (like the CMU) are at once insufficient and stigmatising'. We might expand on Moulier Boutang's remark to offer the following hypothesis: the corporatist and highly dualised nature of the French labour market and social welfare system means that the proliferation of flexible and precarious forms of employment is frequently experienced not merely as threatening French workers' material well-being but also as undermining their social identities as full citizens of the Republic. The republican–corporatist model has thus decisively influenced the ways in which French workers typically understand and respond to the rise of flexible, insecure, and precarious forms of employment characteristic of post-Fordism.

14   *Republican Citizens, Precarious Subjects*

Once again, it is important to stress that we are not arguing that French reactions to precarity are hence all or predominantly corporatist in the negative sense of that term, aimed merely at defending rights and privileges specific to particular professional groups or corporations. On the contrary, as we have shown, struggles to defend republican–corporatist structures are struggles to defend the general interest, to preserve progressive and inclusive notions of social solidarity and the republican pact. It is of course the case that not all those who protest against rising precarity adhere to the ideals of French republican–corporatism. For example, in their 2003 documentary *Attention Danger Travail*, Pierre Carles, Christophe Coello and Stéphane Goxe interview a range of French citizens who have responded to exploitative labour conditions by withdrawing from the labour market altogether, by engaging in various forms of the refusal of work. Experiments in communal living, such as that at Tarnac, have sought other ways to escape the nexus of salaried employment and mass consumption. Calls for the establishment of a generous and unconditional guaranteed social income, voiced by the *neo-operaïste* economist Yann Moulier Boutang (2007), reflect a wholesale rejection of the French corporatist tradition and its unquestioned faith in the intrinsic value of salaried labour.

However, while these various more radical initiatives are thought-provoking, even inspiring, they remain, by definition, marginal or minority phenomena. Indeed, one of the most striking characteristics of recent French debates about work is the remarkable frequency with which the ideals and values embodied in the republican–corporatist model form a kind of benchmark against which the contemporary situation is judged and found to be lacking. For our present purposes, it will be sufficient to provide a few examples of this phenomenon, each of which will be examined in greater detail in the main body of this book. Thus, in 2017 the *Conseil d'État* (the Council of State) published a report into 'uberised' forms of employment in the platform economy. The report adopts the vocabulary of Durkheimian corporatism to lament the ways in which the atomising tendencies inherent to platform work risk eroding 'the forms of social bond and the social solidarity produced in industrial society' in the 'factory/firm', itself defined as 'the centralised space in which human bonds were created and collective organisations defending the interests of workers were formed' (Conseil d'État 2017:90). One of the catalysts to the *Nuit debout* protests against the El Khomri labour reforms in 2016 was the challenge those reforms posed to the so-called 'principe de faveur', according to which terms and conditions of employment in individual firms could not be less favourable than those negotiated between trades unions and employers at the level of the 'branche d'activité' or industrial sector. In other words, a key bone of contention here was the refusal of the protestors to accept an erosion in the role accorded to the 'intermediary bodies' under the terms of France's republican–corporatist post-war settlement. Numerous commentators on the *gilets jaunes* movement have also focused on the key role played by the 'intermediary bodies', arguing that it was Emmanuel Macron's insistence on bypassing those 'intermediary bodies' that forced the movements' participants to engage in direct action on provincial roundabouts and city centre streets (Duhamel 2018; Frémeaux 2018; Lipietz 2018). In the late 2000s and early 2010s, the *sans papiers* or undocumented migrants brandished evidence of their record of contributions to occupational social welfare schemes in support of their demands that the State live up to its stated commitments to social solidarity through salaried employment and hence accord them full residency rights.

As this brief survey indicates, the values and ideals embodied in the French republican–corporatist model have thus served as important points of reference in a wide range of protests and debates about the nature of salaried labour in France today. Indeed, this is true also of those commentators arguing in favour of the increased de-regulation and liberalisation of the French labour market. Thus, in their prize-winning 2012 study, *La Fabrique de la défiance ... et comment s'en sortir,* economists Yann Algan, Pierre Cahuc, and André Zylberberg argue that the corporatist structures of the French labour market produce rigidities and self-interested forms of behaviour by competing professional groups that are barriers to economic efficiency and full employment. In opposition to republican–corporatism, they advocate a more liberal, individualised model of professional identity, with terms and conditions negotiated through looser forms of 'social dialogue' at the level of the individual firm. It is this more liberal, individualistic philosophy that has inspired many of Macron's labour reforms, which seek to foster greater 'social dialogue' precisely by bypassing the traditional role accorded to the 'intermediary bodies' or trades unions in representing workers' interests.

Thus, the republican–corporatist model represents a fundamental point of reference both for those pushing for more labour market

16   *Republican Citizens, Precarious Subjects*

flexibility and for those protesting against its negative effects. It is, therefore, essential to recognise the specificities of that model in order to understand the nature of French responses to a labour market increasingly characterised by flexible, insecure, and precarious forms of employment. Indeed, the centrality of republican–corporatist values and assumptions to French debates concerning work highlights the benefits of adopting a so-called 'varieties of capitalism' approach to these issues. The premise of such an approach is that capitalism has developed in different ways in different national settings as it has been mediated through and inflected by the particular institutional forms and structures characteristic of each nation state (Hall and Soskice 2001). Hence, it is possible to identify a specifically 'French model' of socio-economic organisation, a peculiarly French form of compromise between capital and labour that emerged in the decades immediately following 1945, in short, a specifically French form of Fordism. If republican–corporatism represents one of the characteristic features of that model, another is surely the generosity of the French social model.

French Exceptionalism?

One of the most widely held beliefs about the French social model reflects its apparently exceptional generosity, particularly in comparison to its British or American counterparts. This, in turn, has encouraged the tendency to understand labour market de-regulation to be the product of the hegemony of a so-called 'Anglo-Saxon model' of socio-economic governance, characterised by a preference for a small State, minimal welfare protections, and unchecked market forces. Certainly, there is clear evidence that, overall, the French model is more generous that those in place in many comparable developed economies. Thus, for example, in 2016 French overall public spending as a proportion of gross domestic product (GDP) was 10.1 percentage points higher and its expenditure on social welfare 5.3 percentage points higher than the European Union (EU) average (Maurin 2018:16). Public pension provision is also more generous in France, representing on average two-thirds of net average wage, as against just 41 per cent in the UK and 45 per cent in the US (OFCE 2013:38). Further, according to the Organisation for Economic Co-operation and Development (OECD) index of protection against individual redundancy, French workers are

Much better protected than their British or American equivalents, with an index of 2.5 for French workers, as against 1.1 for British and just 0.5 for American workers. Thus, as Bruno Amable (2017:27) has shown, although inequality, as measured by the Gini coefficient, has increased in France from the 1980s onwards, it has risen at a slower rate than in other developed economies, particularly the UK or the US. Taken together, these phenomena have encouraged the widespread belief in France that such differences reflect something intrinsic to the French national character, an essential commitment to social justice delivered through the institutions of the Republican State.

The establishment of this relatively generous welfare system was accompanied, in the post-war decades, by a particularly high level of direct State intervention in the national economy, through both State planning and a large nationalised sector, comprising finance, industry, and public utilities. These post-war decades are widely remembered in France as an era of unprecedented national prosperity, characterised by stable employment, increasing incomes, and consequent social mobility. Indeed, the '*trente glorieuses*' or 'thirty glorious years' between 1945 and 1975 represent a period during which French GDP growth regularly outpaced that of Germany, the UK, and the USA, being placed second only to Japan among the OECD nations (OFCE 2018:19). This era of apparently triumphant economic interventionism is often itself seen as being peculiarly French in character, dubbed 'colbertisme' in memory of Louis XIV's interventionist Minister of Finance, in a manner that suggests it forms part of an unbroken tradition that defines itself by its opposition to an inherently Anglo-Saxon model of economic liberalism. Further, the successes of 'colbertisme' in the post-war decades lend credence to the notion that it also forms an intrinsic part of that specifically French Republican tradition according to which the State acts as guarantor of 'the general interest', hence securing the 'republican pact'.

In one sense, this tendency to set up a straightforward opposition between a 'good' French model and its 'bad' Anglo-Saxon nemesis corresponds to an observable reality. For it is certainly the case that following the Thatcher and Reagan revolutions of the early 1980s, the UK and the US became standard bearers for neo-liberal deregulation throughout the world economy. Moreover, the liberalisation of the French capital markets, from the late 1980s onwards, has seen UK- and US-based pension funds exert a disproportionate influence over French

18 *Republican Citizens, Precarious Subjects*

industry and employment, often acting as prime movers behind calls for French companies to reduce their labour costs and hence boost their dividend payments. Since the majority of French pensions are paid out of current contributions, rather than from revenue generated from capital investments, French pension funds have not played such a conspicuous role in eroding the terms and conditions of French workers. As El Mouhoub Mouhoud and Dominique Plihon (2009:45) have pointed out, France has one of the highest proportions of foreign share ownership of all the developed economies. In this context, the temptation to attribute any degradation in working conditions to the malign influence of foreign or Anglo-Saxon forces is understandably strong.

From Socio-economic Models to National Stereotypes

The role of the UK and USA as standard-bearers for neo-liberalism, the relative generosity of the French social model, and the successes of post-war 'colbertisme' have all thus contributed to an observable tendency in France to figure labour market de-regulation, flexibility, and precarity as inherently Anglo-Saxon in origin and inspiration. Nonetheless, it might be argued that such an approach ultimately relies more on national stereotype than it does on detailed historical analysis. In short, there is a risk that the progressive characteristics of the French model will be interpreted as expressions of an essentialised national identity or unchanging national character. That national identity or character is then assumed automatically to produce a commitment to egalitarianism and social justice that is defined by its opposition to the unbridled pursuit of material gain that supposedly characterises Anglo-Saxon social and cultural mores.

As Sarah Waters (2012:88–111) has shown, this tendency is certainly evident in a significant amount of French anti-globalisation and anti-neo-liberal discourse. This discourse relies on what Waters (2012:90) terms 'an essentialist vision of globalisation that linked it to predetermined cultural factors [...], to a *monde anglo-saxon* defined by a dominant set of cultural characteristics and traits'. This dichotomy between a 'good' French model and its Anglo-Saxon nemesis also structures the narratives of many recent filmic and novelistic representations of the contemporary French workplace. Here British or American institutions and individuals are figured as the bearers of management values and practices that are fundamentally destructive of established French forms of solidarity and social justice. For example, the narratives of the two films *Violence des échanges en milieu tempéré* (2003) and *Crime d'amour* (2010) both turn on the seduction of young French executives by the mercenary values promoted by their American employers, two fictional US consultancy firms, a seduction that has profoundly destructive effects both on these embodiments of French innocence and on wider French society. In Laurent Quintreau's novel *Marge brute* (2006) the ruthless executive responsible for implementing a wave of redundancies among his co-workers is himself French. Nonetheless, we learn that he spent several years studying at Harvard and working in New York and it was there that he learned his exploitative management techniques (Quintreau 2006:18–19). This trope is echoed in Nathalie Kuperman's novel *Nous étions des êtres vivants* (2010). Again, the executive responsible for the violent restructuring of a previously convivial children's publishing firm is French. Yet, we are told he 'loves America' and hence that his French employees will henceforth be 'managed in the American way' to predictably negative effect (Kuperman 2010:18). The fictional account of workplace suicide, featured in Nicholas Silhol's film *Corporate* (2017), centres on a Human Resources (HR) executive who attempts to bully certain employees into resigning as a way of bypassing strict French legal protections against redundancy. This is a tactic that pushes one middle-aged executive to take his own life. Again, the HR executive is French. However, we learn that she is married to an Englishman and spent ten years working in London prior to being recruited by her French firm. Indeed, the film implies, she was recruited precisely in order to employ the ruthless 'Anglo-Saxon' techniques she learned in London. In fictional representations of the contemporary French workplace, therefore, threats to jobs and livelihoods are frequently embodied by 'Anglo-Saxon' characters or institutions. Insofar as any French characters are portrayed as being complicit in such exploitative practices, this is attributed to their having been seduced, somehow tainted or contaminated, by their exposure to 'Anglo-Saxon' values and mores.

As we have noted, to set a progressive French model against its Anglo-Saxon nemesis in this way does reflect a certain reality; however, this is to reflect that reality in a distorted, highly ideological way. A slippage has taken place here, whereby the focus on the

20   *Republican Citizens, Precarious Subjects*

different institutions that shape the particular model of socio-economic governance in any given nation state has been replaced by an appeal to essentialised conceptions of national identity. As we have argued, the 'varieties of capitalism' approach understands each national model to be the contingent product of the historical, economic, and political forces in play both within the nation state in question and internationally at a particular moment or period in time. The films and novels referred to above, however, imply that the progressive nature of the French model is an expression of the French national character itself and hence that the key to safeguarding social rights lies in defending the integrity of French identity against contamination by foreign influences. Such, at least, is the implied message of films and novels from *Violence des échanges en milieu tempéré* and *Crime d'amour* to *Marge brute, Nous étions des êtres vivants* and *Corporate,* all of whose French protagonists would have been better off had they not fallen under the malign influence of 'Anglo-Saxon' ideas and institutions. The role played by the UK and the USA as standard bearers for neo-liberal de-regulation is hence interpreted not as the product of contingent political and socio-economic developments in those two nations from the 1970s onwards, but rather as something inherent to Anglo-Saxon culture and civili-sation, the expression of some essential Anglo-Saxon identity. French national identity, by contrast, is then assumed to be characterised by a fundamental and unchanging commitment to social justice, as evident in republican policies and practices pursued in an unbroken chain from 1789 to the present day.

As Thomas Piketty has pointed out, however, France has not always been a pioneer where social justice is concerned, and French republicanism cannot always be relied upon automatically to produce socially progressive outcomes. He shows that during the *belle époque,* the UK and USA led the way in introducing progressive redistributive tax regimes, while successive French governments justified their failure to follow suit by claiming, hypocritically, that since France was an egalitarian republic it had no need to adopt equivalent measures (Piketty 2019:186–87). As he concludes, 'there is no such thing as a culture or civilisation that is essentially egalitarian or inegalitarian', in spite of what certain forms of French republican discourse might have us believe (532).

Claims regarding the inherent moral or political superiority of the French model can thus sometimes descend into both essentialism

Introduction 21

and myth-making. Moreover, to oppose a 'good' French model to its 'bad' Anglo-Saxon nemesis is always to risk overlooking the contradictions, flaws or injustices inherent to that French model itself. We have already noted the highly dualised and hence inegalitarian nature of the French model of social welfare. We might also mention here the centrality to the post-war French model of large industrial concerns, often partly or wholly State owned, in strategically important areas such as petrochemicals, nuclear energy, aeronautics, and so on. These so-called 'national champions' did contribute to both French prestige and national wealth, but they also frequently relied on fostering highly exploitative relationships with France's colonies and former colonies in order to exploit their natural resources. Hence, as Moulier Boutang (2010:237) remarks in relation to French anti-globalisation discourse, 'it is all very well wagging our fingers at multinationals, telling them they are disgusting, but our multinationals, in which the State is involved, are worse still'.[4]

It might be argued that France's exploitative relationships with its colonies and former colonies have been mirrored in the treatment it has afforded its postcolonial immigrants. Indeed, one of the often-overlooked features of the French model is the very high number of jobs it reserves exclusively for French nationals. All legally resident immigrants were for a long time prohibited by law from accessing a whole range of jobs from the civil service, through various liberal professions, to tobacconists and undertakers. After the Maastricht Treaty of 1992, these jobs were opened to all EU citizens, but non-EU immigrants are still debarred from an estimated 21 per cent of all jobs in France, including those that are the best protected (Tévanian 2013:31–32). For Étienne Balibar (1998:105), it is precisely this linkage of social and employment protection to national identity that means the French post-war model corresponds to what he provocatively terms 'a national social State'.

Fordist Nostalgia

The final risk inherent in the tendency to idealise the French model in opposition to its Anglo-Saxon counterpart is to overlook the exploitative and alienating nature of the Fordist mode of industrial production on which the former was based. This can generate what

22   *Republican Citizens, Precarious Subjects*

Robert Boyer and Jean-Pierre Durand (1993:10) have named 'Fordist nostalgia' – the tendency to idealise Fordism for the job security and prosperity it secured, while overlooking its more negative aspects. In the French context, Fordist nostalgia frequently takes the form of a lament at the passing of the *trente glorieuses*, that thirty-year period of economic growth that is widely remembered in France as an era of unprecedented national prosperity, characterised by stable employment, increasing incomes, and consequent social mobility. Thus, for example, in her account of working undercover in a variety of poorly paid temporary cleaning jobs in the deindustrialised areas of Normandy, the journalist Florence Aubenas (2010:63) laments the passing of the post-war decades in which 'more than 20,000 jobs were shared out between eight huge factories that formed a necklace around Caen and were shown off as examples of a France that was able to marry her fields of potatoes to her coke ovens, a France that was taking off again after the War and decentralising its industries, situating them in the midst of its marshes, its ducks and its bombed-out buildings'.

In her evocation of the harmonious marriage between Caen's potato fields, ducks, and marshes, on the one hand, and its post-war factories, on the other, Aubenas fundamentally misrepresents the history of French post-war economic development. For France's embrace of Fordism in the post-war decades was far from involving the kind of harmonious marriage between industry and agricultural life that she imagines here. On the contrary, the movement of literally millions of French citizens from rural areas and occupations into industrial work in the cities, the so-called 'rural exodus', was experienced as profoundly disruptive, as posing a challenge to the very nature of French national identity through the apparent destruction of the peasant way of life it threatened. Furthermore, working conditions in the new Fordist factories were frequently denounced as being profoundly alienating and exploitative (Friedmann 1964). As classic contemporary accounts such as Claire Etcherelli's novel *Élise ou la vraie vie* (1967) or Robert Linhart's reportage *L'Établi* (1978) highlighted, institutionalised forms of racism and sexism were endemic in the recruitment, promotion, and personnel management practices employed in French factories throughout the so-called *trente glorieuses*.

The Fordism of the *trente glorieuses* clearly did secure greater national prosperity, more stable employment, and hence better prospects for the majority of French people than is the case in the current economic

Introduction 23

conjuncture. A certain nostalgia for those years is thus understandable. Indeed, such nostalgia might be interpreted as, at one level, expressing fundamentally progressive impulses, in the form of an implicit lament at the waning of that period's promises of greater prosperity and equality for all. Nonetheless, there are dangers in idealising Fordism, in overlooking the many negative aspects of the *trente glorieuses*, forgetting that these years were characterised by a profoundly unequal distribution of the benefits of national growth that fostered extremely conflictual and sometimes violent industrial relations. As Robert Castel (2009:15) has argued, the expression 'trente glorieuses' is thus 'highly questionable', fostering, as it does, 'the most suspect forms of nostalgia' for a period in which 'French society certainly modernised itself' but 'remained marked by severe inequalities and many injustices', as manifest in 'the almost insurrectional strikes at the end of the 1940s or the "events" of 1968'.

The highly conflictual industrial relations Castel mentions here are significant not merely insofar as they highlight the exploitative and alienating realities of Fordist labour. These strikes and protests are also important inasmuch as they exemplify the extent to which worker resistance was itself one contributory factor in hastening Fordism's decline and hence undermining the economic bases of the French post-war model. The wage increases secured in the wake of the May 1968 strikes, for example, contributed to eroding the profitability of Fordist modes of production. Further, in the decades following 1968 French industrialists sought ways to curb labour militancy by breaking up the massive Fordist factories, whether by off-shoring production plants or by reorganising production processes into smaller, more collaborative teams and adopting management techniques that aimed to capture workers' personal attributes, their affective and communicative capabilities to an unprecedented degree (Linhart 2015:106–7). This was not so much a matter of 'recuperating' the energies of May 1968, as Luc Boltanski and Eve Chiapello's (1999) rather functionalist account of the genesis of 'the new spirit of capitalism' would have it. Rather, it was a matter of employing a variety of tactics to try to mitigate, circumvent, and defuse those energies. In this sense, then, the crisis of the French post-war model cannot be attributed solely to the hegemony of an Anglo-Saxon model of neo-liberal economic organisation. A more nuanced, dialectical grasp of the various factors in play is required.

24   *Republican Citizens, Precarious Subjects*

That more nuanced, dialectical approach will also be vital when accounting for the ways in which the peculiarly gendered aspects of Fordism have been gradually eroded. As we have noted, one constituent element of post-war Fordism was the central role accorded the nuclear family, with the male breadwinner at its head, as primary unit for both mass consumption and the reproduction of the labour force. This relegation of women to the role of wives and mothers, typical of Fordism in all developed economies, was, in the French case, mediated through and arguably reinforced by a longer history of so-called 'natalism', according to which the health of the nation itself is dependent upon maintaining a high birth rate. Hence, the French social security system offered generous child benefits to those who had large families, in an effort to encourage women out of the workplace and back into the home (Palier 2005:96–97). The erosion of this element of Fordism owes at least as much to the struggles of women themselves both for control over their own bodies and for equality in education and employment as it does to the perceived hegemony of Anglo-Saxon capitalism. The erosion of the patriarchal nuclear family, that other bedrock of post-war Fordism, owes a similar debt to progressive movements that have struggled to achieve equality for sexual minorities and legitimacy for alternative family units. Reliance on too straightforward a dichotomy between a 'good' French model and its Anglo-Saxon nemesis can lead us to overlook the role played by such progressive movements in challenging the more conservative characteristics of the French post-war model.

The French post-war model was hence characterised both by its republican–corporatism and by a particular nexus of gender, family, and nation. Our working hypothesis is that French reactions to the proliferation of insecure and precarious forms of employment have been decisively shaped by the nature of that model. This is a model that embodies certain fundamentally progressive and egalitarian values, notably through the conceptions of social solidarity, the republican pact, and social justice inherent, at least in theory, to the republican–corporatist model of work and welfare. Yet it is also a model whose national and gendered aspects have sometimes generated more conservative assumptions and attachments. In the main body of this study we will examine the various challenges to the French model posed by post-Fordism, the forms of precarity these have generated, and the threats they represent for that model, in its gendered, familial, and national aspects, as much as in its republican–corporatism.

Part One, entitled 'Theoretical Preliminaries', seeks to delineate more precisely the nature and origins of the challenges to the French model posed by the crisis of Fordism. This will provide the interpretative framework that we will then apply to our close readings of a variety of films and texts in Part Two, 'Character Types, Trajectories, Uneven Geographies'. In this second part we will thus examine the different ways in which French authors and filmmakers have represented the effects of the crisis of Fordism on workers of different ages, sexes, social classes, and ethnicities as they pursue different trajectories through the various spaces of contemporary France.

Our first chapter examines the range of political, economic, and technological developments at international, national, and regional level that sparked the crisis of Fordism. It then reviews a range of competing diagnoses of this crisis, seeking to adjudicate between those commentators who understand it to be primarily the product of neo-liberalism as an exogenous ideological project and those who place greater emphasis on its endogenous determinants within the contradictions of Fordism itself. This will not only give us a clearer understanding of the nature of the transition from Fordism to post-Fordism, it will also help us to explain why debates and protests about work should have come to a head over recent decades, from the turn of the twenty-first century onwards. The chapter will also establish clearer conceptual distinctions between, for example, 'post-Fordism', a term we take in a general sense to refer to the unstable set of economic arrangements emerging from the crisis of Fordism, and 'neo-liberalism', understood as an ideological project that has exploited that crisis to push for the scaling back of the welfare state and various forms of labour market deregulation.

Having thus clarified the nature of the crisis of Fordism and its impact on the national labour market, in our second chapter we switch focus to the level of individual firms. Here we examine a representative sample of changes to management practices, State-sponsored employability training, and the legal regulation of work and welfare implemented under the successive presidencies of Nicolas Sarkozy, François Hollande, and Emmanuel Macron. Employing Gilles Deleuze's (2003:240–47) distinction between a disciplinary 'mould' and the more 'modulated' forms of power characteristic of 'societies of control' as its overarching interpretative framework, the chapter will argue that these changes all

26   *Republican Citizens, Precarious Subjects*

obey the same logic of *modulation*. They work together to fundamentally challenge traditional republican conceptions of corporatist identity and social solidarity, replacing these with a notion of the worker as constantly modulating her professional identity and status in response to changing economic demands, cultivating and updating her individualised stock of human capital, as she moves between periods of employment, training, and unemployment.

Over the course of our first two chapters, we will thus refine our interpretative framework before then applying this to our close readings of a sample of feature films, testimonials, documentaries, and workplace novels in the chapters that form the book's second part. The successive chapters that make up Part Two will focus on certain recurrent character types, their educational and career trajectories, their struggles to modulate their professional identities as they navigate regional, national, and international spaces whose varying levels of economic prosperity reflect the uneven geographies of post-Fordism.

Chapters Three and Four examine the recurrent tropes of, respectively, middle-aged male workers struggling to modulate their personal and professional identities to meet the demands of the post-Fordist workplace and *femmes fortes*, or strong working women, whose professional lives seem to demand they renounce any more traditional feminine or maternal role. These two chapters thus focus on the nexus of gender, family, and nation that was at the core of the French post-war model, examining how authors and filmmakers have responded to a series of challenges to a model of republican citizenship embodied in the figure of the male breadwinner.

Chapter Five turns to look more closely at the roles played by education and employment in integrating France's younger generations into the Republic. Here we consider representations of two categories of young French citizens, graduates of France's elite *grandes écoles* and ethnic minority youth from the nation's socially deprived *banlieues*. Although these two categories are situated at opposing poles of France's social and educational hierarchy, we will show that they are depicted as facing equivalent problems in charting a course through education into stable, rewarding forms of employment. These 'doomed youth' are represented as struggling to modulate their personal and professional identities in accordance with the changed demands of a labour market that now rewards intangible 'soft skills' and an entrepreneurial spirit over the academic qualifications and universal truths formerly delivered by the Republican School. This chapter thus switches focus from the questions of gender, family, and nation raised in Chapters Three and Four to consider shifts in the role of republican education and employment in securing the integration of France's young citizens into the Republic.

Our sixth, and final, chapter considers this issue of work and republican integration as it relates to the *sans papiers* or undocumented migrants in France. The situation of the *sans papiers* is normally understood to be determined primarily by questions of racism and the problematic legacies of French imperialism and colonialism. These questions are typically considered to be quite distinct from the issues concerning work and welfare that, as our earlier chapters have demonstrated, have become central concerns of France's indigenous population. This chapter challenges such assumptions, arguing that the changes in global and national economic governance that have so transformed French society and political economy have proved to be key drivers of undocumented migration from developing nations, while decisively influencing the positions occupied by the *sans papiers* within the French labour market. The chapter examines a series of representations of the *sans papiers*, in feature films, novels, and documentaries produced by the migrants themselves, distinguishing between those that tend to elide these key questions of political economy, in favour of forms of apolitical humanitarianism, and those that engage directly with the status of the *sans papiers* as flexible, precarious, post-Fordist workers par excellence. As we will show, the *sans papiers* themselves have highlighted their specific role within the political economy of post-Fordism in support of their demands to be better integrated into the French Republic.

The path taken over these six chapters, through the mass of films, novels, testimonies, and theoretical analyses of work in contemporary France represents only one of any number of alternative routes that might be charted. The range of material covered cannot claim to be exhaustive. Nonetheless, it is hoped that this study's chosen pathway does at least do justice to the range of different social categories, of classes, ethnicities, genders, and age groups, who have been affected by recent developments in the French workplace and labour market. For it is a path that takes us from the centres of financial power in La Défense to the deindustrialised communities of Alsace and the deprived *banlieue* of Paris; it introduces us to a diverse range of precarious subjects,

28 *Republican Citizens, Precarious Subjects*

from powerful female executives to struggling Uber drivers, from unemployed machine-tool operators to disaffected young management consultants and exploited cleaners. Through its readings of a sample of theoretical, fictional, and documentary sources, this study aims to sketch an account of the often incisive, sometimes contradictory or politically ambiguous ways in which French thinkers, authors, and filmmakers have responded to radical changes in the labour market that are provoking a wholesale reordering of French culture and society, posing fundamental challenges to the forms of republican citizenship that had been institutionalised in the French post-war model.

Notes

1   Since they are Belgian nationals and since the action of their films typically unfolds in Belgium, the Dardenne brothers have been excluded from our corpus, despite the thematic relevance of their work.

2   Our corpus tends to focus more on accounts by outsiders – journalists, novelists, professional filmmakers – than on the growing number of testimonial texts produced by workers themselves. This is largely for pragmatic reasons. First, we lack the space to do justice to the formal characteristics specific to testimonial literature. Second, this body of work has already produced an important critical literature by Jackie Clarke (2011) and Audrey Evrard (2018).

3   Important contributions to these debates in the English-speaking world have been made by, among others, Peter Fleming (2015; 2017), Andrew Ross (2009), Ivor Southwood (2011), and Guy Standing (2011).

4   Raphaël Granvaud's (2012) account of the role of French nuclear giant Areva in supporting 'vassalised' and 'authoritarian' regimes in Niger, in order to secure access to its uranium deposits, might be taken as exemplary in this respect (Granvaud 2012:12; 23). At a more general level, the extensive literature on 'la Françafrique' has emphasised how central to the French model was the maintenance of exploitative relations with France's former African colonies. See, for example, Verschave (2003).

Part One

Theoretical Preliminaries

Chapter 1

The Crisis of Fordism

Symptoms and Diagnoses

In common with numerous other developed economies, France today offers many striking examples of the crisis of Fordism, emblems not merely of the waning of a dominant paradigm of industrial production but also of the erosion of that paradigm's associated political, cultural, and social forms. One such example can be found on the Île Seguin in the Seine, on the western edge of Paris. From the late 1920s on this was the location of Renault's massive Boulogne-Billancourt factory, a byword for both French industrial productivity and working-class identity and militancy. In the 1950s, as a fellow traveller of the French Communist Party, Jean-Paul Sartre was famously alleged to have declared 'we mustn't demoralise Billancourt' to justify his silence regarding the failings of Soviet communism. In May 1968, protesting students marched to Billancourt from the Sorbonne in an attempt to seal the alliance of the student and workers' movements. The factory closed in 1992, the same year in which, just forty or so kilometres to the east, Disneyland Paris was opened. Today, the Île Seguin has been transformed, the factory largely dismantled to be replaced by luxury flats and a planned sports, musical, and cultural complex.

Three years before the closure of Boulogne-Billancourt, the transformation of a former steel plant at Maizières-lès-Metz, in the Lorraine, into a Smurf-themed amusement park offered an equally poignant symbol of the decline of French heavy industry and its replacement by service-sector activities. The closure of French textile mills around the northern cities of Lille and Roubaix from the 1970s onwards offers one further example of this shift from Fordist industry to post-Fordist tertiarisation. As Gilles Balbastre shows in his documentary *Fortunes et infortunes des familles du Nord* (2008), the

32   *Republican Citizens, Precarious Subjects*

textile industry had been dominated by a close network of wealthy Catholic families, the so-called '*grandes familles du Nord*', who socialised and intermarried to preserve their Catholic faith and consolidate their industrial power. Devoutly religious, these families not only provided employment for local workers in huge textile mills, they also sought, in paternalistic fashion, to look after the physical and spiritual welfare of their employees, setting up hospitals, schools, libraries, and sporting clubs for their benefit.

As early as 1961, one of the leading members of this northern industrial dynasty, Gérard Mulliez, opened the first branch of a now global supermarket chain, Auchan, in Roubaix. In 1976, Mulliez's first cousin Michel Leclercq founded Decathlon, a company that specialises in the production and sale of sports clothing and equipment. It currently has more than 1,000 stores in 34 countries, as well as production facilities in France, Eastern Europe, Latin America, and Asia. Through a family holding company, Mulliez and Leclercq hold controlling interests in a wide range of retail and catering chains that are household names in France, including Auchan, Decathlon, Saint Maclou, and Flunch. Industrial production, rooted in a particular location and supporting a ramified network of social and cultural institutions, has thus been replaced by a globalised retail consortium, frequently relying on cheap, offshore production facilities and offering more precarious, service-sector employment to its French employees. In 2019, Auchan announced it was embarking on a major round of supermarket closures and job cuts, in response to changed consumer habits and the rise of Internet shopping. This suggests that poorly paid jobs in retail may now be replaced by what are often even more exploitative forms of employment in Internet warehousing and distribution.

The closure of Renault's Boulogne-Billancourt plant, the decline of steel production in Alsace-Lorraine, and the shift by Mulliez and Leclerq from textile production to retail and catering can all be taken as emblematic of what is at stake in the crisis of Fordism and the shift to post-Fordist forms of accumulation. At the simplest level, all of these examples involve a shift away from industrial production to tertiary activities, activities that often involve more flexible and less well-paid forms of employment. In each case, these shifts are spatialised in particular ways. In the case of the decline of France's steel and textile industries, deindustrialisation has produced pockets of severe socio-economic deprivation in peripheral regions of France.

As for the Île Seguin, this is less a case of impoverishment through deindustrialisation than of a shift away from industrial production to financial speculation on rising property values, accompanied by gentrification and the marginalisation of the Parisian working class. In all three cases, these developments are not merely economic but also political and socio-cultural: they have involved the disappearance of established working-class ways of life, forms of sociability, and identity; they have been accompanied by the decline of strong trades unions and the French Communist Party, which had together defended workers' interests.

This chapter sets out to demonstrate that our three chosen examples are representative of much more general shifts affecting the French economy as a whole, from the 1970s onwards. The chapter seeks to identify and anatomise the symptoms and causes of these shifts with greater precision, showing how they have contributed to the widespread anxieties concerning salaried employment in France today. Fordism is generally understood to have entered into crisis from the mid- to late 1970s onwards, while the deindustrialisation of French regions such as the North or Alsace-Lorraine has been a long-drawn-out affair, extending from the late 1970s through the 1980s, 1990s and on into the 2000s. This raises the question of why anxieties concerning work should have reached a peak in France from the late 1990s and early 2000s on, as evidenced in the profusion of political struggles, theoretical studies, and fictional and documentary representations we identified in our Introduction. Examining a range of developments, from changes in global financial governance, through national political decisions, to new initiatives in the organisation of work at the level of individual firms, we hope to show why this should be so. We conclude that a variety of different national and international political, social, and economic factors combined to render salaried employment in France much more precarious by the 2000s. Here we apply the distinction we identified in our Introduction between two different, but by no means mutually exclusive, forms of 'precarity', the 'objective precarity' experienced by France's growing numbers of unemployed and low paid and the more 'subjective precarity' experienced by those whose working conditions have deteriorated, who are subject to ever more intrusive forms of auditing and appraisal, and who live with the constant threat of unemployment if they fail to meet their targets or if economic conditions change.

34   *Republican Citizens, Precarious Subjects*

Having identified the causes of these new forms of precarity, we then turn to consider competing diagnoses of this situation. Here we distinguish and begin to adjudicate between two broad schools of thought. The first interprets these developments as being primarily the product of exogenous political factors, in the form of the hegemony of a global financial elite pursuing a neo-liberal agenda in the hope of reversing the social gains of the post-war decades and hence appropriating an ever greater share of global wealth for itself. The second places greater emphasis on endogenous factors to argue that the crisis of Fordism was provoked by its own internal contradictions, as manifest notably in the extent of worker resistance to its hierarchical, alienating, and exploitative characteristics.

By engaging critically with these competing diagnoses, the chapter will begin to sketch an interpretative framework of its own. This framework will, in turn, allow us to clarify such questions as what, more precisely, is meant by 'the crisis of Fordism' and how that crisis has generated new forms of both subjective and objective forms of precarity in relation to salaried employment in contemporary France. This new interpretative framework will also clarify the distinction between 'post-Fordism', understood as referring to the unstable set of economic arrangements emerging from the crisis of Fordism, and 'neo-liberalism', understood as an evolving ideological project that has exploited that crisis to push for reductions in social welfare payments and the liberalisation of global flows of goods, labour, and capital, among other things. Finally, as we continue to refine this interpretative framework over succeeding chapters, we will be able to show more clearly how and why these developments have undermined the terms of the post-war compromise, eroding established notions of French republican citizenship and replacing these with more precarious forms of subjectivity.

From Fordism to Deindustrialisation

As we noted in the Introduction, the increasing precarisation of salaried employment in France can be interpreted as a symptom of the long-drawn-out crisis of the Fordist regime of capitalist accumulation that emerged in France in the post-war decades and of the gradual unpicking of the post-war compromise that rested on that particular

The Crisis of Fordism   35

regime. In our Introduction, we identified a number of key elements that characterised Fordism as a successful regime of accumulation. Very briefly, Fordism was based on a dominant industrial paradigm that operated within a significantly regulated national and international market.

Under Fordism, the dominant industrial paradigm, the primary source of surplus value was the mass production of standardised consumer goods on assembly lines operated by low-skilled workers. Such workers were typically employed in large factories organised in hierarchical structures, according to the principles of Taylorist 'scientific management'. That is to say that workers' tasks were broken down into 'parcellised', repetitive gestures in accordance with rigorous time and motion studies. A strict distinction between command and execution meant that assembly-line workers were required to invest little of their own intelligence, initiative, or enthusiasm in their labours, the meaning and purpose of their actions being rigidly prescribed by a distant management. The tedious, alienating nature of such work was compensated by the guarantee of stable, relatively well-paid employment, as well as by the much-improved forms of social insurance put in place after the Second World War. As a regime of accumulation, Fordism rested on a virtuous circle of increased productivity based on economies of scale and technological efficiencies, rising profits redistributed to workers through wage rises, consequently buoyant consumer demand that itself fed into further profits and further productive investment.

At the institutional level, and particularly in the case of France, the State was extremely active in intervening in the economy in the immediate post-war decades, nationalising banks, insurance companies, and major French firms at the Liberation, as well as establishing a central planning commission that channelled both domestic investments and American Marshall Aid into certain strategic industries that became symbols of French technological achievement. These so-called 'national champions' secured national pride and economic prosperity in equal measure. Operating within the Bretton Woods system of fixed exchange rates and with an economy that remained relatively closed to foreign capital, successive post-war French governments were able to subsidise and build up strategic industries in this way, free to engage in bursts of Keynesian deficit spending at times of slowdown or managed devaluations in response to any inflationary pressures (Boyer 2015:65–66).

36   *Republican Citizens, Precarious Subjects*

As we noted in the Introduction, in the immediate post-war decades these arrangements secured unprecedented levels of national economic growth. However, as we also noted, the spoils of that growth were unevenly distributed and those decades were marked by highly conflictual industrial relations, as evidenced most strikingly by the millions of workers who downed tools in May 1968 demanding a complete transformation not only in their pay but also in their working conditions. Indeed, the concessions secured by workers in the wake of May 68 formed one of the factors that sparked the crisis of Fordism from the early 1970s on. The productivity gains and rising profits that had initially been achieved by the introduction of new mechanised production techniques were beginning to slow as Fordist technologies came to maturity. Increasing wage demands by French workers further eroded rates of profit. Meanwhile, French consumers were becoming disillusioned by the standardised and often poor-quality goods produced in French factories and were turning instead to higher quality and more diversified imports, notably from Japan. These problems were then exacerbated by the two oil crises of 1973 and 1979, which further fuelled inflation, as unemployment rose and gross domestic product (GDP) growth faltered.

The crisis of Fordism from the 1970s onwards was, over succeeding decades, to impact the French jobs market in two principal ways. First, France would see a significant reduction in the number of stable, relatively well-paid industrial jobs. From the 1980s to the present day, the country has thus suffered from stubbornly high overall unemployment and youth unemployment rates. Second, there would be a series of fundamental transformations to the nature of those jobs that did remain, with work often rendered less well-paid, more intensive, and more stressful as employers sought to boost their competitiveness, productivity, and profitability.

In terms of the nature and volume of employment in France, perhaps the most conspicuous shift has been the decline in the number of relatively stable and well-paid industrial jobs and the rise of less secure employment in low-level tertiary jobs. Between 1977 and 2011 the share of industrial jobs as a proportion of total employment in France dropped from 25 per cent to 12 per cent (OFCE 2012:65). In 2011, 24.6 million workers were employed in France's service sector, as against just 3.2 million in industry (51). A significant proportion of this shift can be attributed to firms concentrating, in the name of financial efficiency, on their core activities and, hence, outsourcing their peripheral functions. It is estimated that 28 per cent of industrial jobs lost in France between 1980 and 2001 can be accounted for by a combination of outsourcing and recourse to agency workers, two phenomena that typically involve deteriorations in the terms and conditions of the affected workers (ibid.).

In common with many developed economies, France has thus seen a profusion of more flexible, precarious, and short-term forms of employment since the 1980s. One useful measure of this, in the French case, is provided by the proportion of fixed-term contracts, or CDDs, as against permanent contracts, or CDIs. In 2017, a clear majority of jobs in France, 88 per cent, took the form of permanent CDIs, although this had dropped from 94 per cent of CDIs in 1982. Thus, over the last 25 years, the share of CDDs in the total French jobs market has doubled. More significantly, the majority of new hires in France now take the form of these temporary contracts, so where only 9.6 per cent of all workers are employed under a CDD, 30.4 per cent of workers aged 15 to 24 have these fixed-term contracts. Further, their average length has shortened dramatically. In 1998, just 57 per cent of CDDs were of less than one month; by 2017 that percentage had risen to 83 per cent, with fully 30 per cent of CDDs now being of just one day's length (DARES 2018). Short-term temporary contracts have now become the norm for new entrants into the labour market, for the young.

The offshoring of manufacturing plants, in search of lower wage costs in Eastern Europe or the developing world, is often also cited as a major contributor to the destruction of French jobs and was certainly facilitated through the 1980s, 1990s, and into the 2000s by those developments that fall under the general rubric of 'globalisation', namely a combination of trade liberalisation, the integration of former Soviet bloc countries into the EU, and the economic development of China. In fact, it is estimated that between 1995 and 2001 only 2.5 per cent of all industrial jobs lost in France were directly attributable to offshoring (Mouhoud 2013:81). Nonetheless, as El Mouhoub Mouhoud (2013:74–77) has shown, the effects of offshoring have been concentrated in spatial and sectoral terms, hitting above all low-skilled workers from French regions traditionally reliant on heavy industry, workers who lack the skills, funds, and social networks to enable them to move to areas where new employment opportunities have opened up.

38 *Republican Citizens, Precarious Subjects*

The negative effects of deindustrialisation and offshoring have thus been highly regionally concentrated, exacerbating disparities in wealth and power between the formerly heavily industrialised North and East, on the one hand, and the Île de France, with its concentration of tourism, banking, insurance, and legal services, or the area around Toulouse, with its specialisation in high-tech space and aeronautical industries, on the other (OFCE 2010:27–31). As Florence Weber has noted, this phenomenon of economic polarisation has been further exacerbated in the wake of the global economic crisis of 2008, as France's metropolitan areas suffered least from the resulting economic downturn and spike in unemployment (in Beaud and Mauger, eds. 2017:189–91).

Nonetheless, although France's major cities are now characterised by their concentration of economic power, pockets of significant urban deprivation have emerged in and around them, as exemplified by their *banlieues* or socio-economically deprived suburban social housing projects. Indeed, the emergence of the *banlieues* as so-called problem areas through the course of the 1980s and 1990s epitomises the extent to which the crisis of Fordism has produced effects that are not merely economic in nature but also social and political.

France's large, suburban housing projects were built on the edges of major cities in the 1960s and 1970s, first, because of the availability of cheap land in such areas and, second, because this enabled workers to be housed near to those industries that were also often situated in these suburban areas. With the closure of so many factories throughout the 1980s and 1990s, the *banlieues* became concentrated sites of high unemployment and socio-economic deprivation. From the 1980s onwards, they also gradually came to be home to relatively high concentrations of ethnic minority inhabitants, a phenomenon itself caused by the crisis of Fordism.

The successive French governments that actively encouraged immigration from their colonies and former colonies in the 1950s and 1960s had always assumed, in common with the immigrants themselves, that this would be a temporary phenomenon, that once they had worked in France for a few years, these non-European immigrants would return to their countries of origin. However, in 1974, in the wake of the economic downturn, the government suspended all further labour migration into France on the questionable basis that there were no longer enough jobs for French citizens, let alone for significant numbers of new immigrant arrivals. This presented those immigrants already legally resident in France with a stark choice. If they returned to their countries of origin, they risked never being able to enter France to work again. If they remained in France, they would have to abandon their plans to return home and settle permanently there. The vast majority of non-European immigrants already in France chose the second option and, as a result, decided to bring any wives or children they might have left behind in, for example, North Africa over to live with them. Thus, the profile of France's immigrant and ethnic minority populations changed significantly over the succeeding decades (Bernard 2002:63–108). No longer composed primarily of single men working in France on a temporary basis, these populations were now swelled by wives and children who could no longer be housed in male-only hostels or in the shantytowns that existed on the edge of all major French cities, where their menfolk had thus far typically lived. Since they were predominantly employed in low-skilled, low-paid jobs, ethnic minority groups often qualified for social housing. As a result, they came to be housed, in disproportionate numbers, in the *banlieue*, at the very time at which neighbouring factories were closing and low-skilled industrial jobs disappearing. Their children and grandchildren would thus grow up in areas of high unemployment and severe socio-economic deprivation, suffering from an absence of employment opportunities exacerbated by discriminatory recruitment practices (Hajjat 2013:19–44).

The emergence of the *banlieues* as areas around which broader anxieties concerning unemployment, delinquency, crime, and the integration of France's ethnic minorities have coalesced is thus inseparable from the crisis of Fordism. These phenomena have also had a directly political impact, insofar as anxieties about the *banlieue* and its inhabitants have been successfully exploited by the French Front National, renamed the Rassemblement National in 2018. In recent decades, the Front National has also successfully tapped into the grievances generated by the disappearance of stable employment in France's formerly heavily industrialised North and North East. The most significant political phenomenon in such areas has been the very high rate of political abstention in working-class communities that were previously marked by a strong adherence to the French Communist or Socialist parties. This has been accompanied by the smaller but more troubling phenomenon whereby the minority of working-class voters

40   Republican Citizens, Precarious Subjects

who *do* continue to vote have increasingly turned to the populist and xenophobic solutions offered by the Front National (Collovald 2004). A number of former solidly left-wing towns in Alsace-Lorraine and the Pas-de-Calais have thus become Front National strongholds in recent years. Hence the exacerbated polarisation of economic power inherent to the crisis of Fordism has had effects that radiate far beyond the purely economic, reshaping the economic geography of France while fomenting debates about ethnicity and national identity in ways that the Front National/Rassemblement National has successfully exploited.

At a more general level, the exacerbated socio-economic polarities between wealthy metropolitan centres and the deindustrialised periphery have been perceived as a threat to France's republican model itself. This much has been highlighted by the influential nature of Christophe Guilluy's analyses, in his best-selling book *Fractures françaises* (2010). Guilluy argues that the marginalisation of France's provincial and deindustrialised regions in the face of the rising power of its metropolitan centres risks undermining the unity and cohesion of the Republic itself. However, Guilluy's analyses suffer, first, from exaggerating the disparity between metropolitan centre and periphery, hence overlooking the existence of significant pockets of urban deprivation. Second, the manner in which Guilluy sets the white population of France's marginalised periphery against ethnic minorities in the *banlieue*, whom he alleges to be recipients of excessive media and political attention, has some troublingly xenophobic implications (Guilluy 2010). In a subsequent section of this chapter, we turn to the work of El Mouhoub Mouhoud and Dominique Plihon for an account of these uneven geographies that eschews Guilluy's questionable ethno-nationalist biases.

Nonetheless, Guilluy's work remains significant insofar as it represents an extreme example of the more widespread cultural anxieties generated by the geographic and socio-economic shifts characteristic of post-Fordism. Similarly, the offshoring of manufacturing plant from France's traditional regions of heavy industry is often experienced as a threat not only to economic prosperity but also to French national prestige and vitality. Thus, for example, during the national elections of 2012 the threatened closure of the blast furnaces at Florange, in North-Eastern France, became a talisman for the aspirant socialist administration's commitment to preserving France's industrial base, in contrast to incumbent Nicolas Sarkozy's alleged indifference. In the event, François Hollande's promise to save the Florange plant was broken once he was in power.[1] The inability of a socialist president to intervene in the French economy to save a strategically important industry stands in striking contrast to the post-war decades of full-blown State interventionism, a contrast that itself reflects fundamental shifts in the governance of the global financial system.

From Industrial to Financialised Capitalism

As we have pointed out, post-war Fordism operated within a highly regulated global financial system characterised by the fixed exchange rates of Bretton Woods, capital controls, and limits on the foreign ownership of French firms. This system gave French national governments considerable autonomy as regards the valuation of its own currency and decisions concerning public spending and strategic industrial investment. However, in 1971 Richard Nixon suspended dollar–gold convertibility, unable to maintain the value of the dollar in the face of a national deficit swelled by the expense of the Vietnam War and his reluctance to cut costly domestic welfare programmes for fear of the social unrest that this might provoke. This would prove to be the first step in the process that led to the end of the Bretton Woods system of fixed exchange rates in March 1973 and hence to the emergence of a massive global market composed of foreign exchange traders speculating on and hedging against fluctuations in the value of national currencies. French governments would henceforth have to be much more circumspect as regards their spending commitments for fear of incurring the displeasure of the currency markets and sparking a run on the franc.

Over succeeding decades, the post-war system of capital controls would also be dismantled. Again, the crisis of Fordism proved decisive here. As growth rates dramatically slowed in the 1970s throughout the developed economies, neo-liberal thinkers and think tanks exploited the downturn to discredit the doctrines of economic interventionism and regulated global and national financial markets that had held sway in the post-war decades. They argued that the market was a far more efficient mechanism of resource allocation than any national government and hence advocated the liberalisation of finance and

42   *Republican Citizens, Precarious Subjects*

trade, both globally and nationally, as a means of securing economic growth.

One further way in which national governments began to lose power to the global financial markets related to their increasing recourse to the bond markets to fund their spending commitments. With the slowing of economic growth and the advent of mass structural unemployment, tax revenues were falling at the very moment when spending on welfare was rapidly increasing. At the same time, inflationary pressures were eroding the value of both the savings and the wage rises of influential cohorts of middle-class voters. Politically, then, the tide was turning against tax rises or more progressive tax regimes, while the primary goal of macro-economic policy shifted from the maintenance of full employment to combatting inflation. As Vincent Duchaussoy has shown, the French government therefore had increasing recourse to the international bond markets to fund its spending after the second oil crisis of 1979, preferring this option to monetising the national debt by printing money, a practice now discredited by the monetarist belief in the need to combat inflation through strict control of the money supply. However, he argues that it was only from 1984 onwards that French government borrowing on the bond markets really took off, as the Socialist government abandoned its earlier attempts at Keynesian reflation, opting instead for fiscal austerity, competitive disinflation, and monetary stability through convergence with the constraints of the European Monetary System (Duchaussoy 2014).

The Socialists' 'turn to austerity' in 1983–84 had provided the first, stark demonstration of the extent to which the post-war Fordist mode of regulation had indeed broken down. François Mitterrand had been elected in 1981 on the promise to combat France's slow growth and high unemployment by initiating a programme of Keynesian reflation – a new wave of nationalisations would bolster strategic national industries, while increased spending on welfare benefits and a rise to the minimum wage would boost effective demand. However, such measures sparked an immediate negative response among global investors, provoking capital flight, a run on the franc, and three devaluations before the French government ceded to the demands of the new global financial order, embracing competitive disinflation and fiscal austerity. In addition to having increasing recourse to the bond markets, from 1984 onwards the Socialist Minister of the Economy Pierre Bérégovoy initiated a series of banking and financial reforms that deregulated the Paris stock market with the goal of tapping into new sources of foreign investment to replace falling levels of domestic or State investment (Thesmar 2008). The waves of privatisations engaged in under the premierships of, first, Jacques Chirac (1986–88) and then Lionel Jospin (1997–2002) offered further opportunities for foreign investors to gain control of major French firms. As François Morin has shown, initially these reforms and privatisations led to the emergence of a pattern of share ownership based on cross-holdings whereby major French companies held controlling stakes in one another's firms and the State often maintained a 'hard core' of shares, so that foreign ownership remained limited. However, by the late 1990s this cross-shareholding model had given way to an ever greater involvement of foreign investors, so that by 1997 'foreign capital penetration of the French market' had reached levels that were 'clearly higher than in comparable countries', with the result that the Paris Stock Exchange had become 'the most open and most receptive to foreign investors' of all its direct counterparts, the UK and USA included (Morin 2000:42). Further, many of these foreign investors were US and UK pension funds demanding high and rapid rates of return on their investment that could only be delivered by French firms bearing down on wage costs or shedding labour (43–46).

The liberalisation of the French stock market through the 1980s and 1990s exemplifies the shift away from a Fordist model, based on promoting national industrial growth, to a model in which the interests of international shareholders and global finance would now predominate.[2] This shift from a national industrial model to a form of globalised financialised capitalism was also reflected in a significant transformation in the nature of the French employers' organisation. In 1998, under the presidency of Ernest-Antoine Seillière, the *Conseil national du patronat français* (CNPF or National Council of French Employers) became the *Mouvement des entreprises de France* (MEDEF or Movement for French Enterprise). The CNPF had been founded in 1945 to represent employers' interests in negotiations between business, unions, and the State that aimed to deliver a unified strategy to boost industrial production and hence secure national prosperity. Seillière's presidency and the name change he initiated marked a decisive shift away from this emphasis on national industrial strategy. For Seillière himself was the inheritor of a major iron and steel firm, Wendel, which he had saved from bankruptcy in 1978 by transforming it into

44   *Republican Citizens, Precarious Subjects*

a successful investment fund (Moulier Boutang 2010:75). His decision to replace the old CNPF with the MEDEF in 1998 signalled a more general turning away from the post-war model of managed national industrial growth in favour of a new mode of globalised, financialised capital accumulation.

This shift also involved the French State losing its capacity to intervene to support domestic industries and jobs, ceding its powers in this respect to global financial markets and foreign investors. These tendencies were strengthened throughout the 1990s, as France committed itself to ever closer integration within the EU. When the Maastricht Treaty came into force in 1993 it gave independence to the Banque de France, definitively removing the possibility of France monetising its national debt by printing money. The process of EU integration also set strict limits on French national debt and spending deficits, while making it illegal for the French State to give direct subsidies to its struggling national industries. When France joined the Eurozone in 1999, all possibility of competitive currency devaluation was removed, leaving nation states with only a single option as regards increasing their economic competitiveness, namely, as Wolfgang Streeck (2017:174) has argued, '*internal devaluation*: that is the raising of productivity and competitiveness through more flexible labour markets, lower wages, longer working hours, higher labour market participation, and a welfare state geared to recommodification'.

Under Fordism, relatively good salaries and generous welfare benefits were considered positive phenomena, key to the maintenance of effective demand and full employment according to broadly Keynesian macro-economic principles. Today, by contrast, wages and welfare payments are seen in a very different light, at best as variables to be adjusted downwards to boost competitiveness, at worst as simply drains on the resources of firms and nation states. This fundamental shift in thinking exemplifies the way in which neo-liberal thinkers and think tanks have been able to exploit the crisis of Fordism to secure the hegemony of their economic doctrines. Indeed, following the Socialists' turn to austerity in 1984, none of the governing parties in France has offered a serious alternative to these neo-liberal assumptions.

Neo-liberalism often presents itself as working to reduce State intervention and economic regulation, hence setting markets, entrepreneurs and consumers free to interact in the most creative and economically efficient manner. In fact, as Pierre Dardot and Christian

Laval argue, far from reducing the overall amount of regulation, neo-liberal economic and social policies involve a whole new set of regulations aimed at creating markets or pseudo-markets where none previously existed. This, in turn, involves transforming the manner in which citizens and workers understand themselves, in a concerted process of subject formation or re-formation that aims to turn all citizens into active consumers and competitive 'entrepreneurs of the self' (Dardot and Laval 2013). This attempt to instil a spirit of competitive individualism into every worker and citizen is clearly discernible in a series of changes to the organisation and management of individual firms.

Shareholder Value and 'Fair Value' Accounting

The crisis of Fordism and gradual shift to a more globalised and financialised regime of capital accumulation has not only undermined the capacity of the French State to intervene into its national economy to support economic activity and employment; it has also had a direct effect on the ways in which individual firms are managed. As Michel Feher (2017:49–54) has argued, the crisis of Fordism and consequent fall in the rate of profit was exploited by neo-liberal thinkers to promote their preferred doctrine of shareholder value. Under Fordism, a distinction had opened up between the ownership and the management of large firms. Large firms were typically managed by a cadre of business managers, who owed their position not to their ownership of the firm but to their possession of a set of high-level technocratic skills. For neo-liberal thinkers, this posed a risk to the efficient governance of any corporation insofar as such managers might be tempted to run the firm in accordance with their personal, vested interests in bolstering their own professional position, rather than maximising profits. The doctrine of shareholder value responded to this perceived risk by insisting that firms be managed primarily in the interests of their shareholders. The deregulation of financial markets, the consequent facilitation of hostile takeovers, and the increasing role of foreign institutional investors in company ownership all gave more power to shareholders over managers. That increased power was reinforced by indexing managers' remuneration to their company's share price and increasing the power of corporate boards, composed of

46   *Republican Citizens, Precarious Subjects*

supposedly independent representatives of shareholders, over managers or employee representatives (Feher 2017:65–66).

This shift to shareholder value has had two direct impacts on the working lives of ordinary employees. First, the imperative placed on managers to deliver high dividends to shareholders could most easily be obeyed by bearing down on wage costs, through redundancies, outsourcing, or more general erosion of established terms and conditions. Alternatively, managers could engage in share buybacks, hence diverting any profits away from productive reinvestment and towards speculative accumulation instead. Second, the emphasis on shareholder value provided the impetus behind a shift in accounting standards to so-called 'fair value' accounting. All French listed companies, indeed all listed companies within the EU, have had to comply with the International Financial Reporting Standards (IFRS) regulations on fair value accounting since 2005. Fair value accounting standards demand that all of a firm's assets and activities, tangible and intangible alike, be accorded an up-to-date market value, precisely to enable shareholders to make informed, rational investment decisions. As Michel Aglietta and Antoine Rebérioux (2004:37) have shown, one effect of this has been to designate each of any firm's separate departments a 'profit centre', with its own strict financial targets. As a result, ever more employees are impelled to meet those financial targets, finding themselves subject to the kind of constant auditing that has been rendered possible by the spread of computing technology.

Gaëtan Flocco's study of junior executives and middle managers in various French industrial sectors highlights this impact of financialisation on employees' working lives. For example, his fieldwork in the French nuclear industry reveals that junior and middle managers are increasingly devoting their time to financial-managerial tasks that distract them from the more traditional technological-scientific work they were educated to perform and that define their own sense of their metier. The executives in the nuclear industry Flocco interviews thus lament the fact that they are no longer 'really carrying out the job [*le métier*] for which they had trained during their studies as engineers'; 'still passionate about technology […] physics, mathematics, and mechanics', they now spend 'entire days in front of a screen "filling in Excel spreadsheets", […] carrying out tasks that are most often abstract and dematerialised' (Flocco 2015:52). Flocco suggests that this partly reflects the spread of information technology, the winnowing out of secretarial support staff, and the consequent demand that managers perform their own administrative-secretarial tasks. Yet he also notes the increasing hegemony of short-term financial imperatives over longer-term technological ones, a hegemony contingent on the opening up of French share ownership to institutional investors: 'Every respondent remarks on the ascendancy of financial objectives, which now make themselves felt all the way down the professional hierarchy, with the imposition of measures to reduce labour costs by decreasing the number of "days budgeted" and of staff attributed to each project. […] "Budgetary criteria" are now "tighter" and are "reviewed every three months"' (Flocco 2015:57).

Flocco's fieldwork shows how the logic and imperatives of financialisation permeate down to all employees, who are now placed under greater scrutiny and subject to increased stress. Thus, the shift in corporate governance in accordance with the doctrine of shareholder value has not merely increased the likelihood of redundancies and outsourcing, it has also rendered more stressful the working lives of those who do remain on a company's payroll. These shifts are all the more significant in the case of the French nuclear industry. For that industry represented one of a number of such 'national champions', set up and developed by the French State in high-tech sectors to secure national prestige and economic prosperity and hence serve the general interest. While the French State remains its majority shareholder, the French nuclear industry was opened up to foreign share ownership in 2009 and now operates as a multinational corporation with projects in numerous locations outside France. This transformation from national champion to multinational corporation, with its concomitant diversification in share ownership, thus exemplifies the shift from Fordism to post-Fordism, a shift whose tangible effects are evident in the laments of French employees at the predominance of financial-managerial imperatives over older technological-scientific values.

From Fordism to Toyotism

If financialisation is one source of more stressful working conditions another is the widespread adoption by French companies of so-called 'Japanese' or 'Toyotist' techniques of total quality management (TQM), continuous improvement and just-in-time (JIT) production. Together

48   *Republican Citizens, Precarious Subjects*

these promise to drive down inventory costs while improving the quality and diversity of the products offered by French companies, enabling them to become more reactive to changing demand. As Bob Hancké has shown, these techniques were widely adopted by French companies from the early 1980s on, with the active support of the socialist government who saw this as a means of boosting competitiveness and increasing worker participation. French management, meanwhile, was attracted not merely by the financial benefits such techniques promised but also by their political effects. As Hancké explains, 'what was initially a worker-oriented reform package became a management tool that helped defuse the conflict-ridden formal industrial-relations institutions and allowed for a participative management model integrating workers' skills into the production system without integrating unions in the corporate decision-making structure' (in Hall and Soskice, eds. 2001:325–26).

These new production techniques involve a fundamental break with the kinds of 'scientific organisation of work' that predominated in factories run on older Taylorist-Fordist principles, placing much greater emphasis on assembly-line workers' own initiative and personal implication in the production process. The aim of F.W. Taylor's time and motion studies of workers' movements had been to *deskill* them, stripping them of any autonomy so as to render them more malleable, more easily exploitable. He sought to remove all 'initiative' from factory workers, stating that 'the man who is mentally alert and intelligent' would be 'entirely unsuited' to working in accordance with his principles of scientific management; what was required was a worker 'so stupid and phlegmatic that he more nearly resembles in his mental make-up the ox than any other type' (Taylor 1911:59). As Taylor famously quipped, 'an intelligent gorilla' might thus prove 'a more efficient pig-iron handler than any man can be' (40). The new Japanese or Toyotist methods obey a very different logic, by contrast. They seek not to capture the workers' practical knowledge in order that management can appropriate that knowledge leaving the workers deskilled. Rather the goal now is, first, to capture that practical knowledge and then to enjoin the workers themselves to constantly reflect on and improve it, so that they invest their personal initiative in refining the production process. This necessarily involves soliciting, rather than bypassing, the workers' initiative and, by extension, securing their personal investment in their tasks.

The extent to which Taylorism–Fordism involved the extinction or marginalisation of workers' own knowledge and initiative is perfectly captured in Robert Linhart's classic account, *L'Établi* (1978), of assembly-line work in a Citroën factory in the 1970s. By contrast, 'La Dépossession', the final episode of Jean-Robert Viallet's three-part documentary series *La Mise à mort du travail*, broadcast on French terrestrial television in late 2009, highlights the significant qualitative shift that is involved in the adoption of so-called 'Japanese' manufacturing techniques.

In *L'Établi*'s climactic scene, Linhart focuses on an older worker, who has used his own skill and initiative to fabricate a special workbench or 'établi' with which he is able to first identify and then correct any defects in the production of body panels. A team of 'engineers' or managers then arrives on the factory floor, tasked with rationalising and optimising the production process. They immediately order the worker to destroy his workbench, despite its great effectiveness, and adopt their prescriptions for a more productive mode of work (Linhart 1978:161–71). What this episode starkly illustrates is the strict separation between *command* and *execution* under Taylorist–Fordist conditions: a team of production engineers commands here, determining and prescribing from on high the tasks that workers are then impelled to mutely execute; the workers' own initiative, skill, and knowledge are not simply ignored, in this set-up; these faculties are actively repressed, expelled from the production process.

Ironically, the destruction of the old worker's workbench depicted in *L'Établi* is counter-productive. As Moulier Boutang points out, more typically the Fordist–Taylorist workplace actually depended on allowing workers on the factory floor to employ their initiative and practical knowledge to get round day-to-day problems. What changes with the shift to Toyotism is that such forms of worker initiative change from being 'marginalised and subordinate' to become 'central and hegemonic in wealth and the extraction of value' (Moulier Boutang 2010:117). Hence, workers' 'implicit knowledge' is 'maintained', nourished and solicited, 'and not absorbed' in the production process (Moulier Boutang 2008:101). Workers' cognitive and affective capacities are thus objectified, captured, and exploited in such a way as to not leave those workers deskilled, mutely and unthinkingly executing tasks prescribed by management, but rather constantly investing more of their immaterial labour, of their initiative and affects in their jobs. This second process

50   *Republican Citizens, Precarious Subjects*

is perfectly illustrated in Viallet's 'La Dépossession', a documentary that focuses on the introduction of 'continuous improvement' techniques at French fork-lift truck manufacturer Fenwick in the wake of the company's purchase by a US private equity fund, Kohlberg, Kravis, Roberts and Co. (KKR).

The implementation of these new techniques was primarily motivated by the desire to increase both productivity and profitability, in order, first, to repay the debts incurred in the leveraged buy-out of Fenwick and, second, to make the company more attractive to new buyers when KKR came to sell their own interest. Driven by the demands of a financialised model of corporate ownership, these new production techniques also signal a decisive break with the kind of Taylorist–Fordist destruction of worker initiative illustrated in Linhart's *L'Établi*. For they involve a new imperative that each worker invest her cognitive and affective faculties to an unprecedented degree in the production process, making daily suggestions as to how that process might be made more efficient. As one of Fenwick's directors explains: 'We've put the motivation of our employees at the centre of our strategy.' A series of close-ups then focuses on the noticeboards that have newly appeared on the factory floor, calling for workers to move 'towards 100% involvement', by posting their own 'proposals for improvement'. As the voiceover explains:

> The new credo is that workers should adhere to the firm's objectives. Each employee must propose ideas, knacks, and solutions to improve the productivity and the safety of their workstation every day. This is how the workers become responsible for the intensification of their own work. In order to incite the employees to play along, management constantly evokes the opportunity this presents for them to work in better conditions.

As the tone and content of this piece of voiceover indicates, 'La Dépossession' presents these attempts to capture and exploit workers' cognitive and affective capabilities as entirely negative. However, it is surely questionable whether these new techniques are any more inherently exploitative than the monotonous, unthinking assembly-line labour characteristic of Taylorism–Fordism. In their fieldwork among workers in the automobile industry in Eastern France, the sociologists Stéphane Beaud and Michel Pialoux note that some car-workers welcomed the introduction of JIT and TQM in their factories insofar as the new demands for multi-tasking, flexible working, and greater cognitive input represented a refreshing alternative to the monotony of Taylorist–Fordist assembly-line working (Beaud and Pialoux 2003:144–45, 283). Indeed, many of these techniques were pioneered by the US engineer W. Edwards Deming, who introduced them into Japan as part of the American-sponsored programme of national post-war reconstruction. They were thus intrinsic to Japan's own post-war compromise and the prosperity it secured for that nation's citizens. Further, Deming's own values – a complete rejection of performance-related pay or management by objectives; an emphasis on respecting each worker's pride in their work – stand in stark opposition to what might be seen as characteristically neo-liberal styles of management.

However, as Beverly Silver (2003:42) has pointed out, when TQM and JIT techniques were exported globally in the 1980s and 1990s, they were implemented without the guarantees of job security that Japanese employers had given their workers in return for the intensified workload such techniques involved. Indeed, these techniques were frequently introduced in France as part of corporate restructuring programmes, enabling employers to maintain output in the wake of job losses, precisely by intensifying the workload of those employees who remained on the payroll. In the case of the Fenwick factory depicted in 'La Dépossession', such negative phenomena are intimately related to the liberalisation of the French stock market since it was this that facilitated the factory's buy-out by a US investment fund. In this way, the documentary depicts the financialisation of the French economy, job losses, intensified working patterns, and the adoption of 'Japanese' production techniques as being inseparably linked. As the voiceover informs the viewer, one year after continuous improvement methods were implemented at Fenwick, 100 workers were made redundant. Hence the workers made redundant were confronted by the material or objective precarity inherent to unemployment, while those that remained on the payroll were subject to the more subjective precarity contingent on the intensified exploitation of their affective, cognitive, and physical labour. 'La Dépossession' thus illustrates quite why the adoption of 'Japanese' production techniques is so often seen as an inherently negative phenomenon by French workers and trades unions.

Customer Care

The increasingly widespread adoption of these 'Japanese' techniques in France is demonstrated by the marked increase in the number of accreditations to the internationally recognised standard for quality management, ISO9000. In 1993, there were just 1,586 such accreditations in France, by 2001 that number had risen to 20,919, and it stood at 23,403 at the end of 2016 (ISO 2017). Accreditations to ISO9000 do not merely reflect the adoption of TQM techniques in French manufacturing, of course. Such techniques have also become increasingly common in the service sector, as is manifest in the profusion of 'customer care' policies that prescribe the precise attitude, forms of address, modes of dress and deportment that employees must adopt in their interactions with every customer. As Christophe Dejours (2003:29–30) points out, in an attempt to ensure their employees adopt these prescribed forms of behaviour, French employers have adopted extensive mechanisms of appraisal and audit, mechanisms that are often experienced as highly intrusive and hence stressful by the employees subjected to them. Further, as Danièle Linhart argues, accreditation to the international quality standard ISO9000 involves breaking every task down into its component processes and forcing workers to follow those standardised, prescriptive processes to the letter and this at the very time that management is enjoining those same workers to invest ever more of their personal attributes, affects, and initiative in their labours. This contradiction between the prescriptivism inherent to ISO9000 accreditation, on the one hand, and the imperative for workers to demonstrate their initiative and personal commitment, on the other, has contributed to the proliferation of stress and burnout among French workers (Linhart 2015:37–41).

This contradiction between prescriptivism and the imperative to autonomy is also surely what lies behind the recurrent criticisms of the pressure workers now feel under to *perform* a version of their professional selves, to feign their intense commitment and motivation in even the most menial of service-sector tasks. It might seem that there is nothing new here. After all, in the French context, the classic account of an 'inauthentic' performance by a service-sector worker is surely Jean-Paul Sartre's (1943:82–83) description of the 'bad faith' displayed by a Paris waiter and this dates from the early 1940s. However, if we read Sartre's famous description of a man 'playing at being a waiter in a café' more closely, we come across an observation that might help us understand quite what has changed in the contemporary service sector. Having outlined the 'bad faith' of the waiter's performance, Sartre moves on to consider other categories of service-sector worker. He argues that the public demands of, for example, grocers that they be 'nothing but a grocer', concluding that 'a grocer who dreams is offensive to the buyer' since 'society demands that he limit himself to his function as grocer' (83). What is striking about recent accounts of working in the contemporary retail or service sector is the emphasis that their authors place on the increasing demands by employers that a grocer, for example, be precisely 'a grocer who dreams'. Corporate mission statements and customer care policies increasingly stipulate that grocers, or any other service workers, should, moreover, dream of being not just any grocer but one who works for a particular employer and whose dream is to realise and embody that employer's values.

Far from finding dreams offensive, contemporary service-sector employers thus seem to demand that their employees should dream, before then insisting that those employees show they believe this dream can only be realised by working for a particular chain of supermarkets, hotels, restaurants, or other such. In her account of eight years working at a supermarket checkout, Anna Sam satirises precisely these demands that employees should see working in a supermarket as the realisation of their profoundest hopes, desires, and dreams. She warns any reader about to be interviewed for such a job against stating honestly that they simply need the work, offering a series of alternative responses instead, responses that reflect the contemporary imperative to 'enchant' one's future employer:

> 'Because I've always dreamed of working in a supermarket!'
> If you want to be believed, you should really say this with a lot, a lot of conviction, whilst at the same time as making your eyes shine with amazement. Not easy. [...]
> 'Because, like your brand Champion/Géant/Les Trois Mousquetaires ... I want to be a champion/a giant/the three musketeers!'
> Crazy, it's true, but the winning spirit always goes down well. So, why not? Be careful though; this type of response isn't applicable to all supermarket brands (I want to be a Safeway).
> (Sam 2008:27–28)

54   Republican Citizens, Precarious Subjects

That Sam's experience is not an isolated one would seem confirmed by Florence Aubenas's account of seeking work as a cleaner in the formerly heavily industrialised area around Caen, Normandy. In her various interviews and employability training sessions, Aubenas repeatedly confronts the imperative that she demonstrate and perform the requisite level of 'passion' and 'motivation' for the low-paid cleaning jobs she seeks (Aubenas 2010:164).

The imperative that Aubenas manifest her 'passion' and that Sam show she 'dreams' of working in a supermarket thus stands in striking contrast to Sartre's comment, from the early 1940s, that 'a grocer who dreams is offensive to the buyer'. What Aubenas's and Sam's respective accounts suggest is that, although service work has always involved immaterial forms of affective and relational labour, there has been an intensification of such forms in the contemporary French workplace. Moreover, this is not simply a matter of a quantitative increase; there is also a qualitative shift at work here. Sartre's descriptions of the behaviour of waiters and grocers suggest they are 'inauthentic' or act 'in bad faith' inasmuch as they conceal their true identities, feelings, and motivations behind a mask provided by their collective professional identity, their membership of the corporation of waiters or grocers, with its attendant codified forms of behaviour. This is the implication of his claim that 'a grocer who dreams is offensive to the buyer'. Sartre fails to recognise the positive function performed by such codified professional behaviours, their role as defensive masks behind which employees can conceal their true selves. What Sam's and Aubenas's more recent accounts of service-sector labour suggest, by contrast, is that workers are now compelled to dream, not to hide their real dreams or selves behind the mask of a professional role and identity but to perform that role as though it were the realisation of their most intimate dreams and desires. Corinne Maier (2004:15) captures this shift quite nicely when she remarks: 'My grandfather, a self-made man, a wholesaler, never got up in the morning asking himself if he was "motivated": he did his job [il faisait son métier] and that was it.'

This new imperative that service-sector workers realise their most intimate dreams and desires through their work epitomises what Danièle Linhart terms 'la sur-humanisation managériale', the excessive humanisation of work inherent in contemporary management techniques. As she argues, the imperative to self-realisation erodes an older distinction between the worker's professional and personal selves, a distinction that provided an important form of defence for workers in their working lives. This 'tendency to only see human beings, with their talents, predispositions, and desires, where, in fact, there are professionals at work' is one way to 'oust them as agents' qualified to determine 'the organisation of their own work' and replace them with individualised human beings whose desires and talents can be moulded to the changing demands of the firm (Linhart 2015:43–44). As Moulier Boutang (2010:156–57) points out, the demand that employees realise themselves through work represents 'an intolerable intrusion by the employer, which smashes the classical protections and barriers of the Labour Code'. The French Labour Code protected workers by stipulating what employers could reasonably demand of their employees, the latter themselves recognised as members of a professional group, a *métier*, or corporation with attendant guaranteed rights and social protections. The new imperative to self-realisation relates not to the collective identity of workers as members of a professional group or corporation but to the private selves of atomised individuals now compelled to demonstrate their personal investment in their firm's goals and brand identity. This strikes at the heart of the peculiarly corporatist nature of the French post-war compromise while challenging one of the foundations of French republican citizenship, namely the strict division between the public self of the citizen and the private self of the individual.

The crisis of Fordism has thus involved not merely a quantitative shift in terms of a significant decrease of stable employment in industrial production and an increase in more precarious forms of tertiarised labour. That crisis has also involved a series of fundamental qualitative changes in the nature of salaried employment that has seen an intensified exploitation of immaterial forms of labour. In the executive and managerial positions, financialisation has led to an increased emphasis on managerial-financial imperatives over the more technological-scientific labour typical of Fordism. In service-sector roles, quality management and customer-care policies have increasingly prescribed the nature of the affective-relational labour workers must perform. In a factory setting, the adoption of TQM and JIT techniques has greatly increased the amount of technical-cognitive labour demanded of assembly-line workers. As we have noted, these kinds of technique are not necessarily more exploitative or alienating than repetitive labour on a Taylorist–Fordist production line. However,

56   *Republican Citizens, Precarious Subjects*

they have been implemented in a context of high unemployment, increased global competition, and the pressures intrinsic to financialisation. In this sense, any of their potential benefits, in terms of greater worker autonomy, cooperation, and initiative, have been outweighed by their negative aspects.

In the context of the France of the 1980s, 1990s, and 2000s, then, TQM and JIT production techniques were inextricably linked to the adoption of neo-liberal macro-economic policies at both the global and national levels. Indeed, this link was explicitly articulated in 1993 by Dominique Taddei and Benjamin Coriat in a report they drafted for the then Socialist Minister of Industry and Foreign Trade, Dominique Strauss-Kahn. In their report Taddei and Coriat offered a series of proposals regarding how best to increase the international competitiveness of French industry. They argued that the Socialists' turn to austerity, monetary rigour, and competitive disinflation in 1983–84 had forced French industry to increase its productivity and improve the quality and diversity of its products. With export prices now stable, France could embark on a concerted export drive. However, this export drive would only prove successful provided French industry continued to bear down on wage costs, adopted Japanese-inspired TQM techniques systematically, and exploited tools such as 'the reorganisation/reduction of working hours' (Taddei and Coriat 1993:194n.1). These various measures were seen as essential to ensuring that France equipped itself with the flexible, polyvalent, and personally motivated workforce able to produce the quality products that would guarantee international competitiveness.

Taddei and Coriat's report is instructive not simply because of the direct causal links it posits between fiscal and monetary rectitude, quality management techniques, and national economic growth, but also because of the way in which it presents the reduction of working hours as primarily a tool to render the national workforce more flexible and productive. When, in the late 1990s, the Socialists actually passed their legislation reducing the working week to a maximum of 35 hours, they justified this as a job-creation measure and, indeed, several commentators argue it made a significant contribution to the reduction of French unemployment between 1997 and 2001 (IRES 2009:25; OFCE 2012:27). However, other commentators have emphasised the extent to which the 35-hours legislation also increased stress levels among French workers now obliged to adopt more intensive and flexible patterns of work in order to complete the same amount of work in less time (Dayan 2002:44–46; Caroli and Gautié 2009:110–12).

A whole series of changes at the level of the global and national economy, as well as at the level of individual firms, have thus contributed to what Eve Caroli and Jérôme Gautié (2009:99–107) have identified as 'a marked deterioration over the course of the last twenty years' of working conditions in France. The anxieties generated by this deterioration have surely been exacerbated by the spectre of two further developments, in this case driven by technological change. The first is the threat of the so-called 'uberisation' of the French labour market, that is to say of the spread of precarious and flexible forms of employment for one of the growing number of Internet platforms, of which Uber is perhaps the best-known example. In 2015, 12 per cent of those aged 25 to 34 in France were estimated to be earning more than 50 per cent of their income via Internet platforms (Montel 2017:20). These forms of work in the digital economy may have remained relatively marginal to date, but there is thus some evidence that they are particularly prevalent among social categories, such as the young and ethnic minorities, who find access to more traditional employment difficult (Conseil d'État 2017:57). As a 2017 report by France's *Conseil d'État* (15) has noted, it is possible to understand the rise of 'uberised' forms of work as 'accelerating developments already under way' in the French jobs market as a whole, inasmuch as they epitomise the rise of flexible, less well-regulated jobs that offer none of the legal protections or welfare rights guaranteed by full-time salaried employment.

The second major technological development is the prospect of Artificial Intelligence (AI) or wholesale robotisation destroying vast numbers of jobs. Since such technologies are still in the process of development, estimates of their precise effects on employment remain highly speculative and range from apocalyptic claims that half of all jobs in industrialised economies are at risk from AI to the OECD's more modest estimate of just 9 per cent of such jobs at risk (Standing 2017:105). Given the necessarily speculative nature of such estimates, it is perhaps best simply to note that the spectre of job losses through AI has further contributed to widespread anxieties concerning work in contemporary France.

As we have attempted to show, the series of changes at the level of global finance, national economic policy, and the governance of individual firms help explain the current sense of crisis concerning

58 *Republican Citizens, Precarious Subjects*

salaried employment in France. While the crisis of Fordism itself can be dated back to the mid to late 1970s, a whole range of these changes culminated in the late 1990s and early 2000s – the liberalisation of the French stock market, France's entry into the Eurozone, the 35-hour week legislation, the spike in accreditations to ISO9000, the adoption of 'fair value' accounting methods. The effects of such developments on the increased precarity of salaried employment in France were exacerbated by the global financial crisis of 2008, which sparked increased unemployment, budgetary austerity, and a further bearing down on the terms and conditions of French workers. Enumerating these various changes can thus help us understand both how the crisis of Fordism has occasioned a fundamental deterioration in working conditions in France and why the resulting forms of objective and subjective precarity might have reached crisis point by the beginning of the 2000s. The question remains, however, as how best to account for these phenomena. Is this a fundamentally political process, reflecting the efforts of a ruling elite to reverse the social gains of the post-war decades and appropriate a greater share of wealth for itself, as, for example, Gérard Duménil and Dominique Lévy (2000) have argued? Or, are the causes of this crisis largely endogenous, the product of certain flaws and contradictions inherent to Fordism itself, as Yann Moulier Boutang (2007) argues?

Conflicting Diagnoses

Frédéric Lordon has produced one of the most systematic accounts of the financialisation of the French and global economies that attributes these developments primarily to exogenous political forces. He identifies the emergence of a 'new hegemonic bloc', in Antonio's Gramsci's sense of that term, composed of economic and politico-bureaucratic elites who, he argues, have sought, since the late 1970s, to reverse the social gains of the post-war consensus and dismantle the Fordist regime of accumulation that financed those gains (Lordon 2002:67–68; 2008:18). He locates a fundamental contradiction between the needs of the 'real economy' and the demands of a 'parasitic' financial sphere for high rates of return on investment. The former produces wealth and employment on the basis of productive investment, while the latter demands risky investment that fuels bubbles and provokes recurrent financial crises

(Lordon 2000:80). Lordon interprets the proliferation of subjective and objective forms of precarity that now characterises salaried labour in economies such as France's as primarily the product of this elite class of shareholders seeking to impose ever more exploitative terms and conditions of employment (2010:43–4). He therefore advocates a whole series of measures to rein in global finance and encourage more productive investment (Lordon 2008:166–84). For example, he is an advocate of instituting a so-called SLAM, or Shareholder Limited Authorized Margin, that would set maximum levels of shareholder dividend and hence curtail employers' tendency to seek to boost shareholder value by shedding labour, eroding terms and conditions of employment or engaging in unproductive measures such as share buybacks. More recently, he has argued that democratic control over finance will necessitate a restoration of national sovereignty and French withdrawal from the euro, as a precursor to the construction of some possible future 'common European currency' based on genuinely democratic principles (Lordon 2013). In one sense, then, Lordon might be seen to be arguing for the restoration of the terms of the post-war Fordist compromise. Yet he also seeks to extend and deepen that compromise, advocating transforming firms into worker co-operatives, for example, so as to extend French republican values of freedom, equality, and fraternity into the workplace itself (Lordon 2016).

Lordon's analysis of the parasitic, even destructive power of global finance would seem to have considerable prescience and validity, given the causes and effects of the global financial crisis of 2008. The increasing disparities of wealth in the developed economies to the benefit of senior executives and rentiers, as documented in Thomas Piketty's influential study *Le Capital au XXIe siècle* (2013), seems to substantiate Lordon's claims regarding the fundamentally political motivations behind these developments. Indeed, it might be argued that the response to the global financial crisis, in the form of the bailing out of major financial institutions and the imposition of austerity on ordinary citizens, provides further evidence of Lordon's 'new hegemonic bloc' at work (Hudson 2015).

However, Lordon does tend to project all responsibility for the crisis of Fordism onto malevolent elites, risking idealising Fordist industrial capitalism and the political and social forms it generated as he does so. In this, he tends to overlook the economic flaws and social injustices inherent to Fordism, just as he ignores the extent of

60   *Republican Citizens, Precarious Subjects*

the popular rejection of its rigidities and hierarchies. Lordon hence fails to distinguish between the crisis of Fordism, on the one hand, and the exploitation of that crisis by adherents of neo-liberal solutions, on the other. What is lacking here is a more dialectical grasp of the multiplicity of determinants behind the erosion of the terms of the post-war Fordist compromise.

Moulier Boutang, by contrast, emphasises the extent to which the crisis of Fordism needs to be understood as resulting from a dialectical process. He highlights the determining of the role of opposition to Fordism both as a dominant industrial paradigm and a mode of regulation, focusing on worker resistance to the exploitative nature of the Fordist factory and broader popular resistance to Fordism's hierarchical and paternalist social and political forms. The conflictual labour relations of the 1960s and 1970s are thus interpreted by Moulier Boutang (2010:51–52) as symptoms of a mass phenomenon of refusal of the hierarchies and disciplinary rigidities of Fordism. This refusal also manifested itself in the so-called 'new social movements', in women's struggles to secure their autonomy through, among other things, access to the labour market, or in working-class struggles to gain access to higher education. The crisis of Fordism, according to this account, was provoked not purely by that regime running up against its economic or technological limits. Nor were the gains of the post-war compromise eroded purely at the behest of an exploitative ruling class. By the early 1970s Fordism had become unmanageable in significant part on account of the workers' movement itself. Business owners responded by breaking up the great Fordist factories, outsourcing its peripheral functions, and imposing Japanese production techniques to secure the participation of workers and defuse their militancy (2010:57–58).

From this point, the primary source of surplus labour became no longer the physical labour power of the unthinking assembly-line worker, as under Fordism, but rather the 'immaterial', 'cognitive', and 'affective' forms of labour increasingly demanded of all workers. As we have seen, whether working on an assembly line organised according to the principles of just-in-time production or employed in the expanded service sector, employees are now obliged to invest their cognitive and affective capacities to an unprecedented degree. The different forms of immaterial labour we have itemised in our descriptions of executive, assembly-line, and service-sector work are all taken by Moulier Boutang as evidence of this shift to cognitive capitalism. He gives the example of the manufacture and sale of branded sports shoes, whose surplus value relies less on the *economies of scale* secured by their mass production than on the *immaterial value* embodied in their design, branding, and marketing, activities that rely on capturing and exploiting cognitive and affective forms of labour (Moulier Boutang 2007:50). The development of computing and, latterly, Internet technologies has provided the technological means for fostering, capturing, processing, and exploiting these immaterial stocks of knowledge. This kind of exploitation of immaterial value is exemplified, for Moulier Boutang, by a company like Google, which produces nothing material but captures and monetises the collaborative, communicative, immaterial labour of millions of Internet users, as they post and search for cognitive content (Moulier Boutang and Rebiscoul 2009).

Moulier Boutang argues that the shift to a regime of post-Fordist cognitive capitalism has undermined the bases on which Fordism regulated the labour market, secured productive investment, and shaped the subjectivities of its workers and citizens. From the industrial revolution to Fordism, he argues, surplus value was accumulated according to the principles laid out in the labour theory of value, being generated by a combination of fixed capital invested in plant and machinery and labour power, the latter divisible into and remunerated in terms of measurable units of labour time (Moulier Boutang 2007:79–80). He maintains that industrial capitalism had its own characteristic form of what Michel Foucault termed 'governmentality', defined as 'the manner in which the behaviour of men is steered' in accordance with certain 'relations of power' (2004:192). Industrial capitalism relied on the kinds of 'disciplinary' forms of governmentality Foucault analyses in his *Surveiller et punir* (1975), whereby individuals are transformed into units of productive labour by being subjected to hierarchical management within the temporally and spatially defined space of the factory working day.

According to Moulier Boutang, the intangible, immaterial nature of cognitive labour renders it irreducible to measurement in terms of abstract units of labour time. Further, immaterial labour cannot be disciplined and captured within the finite space of the factory or workplace; it is not separable from individual workers but intrinsic to their whole person and is generated in their social and cultural

62   *Republican Citizens, Precarious Subjects*

interactions across the entirety of society, outside work time as much as during it. This irreducibility of immaterial labour to more traditional, disciplinary forms of measurement and capture poses a problem for business owners, who respond by imposing flexible and precarious work contracts, time-limited and contingent on the completion of pre-defined projects or tasks. Thus, the proliferation of atypical contracts offers employers the 'possibility of reintroducing a generalised system of measurement' of labour value, as well as a new form of 'discipline for workers, who must respect the established criteria' defining the tasks to be accomplished (Moulier Boutang 2007:190).

In a similar vein, Moulier Boutang interprets financialisation as a by-product of the shift to cognitive capitalism. The immaterial bases of this kind of cognitive capitalism are much less predictable and much harder to value, in monetary terms, than were the labour force and labour time of an assembly-line worker producing standardised products. The mobility of speculative finance, its demands for immediate and high rates of return on investment are, according to Moulier Boutang, reflections of the inherent difficulties of predicting the profitability or measuring the market value of these immaterial, affective, and cognitive forms of labour. As he puts it: 'Finance thus proves to be the only means of "governing" the intrinsic instability of cognitive capitalism, even if it introduces new factors of instability' (181).

Finally, Moulier Boutang argues that the shift from Fordism to cognitive capitalism has also demanded a change in the way in which the subjectivities of workers are formed. Where the subjectivity of the Fordist worker was produced in accordance with Foucauldian disciplinary techniques, that of the cognitive worker is now produced in accordance with Foucault's (2004) descriptions of post-disciplinary mechanisms of 'biopolitical' control in his lectures on neo-liberalism. Fordist workers, following Foucault's account, are taken to have been subjected to a process of 'assujettissement', subjected to the hierarchically imposed demands of the productive apparatus, yet also subjectivised as members of a collectivity – car workers, shipbuilders, railway workers, and so on – in whose names political demands could be articulated and social and political rights secured. Cognitive workers, by contrast, are enjoined to become 'entrepreneurs of the self', constantly nurturing and updating an individualised stock of human capital – of intellectual, affective, and immaterial aptitudes – to meet the ever changing demands of the labour market (Moulier Boutang 2007:181–97).

The Crisis of Fordism   63

Moulier Boutang's analyses seem to offer a number of advantages. For he brings together into a single systematic theory the major economic and political developments that we have identified as being key to understanding the crisis of Fordism and its effects on salaried employment in France. As we have noted, he does this in a manner that avoids the pitfalls of ether idealising Fordism or attributing its crisis purely to malevolent exogenous forces. Moulier Boutang's emphasis on the new forms of governmentality and subject formation seems, moreover, to offer a useful interpretative framework through which to make sense of what we have identified as the growing discrepancy between established notions of French republican citizenship and the more precarious forms of subjectivity inherent to the contemporary labour market.

Nonetheless, the hypothesis of a shift to a new regime of cognitive capitalism does seem to rest on some questionable assumptions. As David Camfield (2007:31–33) has pointed out, the notion of 'immaterial labour' is required to do a lot of theoretical work here, covering 'very different kinds of production processes and products', from 'the work of food-servers and salespeople as well as that of computer engineers and teachers', subsuming all of these disparate forms of labour under the single rubric of the 'cognitive'. The immaterial labour performed by a check-out operative in a supermarket is very different, in quantitative and qualitative terms, from the cognitive labour demanded of an assembly-line worker subjected to new TQM and JIT procedures or from the higher-level intellectual skills demanded of a software developer, for example.

Further, Moulier Boutang's hypothesis regarding the interdependency of financialisation and cognitive production surely assumes too neat a relationship between those two phenomena. As we have noted, he presents Google as representing the epitome of cognitive production, of the production of value by means of the kind of collaborative and creative 'pollinisation' of ideas and affects that characterises cognitive capitalism (Moulier Boutang and Rebiscoul 2009). Yet, as Michael Hudson (2015:140–41) has shown, when Google went public in 2004 its senior management took a series of steps to protect themselves against the negative effects of financialisation, limiting the extent to which speculative investors would be able to siphon profits away from productive investment and 'avoiding the usual financial policy [of] yielding management control to Wall Street financiers' by according

64   *Republican Citizens, Precarious Subjects*

their new shareholders limited voting rights. It seems that Google's senior management did not share Moulier Boutang's belief in the symbiosis of financialisation and cognitive capitalism. They appeared to be close to Lordon in this respect, perceiving the finance industry to be parasitic on and hence destructive of the creation of value. Indeed, as Mariana Mazzucato (2018) has shown, the conspicuous successes enjoyed by a variety of global tech corporations, such as Google, Apple, and various biotech firms, have in fact depended more on State funding than on the much vaunted dynamism of venture capital. Mazzucato echoes François Morin (2006) in suggesting that financialisation has in reality proved to be a brake on cognitive production, diverting corporate resources away from investment in research and development towards measures designed to produce short-term boosts to share prices and dividends.

Finally, as El Mouhoub Mouhoud and Dominique Plihon have argued, the interaction between financialisation and contemporary forms of knowledge production is producing economic changes much less uniform than those Moulier Boutang claims to be characteristic of the shift to a regime of cognitive accumulation. Criticising what they term the 'teleological' and 'globalising' tendencies inherent to theories of cognitive capitalism, they argue that the contemporary global economy is characterised by a 'hybridisation' of the productive system according to two logics, a 'cognitive' logic and a 'neo-Taylorist' logic that are both complementary and contradictory (Mouhoud and Plihon 2009:63).

Mouhoud and Plihon thus argue that firms now organise their activities around different 'blocks of knowledge/skills', so that research and development (R&D), design, and marketing are typically concentrated in 'the major centres of technological excellence' and production concentrated either in lower skilled regions within the same nation state or offshored to the developing world (67). Management practices in the centres of technological excellence do indeed follow a model of cooperative, communicative, cognitive labour. Highly speculative venture capital is sometimes required to foster those intangible forms of production in the early stages. However, this only accounts for a minority of speculative global finance, the majority of which is driven by much less productive objectives (42–44). Further, mass production remains governed by Taylorist or, at best, 'neo-Taylorist' logics that may include elements of TQM or JIT but that are organised primarily in terms of low-wage costs and economies of scale. Mouhoud and Plihon's work thus offers a useful interpretative

The Crisis of Fordism 65

tool for making sense of the uneven economic geographies we have identified as being characteristic of post-Fordist France, the increasing socio-economic polarity between metropolitan centres in which cognitive resources and hence wealth are concentrated, on the one hand, and deindustrialised regions marked by socio-economic deprivation, on the other.

Each of the conflicting diagnoses of contemporary political economy discussed above thus has its particular strengths and weaknesses. In interpreting our corpus of representations of the post-Fordist workplace, we will therefore draw on a synthesis of the best of each. From Lordon we retain an emphasis on the destructive and ideologically driven rise of global finance. From Mouhoud and Plihon we take the notion that financialisation is related in contradictory ways to the rising importance of the knowledge economy and has produced a hybridised and hence geographically polarised regime of accumulation. We retain Moulier Boutang's insistence on the need to grasp the dialectical processes behind the crisis of Fordism and his consequent rejection of any form of Fordist nostalgia. We also retain his emphasis on the proliferation of immaterial labour, but interpret this not as symptomatic of a shift to a unified new regime of cognitive capitalism but rather as evidence of the importance now placed by employers on capturing and exploiting the *human capital* of their employees.

This increased emphasis on the exploitation of human capital has a variety of determinants. At the simplest level, it reflects the increase in the quantitative importance of the service sector within the French economy, alongside the adoption of 'Japanese' production techniques in the manufacturing sector. In ideological terms, it reflects the dominance of a neo-liberal theory and practice that seeks to reconceptualise and reshape citizens as embodied stocks of capital to be exploited for commercial gain. These processes of reconceptualising and reshaping have been driven by the search for competitive advantage and facilitated by the weakening of the capacity of the trade unions to protect their members from the most intrusive demands of employers. Danièle Linhart's concept of 'surhumanisation managériale' offers a useful analytical tool for understanding these attempts to exploit various forms of human capital. Nonetheless, as we have argued, it remains important to recognise that the kinds of human capital and immaterial labour in question remain distinct in different sectors of the labour market. This last insight also determines our response to

66   *Republican Citizens, Precarious Subjects*

Moulier Boutang's claim that the advent of cognitive capitalism has necessitated a shift in the dominant mode of governmentality and subject formation, a shift away from *discipline* towards more *modulated, post-disciplinary* techniques. We agree that some such shift in governmentality is empirically observable but insist that it is less homogenous than Moulier Boutang argues. Rather, we suggest that a mixed model of governmentality has emerged, in which older forms of discipline, often intensified by recourse to digital surveillance techniques, now co-exist with more modulated forms of post-disciplinary control. Indeed, it is precisely this mixed model of governmentality, along with the new forms of subjectivity it produces, that poses such a challenge to older notions of French republican citizenship.

In the next chapter, we will seek to demonstrate that this last claim is by no means purely abstract or speculative. Here we will focus on, first, a selection of sociological accounts of contemporary French management practice and, second, a series of recent reforms to the legal regulation of work and welfare. Taken together, these closely related phenomena involve clearly identifiable shifts in the techniques now employed by employers and the State in an effort to transform French republican citizens into 'entrepreneurs of the self', constantly modulating their social and professional identities in response to changing market imperatives. As we will show, the pressure to adopt this new form of subjectivity has proved to be a significant new source of both objective and subjective precarity.

Notes

1   In their 2013 documentary, *La Promesse de Florange*, Anne Gintzburger and Franck Vrignon offer a detailed and moving account of these events.
2   For a more detailed account of financialisation and its effects on the global economy, see Hudson (2015) and Lapavitsas (2013).

Chapter 2

Modulating Work and Welfare

Danièle Linhart (2015:22) has expressed her surprise at the candour demonstrated by the various Human Resource directors of major French companies she has interviewed: all willingly admit to their 'desire to model the subjectivity' of their employees 'more than to develop their professionalism', their 'ambition to extend the firm's hold over their employees so that it dominates the very fibre of their humanity'; managers, she concludes, 'dream of being Pygmalion'. It is this attempt to shape, capture, and exploit employees' most personal attributes that characterises what Linhart terms 'la surhumanisation managériale', the excessive humanisation of management practices. One way of interpreting this phenomenon would be to argue that the proliferation of different forms of immaterial labour we observed in the last chapter has demanded the adoption of new styles of management. In other words, there has been a transformation in the dominant mode of what Foucault terms 'governmentality' among French company managers, a move away from the 'disciplinary' forms characteristic of Fordism towards a post-disciplinary regime that aims to marshal and exploit workers' most personal attributes and intimate sentiments, their human capital, to an unprecedented degree.

As we have already argued, the 'disciplinary' mode of governmentality, analysed by Foucault in his classic *Surveiller et punir*, can be seen to have reached its apogee in the Taylorist–Fordist factory. There workers' subjectivities were moulded into stable forms of collective professional identity, in accordance with a fixed norm attested to by a combination of formal qualifications and time served. Those fixed norms were sanctioned by a distant management that exerted its hierarchical surveillance over the workers within the temporally and spatially

68   Republican Citizens, Precarious Subjects

finite space of a factory's working day. In this way, workers' minds and bodies were disciplined so as to become units of labour power remunerated according to abstract measures of labour time. In his 1978–79 lecture series *Naissance de la biopolitique*, however, Foucault discerned in the writings of various neo-liberal thinkers the emergence of a less hierarchical, more individualised and psychologised conception of governmentality that no longer aimed at subjectivising employees in terms of collective identities, as manual workers, office clerks, managers, or whatever. In the work of theorists of 'human capital', such as Gary Becker, he saw a new, post-disciplinary model emerging in which workers were constructed less as the disciplined members of a collective than as individualised 'entrepreneurs of the self', enjoined constantly to nourish and replenish their portfolio of personalised skills, their stock of human capital.

As we have already pointed out, for Moulier Boutang this transition to a post-disciplinary regime is itself merely one further symptom of the emergence of a regime of cognitive capitalism based on the exploitation of immaterial forms of labour that are not amenable to control or measurement in terms of units of labour time. As we argued in the last chapter, it is not necessary to subscribe to the more teleological and globalising aspects of Moulier Boutang's work to acknowledge the increasing importance of immaterial labour to capital accumulation. Indeed, a number of commentators who do not adhere to the cognitive capitalism thesis nonetheless maintain that there has been a significant change in the manner in which French workers are now typically managed and hence in the subject positions they are enjoined to adopt. Thus, the sociologist of work Vincent De Gaulejac (2005:112–16) contrasts contemporary 'managerial power' with the 'disciplinary' forms of power it has replaced, arguing that where the latter focused on controlling workers' bodies, the former targets their 'psyche'. In her study of the French office of a multinational management consultancy, Valérie Brunel (2008) argues, in similar mode, that the consultants are not so much subjected to disciplinary techniques as they are enjoined to become 'managers of their own souls'. Philippe Zarifian (2009), meanwhile, draws on his fieldwork at Danone, France Télécom, and the French postal service also to suggest there has been a move away from the disciplinary techniques characteristic of Fordism. He turns to Gilles Deleuze's notion of a shift from 'disciplinary societies' to 'societies of control', a notion Deleuze sketched out in his influential

Modulating Work and Welfare   69

'Postscriptum sur les sociétés de contrôle' (1990) that was itself an extrapolation from Foucault's own work on the waning of discipline as the dominant mode of governmentality in the developed economies.

The starting point for Deleuze's analysis of 'societies of control' is his contention that where Foucauldian discipline operated within the enclosed space of, for example, the factory, imposing a 'mould' that defined the roles of workers and bosses, respectively, such enclosures have now broken down. The new forms of 'control' hence function in a manner that is less rigid, more diffuse and open-ended. Control operates less as a 'mould' than as a continuing process of 'modulation' that extends out beyond the workplace to embrace every aspect of a worker's life and identity. Decisions regarding recruitment, promotion, and salary are now increasingly subject to constant modulation in accordance with continuous processes of auditing and appraisal of each worker's most apparently personal of attributes. Deleuze's use of the term 'control' should be understood in its specifically cybernetic sense as referring to control systems incorporating servomechanisms that constantly self-regulate in response to external stimuli, in a feedback loop. In a 'society of control' workers are not so much subjected to the rigid disciplinary injunctions of a hierarchical structure of command as enjoined to forever *modulate* their professional and personal selves, their stock of human capital and hence their employability, in response to changing market conditions, in an analogous form of self-regulating feedback loop (Deleuze 2003:240–47).

As we will show, this shift away from discipline towards control has been an uneven process, generating mixed models of governmentality in which disciplinary mechanisms co-exist with apparently less rigid injunctions to autonomy and flexibility typical of control. Nonetheless, this chapter will employ Deleuze's distinction between 'mould' and 'modulation' as an overarching interpretative framework, by means of which to make sense of a series of recent changes to management practice and the legal regulation of work and welfare in France. The chapter argues that these all show evidence of a shift towards post-disciplinary techniques and characteristically Deleuzean forms of control. Further, these new techniques of control enjoin workers to adopt forms of subjectivity that pose a fundamental challenge to more established notions of French Republican citizenship rooted in the recognition of stable, corporatist identities. The chapter seeks evidence of the pressures now placed on French workers to adopt these more

70   *Republican Citizens, Precarious Subjects*

modulated forms of professional identity in two distinct but closely interrelated fields. In the first instance, we will examine the increasing emphasis placed by French employers on 'compétences', or *skills*, rather than formal qualifications, as the basis on which decisions are made regarding recruitment, remuneration, and promotion. Second, we will examine a series of reforms to the legal regulation of work and welfare in France between 2007 and 2018 under the presidencies of Sarkozy, Hollande, and Macron, changes to the legal regulation of redundancy, the eligibility of the unemployed for welfare benefits, and the administrative structures of France's national employment services. These reforms are intended to offer a representative sample rather than an exhaustive survey of such measures; succeeding one another in historical time, they obey a shared logic that means their combined effects have been cumulative. At the heart of that shared logic is the new priority accorded to ensuring the unemployed are given the opportunity to nourish and modulate their personal stocks of *human capital*. It is this focus on developing and remunerating their employees' human capital that also lies behind French employers' advocacy of the so-called 'skills agenda' from the late 1990s onwards. There has thus been a fundamental shift in the way in which both the State conceives of the unemployed and employers conceive of their workers. The unemployed are no longer seen primarily as victims of economic circumstance with a right to social security based on their status as citizens of the Republic. Similarly, workers are seen less and less as members of a collective professional group, endowed with a status that itself guarantees certain rights. Rather, members of both groups are increasingly considered personally responsible for their own fate, required to render themselves more *employable* by constantly updating their individual portfolio of skills in an open-ended modulation of their professional and social identities.

Deleuze (2003:241–42) argues that this transition to techniques of control should not be seen as a purely negative phenomenon, that control, like discipline before it, embodies 'new freedoms' as well as new forms of what he terms 'asservissements'. This last term is normally translated as 'enslavement', but it also refers in French to servomechanisms that self-regulate in response to feedback. Hence, 'asservissement' might be better translated as 'servo-servitude' in recognition of the manner in which the modulated logics of control place an imperative on workers constantly to self-regulate in response

Modulating Work and Welfare   71

to feedback received from employers and the labour market. Following a suggestion made by Deleuze's close collaborator, Félix Guattari, we understand 'servo-servitude' by analogy with an experienced car driver who constantly and almost intuitively modulates her driving style in response to feedback she receives from changing road conditions, engaging clutch, brake, or accelerator, adjusting steering, changing gears with no need for conscious reflection (Guattari 1980). We argue that post-disciplinary governmentality aims, at its extreme, towards this kind of 'servo-servitude', so that the imperatives inherent to the subject position of the 'entrepreneur of the self' are obeyed almost intuitively, in response to feedback from changing market conditions, with little conscious reflection.

Deleuze argues that the shift to control is itself a symptom of 'a mutation in capitalism' (2003:244), hence implying that any attempt simply to preserve the disciplinary forms of Fordism will prove illusory, while enjoining us to 'search for new weapons' from within the current post-disciplinary conjuncture (242). Nonetheless, as we have mentioned, this new conception of governmentality and subjectivity does pose a challenge to established notions of republican citizenship. Moreover, left-wing parties and trades unions in France have yet to elaborate an agreed alternative model of work and welfare that responds to this new economic conjuncture and around which the labour movement might rally. This chapter will conclude that, in such circumstances, the shift to techniques of control is hence experienced by many French workers primarily as a source of further insecurity and precarity.

From Qualifications to Skills

A number of French commentators have highlighted the transformation that has seen French employers gradually replace formal qualifications with the more intangible criterion of *skills* as the primary basis on which decisions regarding employment, promotion, and remuneration are now routinely made (Paradesie and Lichtenberger 2001; Lallement 2007:107–48; Zarifian 2009). For Michel Kokoreff and Jacques Rodriguez (2012:102), the adoption of 'skills-based management' has been 'pivotal in the "managerial revolution"' that has sought 'to bypass the institutions' that, under the terms of the

72 Republican Citizens, Precarious Subjects

French post-war consensus regulated industrial relations. Deleuze's distinction between 'mould' and 'modulation' proves extremely helpful in making sense of this shift, a shift that exemplifies the emergence of more 'modulated' forms of human resource management. Before turning to these processes of modulation, however, it will first be necessary to clarify what Deleuze has in mind when he characterises earlier management techniques as having imposed a 'mould' on workers' minds and bodies.

If there is one measure, or set of measures, in the immediate post-war period that exemplifies Deleuze's notion of the 'mould' in the context of employment, it is surely the 'Parodi decrees', named after the then Minister of Labour, Alexandre Parodi. The 'Parodi decrees' were a series of decrees passed by the French government in 1945 in an effort to impose wage controls across the labour market, from heavy industry to the service sector. This involved identifying a variety of 'professional fields', then classifying the range of job functions within each field, before stipulating the minimum and maximum salaries of each such function or role (Saglio 2007). As Catherine Paradeise and Yves Lichtenberger (2001:35) argue, the 'Parodi decrees' thus established a stable wage relation based on a causal link between two variables. The first variable was 'the individual capacities' of each worker, attested to by 'the formal qualification (recognising the formal incorporation of knowledge and *savoir-faire* by means of the initial or continuing training) and/or time served (validating the abilities acquired irreversibly through experience)'. These objectively validated 'capacities' then determined the nature and rank of 'the position' occupied by any individual worker, itself 'defined in terms of a supposedly exhaustive description of its prescribed tasks'. Hence, the Parodi decrees exemplified what Paradeise and Lichtenberger term 'a qualifications model' that institutionalised a relatively stable wage relation, based on the equation 'qualification + time served = position = wage' (Paradeise and Lichtenberger 2001:38).

Although the system of wage control initiated by the Parodi decrees would only last until the beginning of 1950, the wage scales and professional hierarchies on which these were based lasted for several decades, not least because that wage structure and those hierarchies were intrinsic to Taylorist-Fordist modes of production and management (Saglio 2007:53). Although apparently specific to the realm of mass production, the dominance of this kind of 'scientific

Modulating Work and Welfare 73

organisation of labour' was such that it became the model also for many other forms of work, including white-collar employment in hierarchical and bureaucratic organisations in the public and private sector alike (Lallement 2007:132–33).

A fairly rigid causal relationship was thus institutionalised in the French post-war labour market between formal qualifications and time served, position in a professional hierarchy, the strictly prescribed nature of the tasks to be performed by the holder of such a position, and the salary that position guaranteed. This relationship exemplifies what Deleuze terms the 'mould', corresponding very closely to Foucault's (1975:201) description of the way disciplinary techniques function by setting up a fixed norm (qualifications/time-served), which subjects must meet by passing some form of exam, overseen by a 'hierarchical gaze' (educational authorities/management). On the basis of their performance in that exam, such subjects are then assigned a status in a social and professional hierarchy. As we have noted, this disciplinary structure also reflects a Taylorist-Fordist organisation of production in which workers occupy a fixed place in a functional hierarchy that operates according to a stark distinction between execution and command, so that assembly-line workers, for example, mutely and unthinkingly execute the commands elaborated by management. Finally, given the corporatist nature of the social security system that emerged in France after 1945, the rigid functional hierarchies characteristic of Fordism related directly to the social welfare rights that were guaranteed by each worker's history of accumulated contributions to one of France's work-based social insurance schemes (Paradeise and Lichtenberger 2001:35). Discipline, Taylorist-Fordist organisation, and the corporatist strand of French republicanism were thus very closely intertwined here. Indeed, the particular form taken by the French post-war compromise might hence reasonably be characterised as 'Fordist–Republican'. However, according to Paradeise and Lichtenberger, by the end of the 1990s the rigid disciplinary 'mould' of the 'qualifications model' had been significantly eroded by the emergence of a new 'skills-based model', a model that corresponds closely to the more 'modulated' forms of management characteristic of Deleuze's 'society of control'.

As the French economy became ever more tertiarised, so French management insisted that the old system of remuneration in accordance with formal qualifications and/or time served was becoming obsolete.

74   *Republican Citizens, Precarious Subjects*

The new service sector economy demanded more personalised, intangible 'skills' of its workforce. Meanwhile in the manufacturing sector, Fordist mass production techniques were proving unprofitable in the face of increased international competition and consumer demands for higher quality, more differentiated products. As we have seen, management responded by differentiating product lines and adopting techniques of total quality management and just-in-time production, in the search for competitive advantage. As we demonstrated in the last chapter, both of these developments have seen an increased recourse to different forms of immaterial labour, whether the affective-relational labour characteristic of service-sector work or the more technical-practical labour deployed by workers in a modernised manufacturing sector. These more intangible forms of immaterial labour cannot be captured or measured by the old fixed norms of formal qualifications plus time served. Hence French employers have sought to replace a now outdated 'qualifications model' with a 'skills-based model' that involves ever more extensive forms of appraisal, of highly individualised mechanisms of 'skills auditing' as the basis on which to make decisions regarding pay, promotion, and retention of staff.

The centrality of this new emphasis on 'skills' or 'compétences' in French management circles was exemplified in 1998 when the French employers' organisation, the MEDEF, dedicated its 'international training symposium' to the theme 'Objectif compétences'. This new 'skills-based model' demanded not only that workers invest much more of their personal selves in their work, but also that they be ready to adapt those selves constantly in response to changing market conditions. The conformity and obedience demanded under the old system gave way to a new emphasis on responsibility, autonomy, and 'multi-tasking', such that, to quote the MEDEF's sixth proposal: 'employees have a responsibility as regards the management of their own skills. They must be able to manage their portfolio of skills or take sufficient control of it as to be able to replenish it and to invest in the acquisition of new skills and commit fully to the training courses they follow' (quoted in Reynaud 2001:13). In accordance with theories of human capital and in just the way that Foucault anticipated, workers are thus conceived as 'entrepreneurs of the self', not as units of labour power in receipt of a wage indexed to a measurement of labour time but as stocks of human capital generating a revenue contingent on the value of that capital, of their skills:

We are at the very antipodes of a conception of a labour force which must sell itself at a market price to a capital invested in a firm. It is not a conception of a labour force, it is a conception of a skills-capital that receives, depending on diverse variables, a certain revenue that is a wage, a wage-revenue such that it is the worker himself who appears to himself as a sort of firm or enterprise.

(Foucault 2004:231)

The skills agenda thus offers one tangible example of the shift from 'mould' to 'modulation', a shift that has not only fundamentally redrawn the terms of the French post-war consensus but also challenged certain core republican values. For, as Lallement (2007:145) has pointed out, the bases on which individualised skills are evaluated are much less transparent or objective than the delivery of formal qualifications through the national school system, a system that, in theory at least, operates according to strictly republican ideals of equality of treatment and objective measures of merit. Further, appraising an employee's formal qualifications represented an attempt to assess their objective knowledge and capabilities, their 'savoir' and 'savoir-faire', to use Lallement's terminology. Assessing that employee's skills, by contrast, involves enquiring into their personal attributes, their 'aptitudes for human relationships', their very sense of being or 'savoir-être' (140). This provides a very concrete example of the manner in which new management techniques threaten to undermine the split between each citizen's public and private selves and hence challenge one of the founding tenets of French republicanism. For to assess employees' personal, intangible 'skills' is to use their private characteristics as the basis on which to make decisions regarding recruitment, retention, and promotion. This undermines the principle that in the public sphere all citizens will be treated equally precisely because their private characteristics will *not* be taken into account, will *not* be used as a basis of discrimination in the allocation of jobs, housing, social or political rights.

Further, the emergence of a battery of new forms of appraisal, audit, and personalised evaluation associated with this 'skills-based model' has played a key role in the increasing incidence of what Christophe Dejours (2003) terms 'workplace suffering' in France, of stress and burn-out among workers. Such techniques set worker against worker

76 *Republican Citizens, Precarious Subjects*

in a constant competition for employment, promotion, and wage rises that has eroded earlier more collective professional identities and sources of solidarity. The shift towards 'a skills-based model' thus institutionalises what Deleuze identifies in his 'Postscriptum...' as 'the modulating principle of "salary according to merit"', exemplifying the way in which the contemporary workplace 'never stops introducing an inexpiable rivalry, presenting it as a healthy form of emulation, an excellent motivation that sets individuals against each other and traverses everyone, dividing them from within' (Deleuze 2003:242–43).

For Deleuze, this 'inexpiable rivalry' is epitomised by the use of 'challenges, competitions and highly comic group sessions', analogous to 'televised gameshows', as the basis on which 'a modulation of every salary' can now be calculated (242). Where, under Fordism, wages were calculated based on a combination of formal qualifications and labour time, in post-Fordism challenges and competitions perform this function, soliciting and evaluating the levels of commitment and enthusiasm, the more intangible skills that constitute each employee's stock of human capital. Their increasing use by French companies has been depicted in two recent documentaries, the second episode of Jean-Robert Viallet's *La Mise à mort du travail* series, entitled 'L'Aliénation' (2009), and Didier Cros's *La Gueule de l'emploi* (2011). Both documentaries include extensive footage of the role plays, games, and competitions in which aspirant and existing employees are compelled to engage, manifesting their enthusiasm, commitment, and adaptability as they do so. The unease that these scenes provoke in the viewer reflects our intuitive understanding that these employees are being *forced* to manifest these feelings, that they are feigning these emotions in a profoundly alienating *performance* of their professional selves. The footage also underlines the fundamental contradiction between the management credo that work should be the locus of workers' self-realisation and the extraordinarily prescriptive definition of the selves that are enjoined to realise themselves in this way. As Ivor Southwood (2011:28–30) has argued, these techniques force every employee or job candidate to transform themselves into 'a contestant in the jobseeking talent show', engaging in efforts to 'improvise the sort of generic character' now demanded by management – 'positive, unquestioning, enthusiastic, extra-mile-going' – then offering this version of their selves 'willingly', adopting a 'suitable emotional orientation' that can 'later be harvested for profit'.

Modulating Work and Welfare 77

In the last chapter we observed this imperative that workers perform a version of their professional selves in Sam's and Aubenas's respective accounts of low-paid service-sector employment in retail and cleaning. Hélène Zimmer has allegorised and satirised these phenomena in her novel *Fairy Tale* (2017), in which Loïc, an unemployed former factory worker, is forced to compete in a televised reality show for the prize of securing a series of job interviews. This basic narrative set-up allows Zimmer to highlight the extent to which a particular *performance of the self* is now an integral part of job-seeking and salaried employment. Hence Loïc must first engage in a performance to convince the producers to feature him in their show, before then performing a version of his self for the television cameras, in accordance with those producers' demands. Having won the reality TV competition, he must then engage in a further performance in his job interviews to win over his potential future employers. All the while, his partner, Coralie, is depicted being compelled to perform her enthusiasm for her low-paid job in a discount retail warehouse.

Through this leitmotif of performance, Zimmer thus highlights that what Danièle Linhart terms 'la surhumanisation managériale' is experienced not as an opportunity to realise our true selves through our labour, as management claims, but rather as an imperative to fashion, feign, and perform an inauthentic version of those selves that accords with our employers' prescriptions. This represents an intensified, highly personalised form of alienation, in which, to reformulate the young Marx's definition, it is no longer merely the inanimate products of our labours that stand over and against us as alien beings, it is now also our very selves, the professional identities we are compelled to perform that take on this alien quality. To quote Brunel, in the contemporary workplace the management of one's emotions hence becomes 'a professional skill', while interiority and the self are transformed into 'objects of labour' (Brunel 2008:88,97). For Brunel, this exemplifies the shift away from disciplinary forms of governmentality: 'Where disciplinary society demanded individuals fulfill a social role and conform to that role, contemporary society will demand of them a capacity for adaptation, transformation, and personal motivation, an extremely intimate investment in the role they are supposed to hold' (37). Zarifian broadly concurs but he emphasises that this is not a uniform process; his fieldwork among workers at Danone, France Télécom, and La Poste reveals rather a kind of mixed model of

78   *Republican Citizens, Precarious Subjects*

contemporary governmentality that combines elements of discipline with aspects of control. One of the clearest examples of this mixed model relates to Zarifian's fieldwork at France Télécom, the company that had originally been France's State-run telecoms provider but was floated on the stock exchange in 1997, becoming fully privatised in 2004, when the government sold its controlling stake.

As Zarifian shows, France Télécom's call-centre operatives are caught between a range of contradictory imperatives – the demanding sales targets set by management, the highly prescriptive scripts they are obliged to use in their interactions with clients, the requirement to master the technical details of rapidly changing packages of Internet and other services, and the need to devote time to delivering a personalised service in order to attract and retain the company's customers. Elements of this work obey a fundamentally disciplinary logic, corresponding to modernised and intensified forms of Taylorism–Fordism – the highly prescriptive scripts, the demanding sales targets, and the use of information technology to surveil every employees' words and actions, sanctioning the taking of unauthorised breaks or any failures to deal with customer queries in the allotted time. These are the kinds of disciplinary technique that some commentators characterise as 'digital Taylorism' (Brown, Ashton, and Lauder 2010:15–17). Other aspects of the work, however, are more immaterial – the cognitive labour of mastering the technical details of the products the call centre operatives sell, the affective-relational labour inherent to delivering quality customer service (Zarifian 2009:19–21).

This second set of more immaterial operations cannot be managed by recourse to disciplinary techniques; here it is no longer a matter of 'imposing the mould of prescribed "tasks"' but rather of a new form of modulated control that Zarifian names 'control of [the worker's] commitment' or 'control of [the worker's] engagement' (88). This second set of immaterial operations relies, of course, as much on each worker's intangible skills as it does on their formal qualifications, and it falls to each worker to cultivate and mobilise those skills:

> The new employees of the era of modulation must constitute their skills as an efficient resource and mobilise them advisedly. Of course, the firm can help them to develop their cognitive resources, if only by providing training programmes. But it will fall to individuals to oversee the development of this resource,

> which they constitute for themselves, to ensure they remain
> sufficiently skilled, to mobilise themselves, turning themselves
> into a form of potential capital. (Zarifian 2009:91)

This, then, is the worker as Foucault's 'entrepreneur of the self', as a form of embodied 'skills-capital', or seen, in Zarifian's words, as 'a microcapital', 'a bit of capital forced to valorize itself by its own efforts' (90).

The value of this 'skills-capital' or 'microcapital' cannot be measured by reference to a one-time assessment of a worker's formal qualifications that render her eligible for a fixed hourly rate of pay. This characteristically disciplinary mechanism, in which salary is based on fixed units of labour power multiplied by labour time, gives way to a modulated system of control in which a significant proportion of every worker's remuneration is *variable* and *contingent*. As a documentary broadcast on France Inter in September 2018 revealed, up to 50 per cent of call centre workers' salaries depends on a combination of sales performance and average scores in customer satisfaction surveys, every interaction with a client being evaluated by an online questionnaire.[1] The immaterial aspects of call centre work are thus solicited by a form of 'asservissement' or 'servo-servitude', which pushes workers to become 'entrepreneurs of the self', forever modulating their behaviour, speech, and personal characteristics in response to regularly updated feedback from customers and the market. The systematic use of online rating sites and customer satisfaction surveys across the service sector means ever more workers are subject to this kind of 'servo-servitude'. These phenomena also affect the manufacturing sector insofar as JIT and TQM techniques seek to transform relationships between different stations on a production line into those between suppliers and customers, hence enabling constant internal evaluations of the performance of, for example, the paint shop by windscreen or engine fitters further down the line. Moreover, *kaizen* or 'continuous improvement' techniques mean that assembly-line workers are now eligible for bonuses that reward the quality of their suggestions for improving the production process.

As we have noted, Zarifian argues that in the contemporary workplace the logics of modulated control that govern immaterial labour co-exist, in a contradictory fashion, with forms of Taylorist–Fordist discipline, whose intensification is facilitated by developments in information technology. Indeed, he suggests that it is precisely

80   *Republican Citizens, Precarious Subjects*

this co-existence of contradictory logics that explains 'phenomena of psychic exhaustion at work'. For France Télécom's call centre operatives are confronted by a series of contradictory injunctions, first, to spend as little time with each caller, second to sell them as many new products as possible and, third, to take the time, to invest sufficient affective and relational labour, so as to cultivate lasting relationships with every customer based on trust (17).

In short, then, Zarifian's fieldwork does uncover a shift away from disciplinary to more modulated forms of control, a shift inherent to the increasing reliance on skills rather than formal qualifications in the contemporary French workplace. However, he emphasises that this is not a simple, linear process but a highly contradictory one and that the inherent difficulties of negotiating such contradictions constitute the primary source of increased levels of workplace suffering, stress, and burn-out. Faced with the increasing incidence of such phenomena, it is, to quote Zarifian (2009:39–40), 'always tempting to lament the passing of older forms (the warmth of the old trades, the reserve of the Taylorised worker)'. However, as he rightly warns, this would be to forget the repressive nature of earlier disciplinary mechanisms and the extent to which they were characterised by precisely their refusal to recognise any forms of worker knowledge or capacity outside those that were prescribed by management or formalised in official qualifications. The problem is that under a skills-based model of management, the personal aptitudes and affects of each worker are not really nurtured and valued. Rather, these are solicited only to be disciplined and submitted to the narrowly instrumentalist tenets of human capital theory. As the co-existence of intensified forms of Taylorist–Fordist discipline with more modulated logics of post-disciplinary control clearly demonstrates, any recognition of workers' skills has taken place in a context still dominated by profit-maximising imperatives and has hence been subordinated to those imperatives. The new emphasis on skills has thus produced paradoxical forms of what Thomas Coutrot terms 'controlled autonomy' (quoted in Kokoreff and Rodriguez 2012:98). This contradictory injunction that workers demonstrate their autonomy in a rigidly prescribed manner has a direct equivalent in the injunctions now placed on France's unemployed to cultivate their autonomy and employability by following rigidly disciplinary prescriptions.

The Jobseeker as Entrepreneur of the Self

Foucault (2004:203) has provided a concise summary of the philosophy behind the French welfare state when it was first established, arguing that it was based on 'the model of national solidarity, a model which consists in asking people neither why what has happened to them happened nor which economic category they belong to. Whatever happens to an individual in terms of a deficit, an accident, or a misfortune of whatever kind must, at all events, be taken care of by the collectivity as a whole in the name of national solidarity'. As we have noted, in France this model of national solidarity was realised through the peculiarly corporatist structures of a benefits system based around contributions to workplace insurance schemes of different kinds, so that welfare was articulated with the disciplinary forms of the Fordist workplace in a very particular way.

Zarifian (2009:80–81) has argued that in its contemporary form, the French welfare system has departed in significant ways from the original model outlined by Foucault. On the one hand, jobseekers and benefit claimants of all kinds are now subjected to intensified forms of discipline that oblige them, for example, to provide evidence they are actively seeking work or risk losing benefits. On the other hand, jobseekers are increasingly subjected to more individualising forms of 'control of [their] commitment' that oblige them to remodel their own selves, to modulate their professional identities and stocks of human capital in accordance with the changing demands of the labour market. The contradictory combination of disciplinary and post-disciplinary techniques Zarifian identifies in the contemporary workplace is thus also observable in the domain of welfare.

If there is a package of legislative reforms that best exemplify Zarifian's point here, it is surely the changes to the rights and responsibilities of the unemployed passed in the early years of the Sarkozy presidency (2007–12). In August 2008, a 'Law Regarding the Rights and Responsibilities of Jobseekers' was passed that stipulated that any jobseeker who refused more than two 'reasonable' job offers would henceforth risk losing their rights to unemployment benefit for two months. 'Reasonable' was defined as corresponding to jobseekers' qualifications and experience and offering at least 95 per cent of their former salary if they had been unemployed between three and six months, a percentage that fell as the length of unemployment

82   *Republican Citizens, Precarious Subjects*

increased. Jobseekers would henceforth also have to draw up 'a personalized plan for accessing employment' with an advisor at France's national employment service, a plan that detailed jobseekers' skills and experience, as well as the actions they committed to undertaking in order to secure employment – training, CV-writing sessions, type and number of job applications, and so on. In December of 2008, ASSEDIC (Association for Employment in Industry and Trade), the organisation that managed French unemployment insurance, collecting contributions and distributing benefits, was merged with the national unemployment service, ANPE (National Employment Agency), to form the new organisation Pôle Emploi, in a move that institutionalised the new emphasis on the conditionality of unemployment benefits on the active search for work. Finally, in the same month a new benefit, the RSA (*Revenu de solidarité active* or Active Solidarity Income), was introduced, open to claimants who lacked sufficient accumulated contributions to qualify for work-based unemployment insurance payments. The RSA was also intended to help avoid poverty traps by providing a supplementary source of income to those unemployed who managed to secure part-time or low-paid jobs, ensuring that accepting such employment would not lead to a decrease in their real income through loss of benefits.[2] RSA claimants have to sign a contract committing them to taking the necessary steps to secure employment stipulated in their 'personalized plan for accessing employment', again with the threat of suspension of payments should those commitments not be met (Grandguillot 2009).[3]

Taken together, these various reforms represent a fundamental shift in the way in which the French State understands the rights of the unemployed and, by extension, in the manner in which it enjoins them to think of themselves. The unemployed are no longer conceived as citizens, who possess rights to social insurance against accidents and risks that are out of their control, in accordance with the principle of social solidarity. Rather, they are figured in a much more individualised fashion as personally responsible for their own employability and hence having the right to welfare benefits only insofar as they demonstrate continuing efforts to improve that employability, to cultivate and replenish their portfolio of skills or stock of human capital. The name of the RSA is revealing in this respect. Its reference to 'solidarity' evokes long-established French republican principles, as elaborated, for example, in Durkheim's *De la division du travail social* in which corporatist

Modulating Work and Welfare   83

structures are posited as guarantees of the Republic's 'organic solidarity'. As we noted in the Introduction, Durkheim's corporatist vision was a fundamental source of inspiration for the post-war French model of social welfare. However, the RSA qualifies that established republican value of 'solidarity' with the adjective 'active', itself an allusion to the rise of so-called 'activation' policies in the developed economies since the 1990s. Activation policies reflect the assumption that governments must implement measures to ensure the unemployed actively seek work, for fear they claim benefits merely as a so-called lifestyle choice (Dermine and Dumont 2014). The very name of the RSA thus exemplifies the inflection of older values of corporatist, collective solidarity that it enacts. In its contractualism, the RSA also embodies the shift to more individualised, modulated modes of governmentality, even as the sanctions it threatens for non-compliance reflect an intensification of disciplinary techniques.

As Nicolas Duvoux argues, these kinds of measure 'confront claimants with a veritable "injunction to be autonomous"', soliciting a paradoxical form of 'disciplined autonomy' (in Paugam and Duvoux, eds. 2008:43–44). The paradoxical nature of the 'disciplined autonomy' inherent to these new activation policies, the extent to which they can engender new forms of subjective precarity in the unemployed, and the manner in which they are intimately related to the shift from qualifications to skills are all captured in a pivotal scene in Stéphane Brizé's 2015 feature film, *La Loi du marché*. The film focuses on the travails of a middle-aged, unemployed, machine-tool operator, Thierry (Vincent Lindon), as he struggles, first, to find a new job in manufacturing and, then, to adapt to the different demands of service-sector employment. In one scene we see Thierry attending one of his compulsory employability training sessions. Thierry has been filmed undertaking a role-play exercise in the form of a practice interview. Under the guidance of an employability counsellor, Thierry and a group of fellow jobseekers are watching the video recording of his interview performance, commenting on his personal appearance, posture, approachability, commitment, and motivation.

Encouraged by the counsellor, the jobseekers thus criticise Thierry's most personal attributes. Thierry himself is obliged to partake in a kind of self-critique, reflecting on his own strengths and weaknesses, transforming his personal characteristics and emotions into 'objects of labour', to quote Brunel once again, engaging in a kind of refashioning

84   *Republican Citizens, Precarious Subjects*

of his own self to align it more completely to the demands of the contemporary labour market. Thierry's *savoir-faire*, his qualifications and experience as a skilled machine-tool operator are ignored here; what matters is his *savoir-être*, the more intangible skills, personal attributes, and immaterial dispositions now routinely demanded by employers. Thus, the employability counsellor invites the assembled jobseekers to assess Thierry's performance using a set of criteria that range from his 'general posture' to more psychological attributes:

> *Counsellor:* As far as his personability goes, what did you think?
> *Jobseeker #1:* A bit cold, I thought, a bit distant. He didn't smile much.
> *Counsellor:* Absolutely. Very good. In real life would you want to speak to the Thierry that we can see in the video?
> *Jobseeker #2:* Personally, no.
> *Counsellor:* Personability is very useful in interviews. The idea here is to establish a good feeling [*un bon feeling*] with the recruiter because, during the interview, the recruiter is trying to imagine you in the job. I don't know what you think yourself?
> *Thierry:* Yes, yes, I agree.
> *Counsellor:* As for his expression, what do you think?
> *Jobseeker #3:* Pensive, as if he wasn't there. He seemed to be avoiding the interviewer's gaze. You felt he wasn't really opening himself up and that he was just answering the questions, not investing himself.
> *Counsellor:* Very good. OK. What about the volume at which he spoke?

That this represents a profoundly alienating, intrusive experience for Thierry is emphasised by Brizé's camerawork. Throughout most of the scene, the camera remains in medium close-up on Thierry, occasionally panning slightly to the left or the right to track the source of the comments of his fellow jobseekers, who nonetheless remain largely outside of the frame. This allows the viewer to focus on Thierry's emotional reactions, his downcast eyes, his evident discomfiture, his largely mute submission to the imperative that he integrate all of this feedback into a refashioned, more motivated, employable version of his old self.

Brizé's fictional depiction of an employability training session thus perfectly illustrates the manner in which a man such as Thierry is

Modulating Work and Welfare   85

enjoined to modulate not only his professional identity but also his personal sense of self in response to the changing demands of the market. As we have argued, this shift from mould to modulation challenges more established French republican notions according to which workers were primarily interpellated as members of a professional corporation, membership of which depended on certain formal qualifications while guaranteeing a range of collective rights. This shift away from the disciplinary, corporatist mechanisms of Fordism to the more modulated techniques of post-Fordist control has been mirrored in a series of reforms to the French Labour Code under the successive presidencies of Sarkozy, Hollande, and Macron. These reforms, which all involve the adoption of forms of so-called 'flexicurity', have further challenged the corporatist bases of the French post-war compromise in at least two distinct ways. First, they have institutionalised a vision of workers no longer as members of a professional corporation with certain guaranteed rights but rather as atomised individuals embarked on an open-ended 'career path', in the course of which they will be expected constantly to modulate their skills, human capital, and terms and conditions, as they move between periods of employment, unemployment, and retraining. Second, this constant modulation has now to be negotiated in a process of 'social dialogue' that intentionally bypasses the tripartite structures of collective bargaining between unions, State, and employers that had formed one of the keystones of the post-war compromise.

Successive governments have justified these reforms by arguing they extend social protection to workers engaged in flexible and atypical forms of work, who have been poorly protected by a corporatist model that was designed for an era of full employment. As we argued in the Introduction, the French model of social welfare is indeed ill-equipped to deal with the proliferation of atypical forms of labour characteristic of post-Fordism. The kinds of flexicurity introduced by successive French governments are thus responses to genuine flaws in that model. However, these forms of flexicurity are dominated by the essentially neo-liberal assumption that labour flexibility holds the key to combatting high unemployment. Hence, rather than simply extending protections to workers in atypical employment, these reforms actively seek to produce a workforce that accepts precarious, flexible employment as inevitable. At the same time, the French left and the labour movement have struggled to unite around an alternative

86   *Republican Citizens, Precarious Subjects*

reform agenda that might produce a more progressive model of work and welfare, better adapted to the current conjuncture.

From Corporatism to Flexicurity

As we noted in the Introduction, the peculiarly corporatist structures of the French welfare state were not much contested in the decades of full employment that followed the Liberation. However, through the course of the 1980s and 1990s, as high long-term unemployment and youth unemployment became apparently permanent features of French society, that changed. Work-based unemployment insurance schemes, dependent on contributions from their members, struggled to cover payments to the massively increased number of unemployed. As a result, over the course of the 1980s, those who had contributed to such schemes saw their entitlement to benefits become more dependent on their history of contributions and more time limited. Those whose poor employment records meant they had never accumulated significant contributions or whose long-term unemployment meant they had exhausted their rights to unemployment insurance came to rely on the so-called 'minima sociaux', of which the RSA is but one example. A secondary or supplementary set of much less generous welfare benefits has thus emerged since the 1980s, financed out of general taxation rather than employee and employer contributions to a work-based insurance fund.

As we saw in the Introduction, this means that the dualisation of the French job market is mirrored and institutionalised in a dualised welfare system that delivers generous benefits to a core of workers with stable employment histories, according to established republican principles of corporatism and *solidarity*. The periphery of workers in more precarious, flexible forms of employment, by contrast, have to rely on the less generous forms of *social assistance* delivered by the 'minima sociaux' (Paugam and Duvoux 2008). The young and the long-term unemployed suffer particularly from this inegalitarian dualisation of the French welfare system since they are overrepresented among those forced to accept 'atypical' work contracts (temporary contracts, agency work, internships) that lack the protections and welfare rights that permanent contracts have typically guaranteed in post-war France.

Modulating Work and Welfare   87

The measures of flexicurity introduced during the presidencies of Sarkozy, Hollande, and Macron purport to address this problem, enabling workers with atypical employment histories to accumulate and preserve welfare rights as they move between periods of employment, sporadic unemployment, or continuing education. As a result, such measures have begun to institutionalise the emerging conception of workers constantly modulating their professional identities, updating their stocks of human capital in periods of unemployment, self-regulating in response to changing market conditions in a feedback loop characteristic of Deleuzean control.

The major labour reform Sarkozy passed in 2008 included two modest steps towards a form of flexicurity. First, a new form of redundancy was introduced, so-called 'contractual redundancy', according to which if workers and their employers come to a mutual agreement then the former can retain their rights to unemployment insurance having been made redundant without the need for judicial scrutiny. Second, rights to health insurance were made more portable and opened to those with a much shorter history of contributions (one year as against the previous three) (Cahuc and Zylberberg 2009:41–66). These first steps in the direction of flexicurity would be extended by two reforms under the Hollande presidency, the 2013 'Law on Making Employment More Secure' and the highly controversial El Khomri Law of 2016.

The 2013 law included a number of measures that clearly attempt to address the greater flexibility of the French labour market and the consequent greater mobility of French workers. It approached these phenomena from two angles, motivated both by the desire to encourage workers to accept such mobility as a positive feature of their working lives and an attempt to provide more comprehensive welfare coverage for those whose employment histories were hence more patchy, characterised by sporadic periods of unemployment or atypical employment. Thus, there were measures that introduced the notion of 'rechargeable rights', so that jobseekers could maintain their former rights to unemployment insurance 'in case of a return to work following a period of unemployment'. Another measure introduced the notion of 'protected voluntary mobility', enabling employees to go to work for another company in order to diversify and extend their 'career paths', protected by the guarantee of a job at their original employer should they wish to return there. The 2013 law also put in place a mechanism to realise the pre-existing right to permanent education or

88   *Republican Citizens, Precarious Subjects*

training, through the establishment of a 'Personal Training Account' that gave all employees and jobseekers the right to a defined number of hours of free training per year, in order to 'encourage them to take a step back, elaborate and undertake a new career plan'.

The most striking concession workers would afford employers in return for these forms of 'security' came in the form of the so-called 'Agreements to Safeguard Jobs'. These allowed agreements to be reached at the level of the individual firm whereby, if that firm was experiencing economic difficulties, employees would agree to unfavourable changes to their pay, conditions, or working hours in return for a guarantee of no redundancies (Ministère du Travail 2015).

The philosophy behind this package of measures is clearly one of an individualised logic of 'modulation'; workers and the unemployed are figured as being engaged in an open-ended 'career plan' or 'path' in the course of which they must constantly modulate their own capacities, expectations, and social statuses in accordance with changing market conditions. The culmination of this logic is, of course, the 'Agreements to Safeguard Jobs'. These agreements are negotiated at the level of the individual firm, rather than the branch or sector of industrial activity, as had been the established convention in the post-war era. They demand workers modulate their conditions and hours of work, alongside their pay, in order to see off the threat of redundancy. Responsibility for maintaining employment and avoiding redundancy has thus been radically invdividualised here, delegated from the managers of either the national economy or the private enterprise to the individual worker.

The logics of individualisation and modulation contained in the 2013 law would be extended and deepened by the El Khomri Law that the Socialists forced through the French Parliament three years later. As regards training, the 'Personal Training Account' created in 2013 was transformed into a new, universal 'Personal Activity Account'. Two existing 'accounts' had enabled those engaged in dangerous or physically demanding work to build up rights to early retirement and those engaged in voluntary work to build up rights to training. Those two 'accounts' were now amalgamated, along with the earlier 'Personal Training Account', into the new single 'Personal Activity Account'. In the words of the French Labour Ministry's website, this was intended to take account of the fact that 'a career path is rarely linear' by ensuring all workers possessed 'the means to anticipate

Modulating Work and Welfare 89

transitions, whether imposed or freely chosen, in order to be able to bounce back' (Ministère du Travail 2016). In one sense, this measure guarantees important rights to groups or workers and citizens who might otherwise be poorly protected by France's corporatist system of welfare. Yet it also clearly partakes of the tendency to view workers as 'managers' of a personalised stock of 'skills' or human capital that must be constantly replenished and updated in an open-ended process of 'continuing education', in just the manner that Deleuze anticipated (2003:246).

This tendency was also evident in a reform that extended the logic of the 'Agreements to Safeguard Jobs' introduced in 2013. Those agreements quickly gained the nickname 'defensive agreements' since they were justified by reference to the need to *defend* existing jobs. They had, however, met with limited success; by 2016 only ten such agreements had actually been signed. The socialist government thus sought to give new impetus to this initiative by allowing, in the El Khomri Law, for so-called 'aggressive agreements', agreements negotiated at the level of the individual firm in the name of increasing that firm's competitiveness. Workers would agree to unfavourable changes to their terms and conditions no longer in return for a guarantee of no redundancies but to allow their employers to develop new product lines and/or gain new market share, hence eventually, it was hoped, leading to the creation of more jobs (Ray 2017). More specifically, the object of such 'aggressive agreements' would be what the French Labour Ministry itself described as 'the modulation of working time', enabling employers to exceed legal limits on maximum weekly hours worked in any 12-week period of increased competition, new product development, or the search for new markets. Under the pretext of improving 'social dialogue' within French workplaces, agreements to this modulation of legal working hours would be negotiated at the level of the individual firm, rather than at the level of the branch or sector of industrial activity.

As such, these new 'aggressive agreements' struck at the heart of two of the keystones of the French post-war compromise. First, they bypassed the tripartite agreements negotiated between the so-called 'social partners' or 'intermediary bodies', the State, employers, and trades unions, agreements that had been at the core of the post-war French model. Second, they eroded the so-called 'favourability principle', according to which agreements negotiated at the level of

90 *Republican Citizens, Precarious Subjects*

the individual firm could not be less favourable to employees than those agreements signed at the level of the industrial branch or sector. Individual employees who refused to be bound by any such 'aggressive agreement' could hitherto find themselves facing 'redundancy for economic reasons' (Ministère du Travail 2016). It was these measures that proved the most controversial, sparking nationwide opposition to the El Khomri Law when it was first presented to the French public. This is unsurprising, given that such measures seem unambiguously to belong to the 'flexi-' side of the flexicurity equation, increasing labour flexibility while offering little in the way of reinforced security in return.

These tendencies were strengthened by the reforms to the French Labour Code contained in the series of 'ordonnances' or decrees signed by Macron in September 2017. These included a new, all-encompassing 'accord de performance collective' that replaced the existing range of agreements negotiable at the level of individual firms, allowing working hours, remuneration, and employee mobility to be modulated to reflect changing market conditions. Once again, under the pretext of improving 'social dialogue', these agreements bypass the trades unions, those 'intermediary bodies' whose role in negotiating the terms and conditions of French workers at the level of the industrial sector had been a key component of the French post-war model. The 'ordonnances' also include measures to make it easier for firms to shed staff, by placing ceilings on compensation payments for unfair dismissal and allowing firms that are experiencing economic problems purely in France, but nonetheless remain profitable at the international level, to make their French staff redundant. Further, Macron has extended the logic behind the 'contractual redundancy' procedures, introduced in 2008 under Sarkozy, by creating a new 'collective contractual redundancy' procedure that will allow groups of workers to come to collective agreements regarding their own redundancy in return for guaranteed access to unemployment insurance. The clear intention here is to introduce a greater amount of flexibility into the French labour market in the belief this will encourage job creation.

Further measures to both encourage labour mobility and update the French workforce's stock of human capital are included in a new labour law, passed by Macron's government in August 2018. The primary stated aim of the 'Law for the Freedom to Choose Your Professional Future' is the creation of a 'new society of skills' by further rationalising the provision of continuing education. The Law also includes measures that move towards Macron's stated goal of a universal system of unemployment insurance financed out of general taxation, measures that might have contributed to ending welfare dualisation in France. Thus, the Law ratifies a measure taken by Macron in January 2018, replacing employee contributions to unemployment insurance funds with revenue from general taxation. Further, the self-employed will now have access to unemployment insurance, as will those who voluntarily resign from their jobs, provided they can show they did so in pursuit of 'a project for professional development of a real and serious character'. The philosophy behind these last two measures seems clear, namely to encourage labour mobility, while fostering a kind of small-scale entrepreneurialism, so that workers will be encouraged no longer to belong to a single professional corporation, with its attendant status and rights, but rather to embark upon an open-ended, flexible, constantly modulating career path. Finally, these reforms have been accompanied by a reinforcement of the sanctions facing jobseekers judged insufficiently assiduous in their search for work, as well as a commitment to reduce expenditure on unemployment benefits by approximately 3.4 billion euros over the next three years (Foulon 2019:8).

Macron's most recent reforms, then, represent the culmination of a process whereby the corporatist bases of the post-war model of work and welfare have been gradually eroded. Since the mid-1970s, French employers have campaigned to have their contributions to social insurance funds reduced, on the pretext that this will reduce labour costs and encourage new hires. The success of these campaigns, combined with the rising importance of the 'minima sociaux' that are funded out of general taxation, has fundamentally altered the bases on which social welfare is financed in France. Thus, in 1990, 80.1 per cent of the total social protection budget was accounted for by employer and employee contributions combined, with just 3.5 per cent deriving from taxation. By 2013, employer and employee contributions had dropped to 61.9 per cent of the total, with the proportion of funding derived from tax having risen to 25 per cent (DRESS 2015:38–40). Macron's replacement of employee contributions to unemployment insurance funds with tax revenue represents a further step in the direction of a less Bismarckian, more Beveridgean system of welfare. His stated aim of establishing a genuinely universal system of unemployment benefit certainly does respond to significant gaps in existing provision.

92 Republican Citizens, Precarious Subjects

However, it seems that in the transition to such a system the overall level of unemployment payments will be reduced downwards, as the link between benefits and former salary is severed.

Indeed, it would be possible to interpret Macron's labour reforms, like those of Hollande and Sarkozy before him, as amounting to little more than an exercise in neo-liberal deregulation. When considered cumulatively, what is so striking about all these measures is the extent to which they seem to have realised the goals of the infamous, but at the time largely unsuccessful project of 'refondation sociale' launched by the MEDEF in early 2000. The MEDEF's plan involved a fundamental break with the corporatism of the French welfare system, replacing national collective bargaining with localised social dialogue, promoting more individualised forms of health and unemployment insurance, for example (Lallement and Mériaux 2003). One of the initiators of this scheme, François Ewald, had been Foucault's research assistant and he appears to have interpreted his master's analyses of neo-liberal governmentality not as a critique but as a recipe to be followed.[4]

What is clear is that the bypassing of the tripartite structures of collective bargaining in the name of greater 'social dialogue' tapped into a long tradition of criticising the corporatist nature of the French post-war compromise, lamenting the divisiveness of the workplace relations it engendered, with rival professional groups or corporations all allegedly fighting to retain their particular rights and privileges. This, it is argued, explains the extremely combative nature of French labour relations and the absence of the kind of genuine 'social dialogue' to be found in Germany or the Scandinavian countries. This thesis has a long history, having been first elaborated in Michel Crozier's 1964 study *Le Phénomène bureaucratique* and then rehearsed in Philippe d'Iribarne's *La Logique de l'honneur* (1993), a comparative study of workplace cultures in France, the Netherlands, and the United States. Yves Algan, Pierre Cahuc, and André Zylberberg further popularised this thesis in their prize-winning 2012 book, *La Fabrique de la défiance .. et comment s'en sortir*. These criticisms of the corporatist, hence conflictual and hierarchical nature of French workplace relations clearly influenced the report on collective bargaining prepared by Jean-Denis Combrexelle for then Prime Minister Manuel Valls in late 2015, a report whose recommendations fed directly into the El Khomri Law. In short, the El Khomri Law's measures regarding local negotiation and 'social dialogue' partake of a long tradition of criticising the corporatist nature of French work and welfare. That tradition has sought to undermine any conception of such workers as endowed with a collective or corporatist identity that guarantees them certain welfare rights, in favour of a more liberal conception of workers as individual subjects, who negotiate their terms and conditions at the local level.

The kinds of flexicurity introduced under Macron, Hollande, and Sarkozy thus all aim at transforming French citizens into 'entrepreneurs of the self', constantly cultivating and replenishing their personalised stocks of human capital in just the way that Foucault envisioned in his lectures on neo-liberalism. The lexicon employed in the recent reforms to the French Labour Code is itself highly revealing of this shift. Any mention of *métier*, of collective identity, or of fixed professional status, with its attendant social rights and protections, has been abandoned in favour of a vocabulary of 'trajectories', 'career paths', and 'projects', a vocabulary that communicates a much greater sense of individualism and mobility. To employ Deleuze's conceptual terminology, the 'mould' of post-war Fordism has been replaced by a constant 'modulation' in response to changing labour demand, as workers are expected to cultivate and replenish their stock of personalised 'skills', as they move between periods of employment, unemployment, and continuing education. This process of continuing education will be open-ended, never ending, so that, to quote Deleuze (2003:243), 'in societies of control, one is never finished with anything – the firm, training [...] being metastable states coexisting in one and the same modulation, like a universal system of deformation'.

On one level, this shift to conceiving employment as a 'path', punctuated by periods of continuing education, need not be seen as inherently regressive. Indeed, this might be viewed as eminently preferable to Fordism, in which workers spent decades performing the same mindless tasks on an assembly line. The problem, however, is the coercive and narrowly instrumental nature of this new model. The education envisaged here is not the disinterested pursuit of knowledge. It is the accumulation of 'skills' or human capital in an 'account' – the economic metaphors are revealing here – as part of an imperative placed on every citizen to render themselves more employable or face monetary sanctions, in the form of the loss of job or welfare benefits. It is in this sense that we can understand Deleuze's (237) claim that the never-ending nature of continuing education represents a 'terrible' prospect.

94 Republican Citizens, Precarious Subjects

Uberisation and Servo-servitude

As we have shown, the shift from a 'qualifications model' to a 'skills-based model' in the French workplace, the invention of the RSA, the creation of Pôle Emploi all share this same logic. Together with recent reforms to the Labour Code, these developments seek to institutionalise a conception of French workers as constantly self-regulating in response to changing market conditions, like servomechanisms responding to external stimuli in a feedback loop. As Michel Feher (2017:142–46) points out, the workers who are obliged to realise this new model of subjectivity most fully are surely those who work on a freelance basis for an Internet platform, as Uber drivers, bicycle couriers, or fast-food delivery workers. Their freelance status gives them few guaranteed legal protections or welfare rights. Their hours and conditions of labour forever vary in response to immediate changes in demand. As 'entrepreneurs of the self' they must constantly manage their personal stock of human or reputational capital since their future income is so dependent on the quality of the permanently updated reviews delivered by their customers via the web.

Licensed taxi drivers are regulated by a characteristically disciplinary apparatus, dependent on municipal authorities to deliver them an operator's licence based on a formal assessment of their capacities against a fixed norm. Uber drivers, by contrast, are subject to no-such hierarchical gaze or single normative sanction. Rather, they are subjected to a form of 'contrôle continu', or continuous assessment, to use Deleuze's (2003:243) term, exerted no longer by a single authority but by a much broader constituency composed of all their past and future customers. In our discussion of the employability training session in *La Loi du marché*, we argued that Thierry was depicted being forced to modulate his personal and professional selves in response to the feedback he received from his fellow jobseekers. For Uber drivers this process of modulation and refashioning is constant, never-ending, as customer ratings are updated daily, even hourly. Like the servo-mechanisms in a control system, Uber drivers must integrate this constantly changing feedback, modulating their speech, behaviour, appearance, their very selves, accordingly. Uber drivers are thus subject to a particularly intensified form of what Deleuze terms 'asservissement' and what we have chosen to translate as 'servo-servitude'.

Modulating Work and Welfare 95

In its 2017 report on the platform economy, the *Conseil d'état* suggests that the best way to regulate these new 'uberised' forms of work is not to draw on the French corporatist tradition by creating a new professional status, with its associated special social insurance funds. Rather the *Conseil* advocates expanding on the logic of the Personal Activity Account created by the El Khomri Law, so that platform workers' welfare rights are attached to their person, rather than their professional status, and they accumulate portable welfare rights in an individual account (Conseil d'État 2017:89). This notion that the corporatist forms of the post-war compromise may not represent the best way of regulating the new forms of salaried employment is echoed by Feher. He argues that the struggles of Uber drivers and bicycle couriers to have their status as employees legally recognised do not reflect their desire to be constrained by more traditional kinds of work contract or professional status. Citing a published interview with Jérôme Pimot, of the French Bicycle Couriers Collective, he shows that the aim of such struggles is not to recreate corporatist forms of professional status and welfare rights, as these risk eroding the freedoms that flexible work patterns nonetheless do offer these workers. Rather, the ultimate goal of activists like Pimot is to drive the platforms to bankruptcy, so that they can then be taken over by their employees and run as cooperatives. The hope is that, through strike action, platform workers will undermine the profitability of their employers by increasing their wage costs, hence provoking the withdrawal of venture capitalists, who only continue to bankroll these firms, despite significant initial losses, because of a combination of low wage bills and the promise of future monopolies (Feher 2017:154–56).

The goals of French uberised workers, as they are described by Feher, represent one attempt to overcome the exploitative nature of contemporary forms of flexible labour not by returning to the corporatism of the French post-war model but by working within and against the terms of the current conjuncture. A different attempt to achieve this can be found in Moulier Boutang's advocacy of replacing existing corporatist forms of welfare with a universal guaranteed income. Set at a suitably high level, not only would this income ease transitions between periods of employment and unemployment, it would also enable citizens to refuse any work contract whose terms and conditions were excessively exploitative. Such a universal income would also allow those not in salaried employment to pursue genuinely

96 *Republican Citizens, Precarious Subjects*

disinterested forms of training or education, rather than the narrowly instrumental forms of skills acquisition promoted by existing forms of flexicurity (Moulier Boutang 2007:221–43).

Christophe Ramaux, by contrast, rejects such calls for a guaranteed income, arguing that, in common with all forms of flexicurity, such proposals rest on the faulty assumption that flexible and atypical forms of work are the inevitable results of immutable economic forces, rather than being the products of a sustained campaign of neo-liberal de-regulation. Ramaux (2006) advocates a return to Keynesian policies of full employment through effective demand management as the only sure way to secure the welfare of all French citizens.

Bernard Friot (2017) is similarly dismissive of both flexicurity and guaranteed income, seeing both as constituents of what he terms 'the capitalist counter-revolution'. He advocates a deepening of the principles on which the French social security system was founded in 1946, calling for the establishment of a series of collectively managed funds, based on the model of the 'régime général' established in that year. Thus, the majority of company profits would be collectively managed in three separate funds, the first of which would channel productive investments, bypassing speculative private finance, the second of which would fund public services, and the third of which would deliver a universal 'salary for life'. The level of that salary would be based on a democratic, objective assessment of 'each worker's qualification', itself a collective recognition of each adult's 'contribution to the production of value', whether retired, employed, unemployed, salaried, or self-employed. Friot's (2017) proposals thus represent both a return to the principles of the corporatist post-war compromise and a radicalisation of those principles in what he himself describes as a 'communist' direction.

The influential sociologist of work, Dominique Méda, meanwhile, has advocated returning to the question of reducing working time and hence more equitably sharing out available employment. In a book she co-authored with Pierre Larrouturou in 2016, she advocates exploring this avenue in preference to seeking to create jobs by pursuing what she sees as the illusory goal of continued economic growth (Méda and Larrouturou 2016). Hence, she signals her disagreement with Ramaux's calls for a return to Keynesian policies of economic growth and effective demand management as the solutions to mass unemployment and precarious forms of labour.

If French left-wing intellectuals appear divided on the issue of how best to respond to the profusion of precarious forms of labour, French trades unions are no more united on this issue. From 2006 on, the centrist union, the CFDT (*Confédération française démocratique du travail*), has supported a form of flexicurity it terms 'la sécurisation des parcours professionnels [making career paths more secure]'. The CFDT thus advocates increasing the portability of accumulated welfare rights and extending workers' rights to continuing education, so that all workers might become the 'agents of their own career paths', able to dedicate sporadic periods of unemployment to renewing and replenishing their stock of 'skills' (Grimault 2008:78–79). The more left-wing, historically communist trades union, the CGT (*Confédération générale du travail*), meanwhile, has adopted a position influenced by Bernard Friot's work. Thus, the CGT advocates what they term 'occupational social security', according to which workers made redundant through no fault of their own would continue to receive a wage and to accumulate welfare rights. This is effectively a wage for life and would be funded out of employers' and employees' contributions to the existing social insurance funds (Grimault 2008:77–78).

This brief survey of the positions taken by a variety of intellectuals and trades unions on these issues is by no means exhaustive. However, it does usefully highlight the extent of the divisions on the French left regarding both how best to respond to the current conjuncture and what the precise terms of any new social compromise might be. In the absence of any such consensus or shared project, behind which workers, the unemployed, and politicians might mobilise, it seems that the shift away from the corporatist 'mould' of post-war Fordism towards the more modulated forms of post-Fordist 'control' is destined to be experienced as profoundly disruptive and exploitative. In such circumstances, these developments are likely to be understood as amounting to little more than the erosion of the apparently more stable forms of republican- corporatist citizenship and their replacement by more precarious forms of subjectivity.

Over this and the preceding chapter we have identified a range of different manifestations of this widening gap between established models of republican citizenship and contemporary forms of precarious subjectivity. In the first chapter we noted how a range of economic and political developments, at global, national, and local level, had undermined the ability of the French Republic to intervene in the

98   *Republican Citizens, Precarious Subjects*

national economy to secure growth and jobs for its citizens. We also noted the ways in which the tertiarisation and financialisation of the French economy, along with the rise in immaterial forms of labour, were placing French workers and citizens under new pressures. In this second chapter, we examined claims that there has been a shift away from a disciplinary mode of governmentality to a Deleuzean 'society of control', analysing the logics of modulation behind a range of changes in both management practice and the legal regulation of unemployment, work, and welfare. We demonstrated that the corporatist terms of the French post-war compromise have been significantly reformulated in a manner that can indeed be seen to have eroded older collective identities and their attendant social rights and protections. In all cases we emphasised the unevenness of these developments – global and financial shifts have enriched some regions of France and impoverished others; the rise of immaterial labour takes different forms, quantitatively and qualitatively, in different sectors of the economy and cannot be subsumed under the rubric of a uniform shift to 'cognitive capitalism'; the advent of more modulated forms of control has gone hand-in-hand with the intensification of disciplinary techniques.

What does unite these varied and uneven developments is that they all pose a threat to established notions of republican citizenship. As we turn in subsequent chapters to analyse cultural representations of these phenomena – in feature films, novels, documentaries, testimonials, and journalistic reportage – it will be possible to see more clearly how this tension between republican citizenship and precarious subjectivity has been narrativised to produce a range of recurrent tropes, of character types, educational and career trajectories that are played out against uneven regional, national, and global geographies. This corpus of cultural representations thus offers important insights into the diverse ways in which authors and filmmakers have made sense of these shifts in their various accounts of the struggles of French citizens of different sexes, classes, ethnicities, and age groups to modulate their professional and personal identities to meet the demands of the contemporary workplace.

Notes

1 'Tous évalués, tous menacés', France Inter, 9 septembre 2018, www.franceinter.fr/emissions/interception/interception-09-septembre-2018, accessed 1 August 2019.

2 This element of the RSA, the so-called 'RSA activité', was replaced in January 2016 by the 'Prime d'activité [Activity Bonus]'.

3 As Tim Vlandas (2013) points out, elements of this kind of conditionality had been included in the earlier benefit that the RSA replaced, the RMI (Revenu minimum d'insertion). However, those sanctions had never been systematically enforced.

4 The precise attitude of Foucault towards neo-liberalism, as well as the role played by his assistant, Ewald, remain contentious topics. For a range of more detailed interpretations of both questions, see Zamora and Behrent (2016).

Part Two

Character Types, Trajectories, Uneven Geographies

Chapter 3

Modulated Masculinities

Benoît Delépine and Gustave Kervern's 2010 film *Mammuth* is a kind of surreally comic road movie that centres on the efforts of the recently retired Serge Pilardosse (Gérard Depardieu) to contact his previous employers in order to collect the proof of employment necessary to qualify for a full pension. As Serge drives along the French Atlantic coast on his classic German 'Mammoth' motorbike, the workplaces he visits represent a compendium of traditional embodiments of French national identity – an abattoir producing charcuterie, a mill producing flour for bread, a vineyard, and a Catholic church, among others. The film suggests that the flexible working practices Serge observes in the workplaces he visits have combined with his own retirement to provoke some kind of crisis in both French national identity and conventional notions of masculinity. On the first day of his retirement, we witness a Serge feminised, as he attempts and fails to control a shopping trolley in the car park of the supermarket where his wife has sent him to do the weekly shopping, while she goes out to work. Later, Serge visits the flour mill at which he had worked as an apprentice miller. He is perplexed to discover that the mill has been painted bright pink and taken over by a firm specialising in 3-D storyboards that glories in the English name of 'Funny Rabbit'. A heated discussion follows via the firm's entry-phone between Serge and a female receptionist. The receptionist tells him she understands nothing of flour milling, before informing Serge that 'everything has been digitised' and that he should therefore 'go onto our site', if he wants to track down his employment records. Misunderstanding the receptionist's reference to the firm's website, Serge replies, bewildered: 'Your site? But I'm already on your site!'

104   *Republican Citizens, Precarious Subjects*

As Cristina Morini (2007:42) has argued, the immaterial skills demanded of workers in the burgeoning tertiary sector, 'capacities for relationships, emotional aspects, linguistic aspects, propensity for care', are widely coded as being inherently feminine. This feminisation of labour is clearly communicated in this scene, in which a form of masculine artisanal labour, rooted in and emblematic of French national identity, is depicted as having been displaced by a feminised, deterritorialised, dematerialised service sector activity carried out by a company with a jarringly 'Anglo-Saxon' name. This displacement is signified visually by the striking contrast between Serge's hulking physical presence, on the one hand, and the bright pink former flour mill from which issues the disembodied voice of the female receptionist, on the other. This contrast between solidity and disembodiment, masculinity and femininity emphasises quite how out of place this working-class man is in the new world of dematerialised, feminised, and tertiarised production.

Recent French films and novels offer a multitude of analogous examples of middle-aged male workers who find themselves displaced, struggling to modulate their masculine identity in accordance with the demands of a contemporary labour market characterised by the profusion of more immaterial forms of work. Often, the effects of these struggles spill over from the workplace, challenging their masculinity and threatening to undermine their roles as heads of their nuclear families. In some cases, as with *Mammuth*, these are workers in late middle age who have taken or been forced into some kind of early retirement. In Robert Guédiguian's *Les Neiges du Kilimandjaro* (2011), the middle-aged trade unionist and committed socialist Michel (Jean-Pierre Darroussin) agrees to take redundancy from a Marseilles shipyard to preserve the job of a younger worker. He is now forced to spend his days looking after his grandchildren and doing the shopping while his wife works as a care assistant. Abdellatif Kechiche's *La Graine et le mulet* (2007) focuses on the travails of Slimane (Habib Boufares), a 61-year-old Maghrebi shipyard worker. Divorced, redundant, and struggling to exert his authority over his wayward sons, Slimane will attempt in vain to re-establish his socio-economic and familial role by setting himself up as a restaurant owner. Stéphane Brizé's 2015 film, *La Loi du marché*, focuses on a slightly younger worker, unemployed machine tool operator Thierry (Vincent Lindon), who struggles to adopt the more open, personable, engaged persona that will enable him

Modulated Masculinities 105

to find a service-sector job and hence support his wife and disabled son. The protagonist of Thierry Beinstingel's novel *Retour aux mots sauvages* (2010) is a middle-aged former telecoms technician who has been forced to accept a new post working in one of his firm's call centres and who experiences this career change as a kind of feminisation. Delépine and Kervern's 2014 film *Near Death Experience* also centres on the travails of a male middle-aged call centre worker. Paul, played by the celebrated novelist Michel Houellebecq, leaves his family home one afternoon, apparently for a brief cycle ride in the country but actually to contemplate suicide.

Depictions of middle-aged male workers in crisis have by no means been limited to those in working-class or petty bourgeois occupations; they have also involved a significant number of French male business executives. In Francis Veber's broad comedy *Le Placard* (2001), Daniel Auteil plays a middle-aged accountant, François Pignon, who is estranged from his wife and teenage son and sidelined in his professional life by the two female colleagues with whom he shares an office. Threatened with redundancy, Pignon is only able to save his job by pretending to be gay, that is to say by performing what the film figures, in a highly conservative manner, as a fundamentally effeminate professional identity. Ostensibly a parody of political correctness, *Le Placard* also works as an allegory of the pressures placed on employees to produce and perform a version of themselves adapted to the demands of feminised immaterial labour. A more serious approach to these issues is offered by Laurent Cantet's *L'Emploi du temps* (2001), the tale of Vincent (Aurélien Recoing), an unemployed financial consultant who hides his lack of job from his family and friends by pretending to be employed in international development at the United Nations (UN), funding his lifestyle by, first, running a Ponzi investment scheme and, second, smuggling counterfeit branded goods into France and Switzerland from Eastern Europe. Like *Le Placard*'s Pignon, Vincent must thus feign or perform a fictive professional identity, and the psychological effort this involves undermines his roles as husband to his wife and father to his teenage son.

One of the most moving recent depictions of the contemporary French workplace is offered by Jean-Marc Moutout's 2010 film, *De Bon Matin*. In the film, middle-aged bank executive and family man Paul Wertret (Jean-Pierre Darroussin) is marginalised and humiliated by a new management regime brought in in the wake of his bank's

106 *Republican Citizens, Precarious Subjects*

disastrous losses in the subprime crisis. His resulting depression first undermines his relationships with his wife and son before pushing him to take violent revenge. Having bought a pistol, he goes to work one morning and shoots two of his tormentors, before turning the gun on himself.

Recent French films and novels thus offer a multitude of middle-aged male protagonists who are struggling to adapt to the demands of the contemporary workplace. In all cases, these men are portrayed as being forced to adopt less stable, more precarious professional, social, and familial identities. The forms of precarity they confront range from the objective or material threat of redundancy and unemployment to the more subjective precarity inherent in the imperative they engage in more immaterial, affective-relational forms of labour. Repeatedly, these immaterial forms of labour are figured as posing a threat to their masculinity and to their roles as the heads of their respective families. Sometimes, these new forms of labour and the management discourses that promote them are also figured as posing a threat to French national identity, insofar as they are depicted as representing the imposition of a fundamentally foreign set of values inimical to French traditions of language, culture, social solidarity, and conviviality.

As we have noted in earlier chapters, the male breadwinner and head of family played a central role in post-war Fordism, a role institutionalised in the form of the generous child benefits that encouraged women to adopt subordinate roles as mothers and housewives. The socio-economic pre-eminence of the male breadwinner and head of family was thus inherent to the terms of the French post-war compromise with its associated forms of republican–corporatist welfare. The significant shifts in the labour market that have undermined that post-war compromise have involved a modulation in men's socio-economic pre-eminence and hence a displacement of their former centrality. At the most general level, then, the striking recurrence of depictions of middle-aged male workers in crisis reflects the anxieties provoked by that modulation and displacement. This reshaping of masculinity and the patriarchal family, along with the anxieties it has generated, is not solely attributable to economic shifts, however. As Robert Castel (2009:47n.2) points out, the breakdown of the model of the nuclear family has accompanied very closely the erosion of stable models of lifelong employment, 'without it nonetheless being possible to establish a strict causal relationship' between these two phenomena.

Modulated Masculinities   107

In other words, the reshaping of the patriarchal family and consequent proliferation of non-traditional family units have a range of different determinants, of which the decline in Fordist employment is but one.[1] Others include those more progressive cultural shifts and political movements that have secured greater equality for women and sexual minorities. That those more progressive forces have contributed to the undermining of Fordism highlights once more the need to eschew any simple Fordist nostalgia, in favour of a dialectical grasp of the full range of determinants in play here.[2]

As we will see, the manner in which the relationships between these different determinants is depicted varies greatly across our corpus of fictional representations of the contemporary workplace. In the most conservative of these narratives a direct causal relationship is posited between deindustrialisation, the rise of feminised forms of immaterial labour, and the consequent threat to male authority. All are figured as sources of a loss of national prestige that, it is suggested, can only be regained through the restoration of the patriarchal nuclear family as bedrock of the French nation. As this chapter will show, this kind of reactionary response to post-Fordism is epitomised by the work of Michel Houellebecq in novels such as *La Carte et le territoire* (2010).

However, by no means all of the narratives that focus on the travails of male workers share Houellebecq's conservative worldview. The focus on middle-aged men can also reflect the fact that they belong to a generation whose professional identities were formed by the disciplinary and corporatist regime of French post-war Fordism. This is hence a generation of workers for whom the imperative to *modulate* their established professional identities in accordance with the changed demands of the contemporary workplace can prove peculiarly challenging. Focusing on that generation of workers can thus highlight the extent of both the changes in working practice this involves and the psychological pressures it entails. By extension, these middle-aged workers can serve as incarnations of the hopes and dreams that characterised the 'thirty glorious years' of post-war Fordist growth, hopes and dreams now betrayed. Alternatively, as is the case of Michel in *Les Neiges du Kilimandjaro*, these middle-aged workers can be the incarnations of a tradition of working-class struggle for social justice that is increasingly embattled and threatened with extinction. Finally, those narratives that appear to lament the loss of the nuclear family are not always motivated by a purely conservative vision of the patriarchal

108 Republican Citizens, Precarious Subjects

family as essential to the maintenance of social order and hence the health of the nation. Perhaps particularly for individuals from working-class or ethnic minority backgrounds, the family can be an important source of shelter, mutual support, and emotional sustenance in the face of hostile socio-economic realities.

As it examines a range of novelistic and filmic representations of middle-aged male workers, this chapter will seek to elucidate the different ways in which these novels and films figure the relationships between salaried employment, gender, family, and nation. In the first instance, we focus on *La Carte et le territoire*, a novel that, as we have indicated, epitomises a fundamentally conservative approach to these questions, by lamenting what it figures as the deleterious effects of deindustrialisation on masculinity, the family, and the French nation. We then turn to the film *L'Emploi du temps*, arguing that, by contrast, Cantet offers a vision of the contemporary *haut bourgeois* French family not as a potential antidote to the disruptions of globalisation and post-Fordism but rather as one of the very institutions that generates the forms of modulated subjectivity appropriate to executive labour in a globalised financial sector. From Cantet's focus on executive labour in *L'Emploi du temps* we then move to a depiction of a skilled working-class employee, in the form of the protagonist of Thierry Beinstingel's novel *Retour aux mots sauvages*, a former telecoms technician who is forced to adopt what are figured as more feminised forms of affective-relational labour when obliged to accept a new job in his company's call centre. Beinstingel portrays these new forms of affective labour as, paradoxically, provoking the most radical kind of *disaffection*, in the form of a spate of workplace suicides. Finally, the chapter turns to the figure of the middle-aged worker of North African origin, focusing particularly on Kechiche's (2007) film *La Graine et le mulet* to examine how the imperative to adopt more modulated forms of masculine working identity has been inflected by questions of ethnicity and the history of immigration to post-war France.

Over preceding chapters, we have noted that what Danièle Linhart terms 'la surhumanisation managériale', the attempt to capture and exploit employees' most personal attributes, is often understood to necessitate those employees engaging in an alienating *performance* of their professional selves. As we will show, the male protagonists of Cantet's, Beinstingel's, and Kechiche's respective narratives are depicted as being subject to precisely this imperative. Moreover, the alienation they experience as a result of having to perform versions of their professional self appears to be closely correlated to various challenges to their masculinity and/or their role as head of their families. However, Cantet, Beinstingel and Kechiche avoid the kind of nostalgic lament at the erosion of individual masculine power and national industrial prestige that seems to characterise Houellebecq's work. Rather, through their depictions of male workers of different social classes and ethnicities, they offer a variety of insights into the interrelationships between contemporary forms of work, gender, family, and the French national community. All of our chosen narratives react to contemporary challenges to the centrality of the male breadwinner and head of family. Yet the political implications of these various responses to more modulated forms of both masculinity and employment vary widely.

Houellebecq's Fordist Nostalgia

Michel Houellebecq's Goncourt Prize-winning novel *La Carte et le territoire* (2010) represents one of the most influential fictional surveys of post-Fordist forms of work and their relationship to masculinity, the family, and French national identity. Houellebecq does not examine the effects of these phenomena by focusing on the working life of any particular salaried male worker. Rather, he focuses on their effects on the life and artistic practice of artist Jed Martin, whose various artworks seek to record the impact of deindustrialisation on French society as a whole. A key moment in the development of Jed's artistic career occurs early in the novel, when he is struck by the 'sublime' nature of a Michelin map of the Creuse, a map that offers a visual representation of a combination of French industrial-technological prowess and the unchanging values of the French *terroir*:

> This map was sublime; overwhelmed, [Jed] began to tremble in front of the display case. Never had he contemplated such a magnificent object, so rich in emotion and meaning [...]. On the map, the essence of modernity, of the scientific and technical attitude to the world was mixed with the essence of animal life. The design was complex and beautiful; absolutely clear, it relied on a limited palette of colours. But in each of the hamlets

110   *Republican Citizens, Precarious Subjects*

> and villages, represented in proportion to their actual size, one
> could feel the pulsating call of dozens of human lives, dozens or
> hundreds of souls, some destined to damnation, the others to
> eternal life. (Houellebecq 2010:51–52)

What fascinates Jed about the Michelin map is its synthesis of transformative human endeavour with the natural world and it inspires him to make a series of highly successful works that take the form of blown-up photographs of those maps, exhibited alongside satellite photos of the French landscapes they represent. These works enjoy a critical and commercial success that secures Jed's wealth and fame, rapidly becoming 'the preferred manner for their viewers to be initiated into what the daily newspaper *Libération* was shamelessly to call "the magic of the *terroir*"' (88).

It is no coincidence that it should be Michelin maps that have this effect on Jed and his public. Under the impetus of its founder, Marcel Michelin, Michelin was one of the first French firms to import Taylorist and Fordist production techniques from America, while providing a network of extra-mural organisations designed to safeguard the moral and physical welfare of its employees (Tesi 2008). Yet Michelin remained, as the novel's narrator tells us, rooted in a particular French locality, 'based in Clermont-Ferrand from its origins', a family firm, 'rather conservative, even paternalist' (Houellebecq 2010:66). Furthermore, in sponsoring maps, culinary and regional guides, to encourage car use and hence tyre consumption, Michelin became a guarantor of specifically French values of gastronomy, of regional identity and history, able, then, to achieve a miraculous articulation between American mass-production techniques and the French *terroir*.

The 'sublime' quality Jed attributes to the company's maps seems to correspond closely to Edmund Burke's understanding of that term. For Burke, the sublime is a masculine, virile force defined by its opposition to a feminised 'beauty'. An object is beautiful inasmuch as it imitates the order found in nature. Beauty generates 'pleasure' by appealing to a shared or universal taste that can thus, by means of sympathy, form the basis of a harmonious social order. The danger, according to Burke, is that the sympathetic feelings engendered by beauty can generate self-satisfaction, stasis, even decadence. The awesome grandeur of the sublime, by contrast, shakes the observer out of such 'lassitude', 'melancholy', and 'dejection', inspiring in him an 'ambition' to strive to

Modulated Masculinities   111

achieve the 'grand and commanding conception' evident in the sublime object or personified by the 'dread and majesty' of the 'Sovereign' ruler. This galvanising 'terror' that strikes the imagination of the cultivated few on perceiving a sublime object or personage is, moreover, analogous in its salutary effects, for Burke (1990 [1757]:59–64; 109–12; 122–23), to 'common labour' for the masses.

Jed's series of Michelin maps appears to lament the loss of this sublime 'grand and commanding conception', formerly personified by the paternalistic Marcel Michelin. Michelin's technological and industrial activities, once rooted in the French territory and depending on working-class productive labour, have now become dematerialised, deterritorialised, and feminised. Michelin is now owned by and beholden to *foreign* institutional investors, notably the Russians and Chinese (Houellebecq 2010:106). Jed's primary point of contact with the firm is not a French male industrialist or engineer but a foreign female PR executive, the beautiful Olga Sheremoyova. Olga is tasked with promoting Michelin's recent acquisitions in terms of French hotels and restaurants to Russian and Chinese tourists. Where the Michelin maps had embodied a sublime synthesis of nature and technology, the synthesis of *terroir* and modern conveniences depicted in the company's new tourist brochures aims merely at a feminised pleasure: 'This juxtaposition of elements of the old France or of the *terroir* with hedonistic contemporary facilities sometimes produced a strange effect, almost an effect of bad taste' (98–99). Michelin's virile, authentically French, sublime project, rooted in material production, has thus been replaced by a feminised, foreign, dematerialised one that relies on hawking a commodified simulacrum of the French *terroir* to the now dominant Russians and Chinese. In the wake of globalisation, the novel implies, France has lost its former industrial might and economic power and is hence reduced to prostituting itself, its culture, historical heritage, and gastronomy, to foreign tourists.

At the level of working-class productive labour, things are little better. Jed's early attempts to locate a plumber to mend his boiler lead him on a frustrating search through the immaterial space of the web, where various Internet sites offer equally false promises of delivering genuinely artisanal levels of expertise (12–13). Ultimately, he will be forced to rely on a foreign, immigrant worker, a Croatian plumber, only to learn, to his dismay, that this man too is planning to abandon productive labour and return to his country to start running a tourist

112   *Republican Citizens, Precarious Subjects*

resort (27–28). Later, Jed embarks on a series of paintings entitled 'the series of simple trades'. The first two of these paintings are dedicated to male workers in stereotypically French metiers: '"Ferdinand Desroches, horsemeat butcher", then "Claude Vorilhon, manager of a *bar-tabac*", to professions that are running out of steam.' The third such painting again emphasises the shift to feminised, immaterial, and deterritorialised labour by depicting '"Maya Dubois, remote maintenance assistant"', whose profession is 'emblematic of the adoption of the just-in-time production methods that had orientated the entire economic restructuring of Western Europe at the turn of the third millennium' (116–17). Significantly, the one disappearing profession Jed really wants to paint, but is unable to, is the Catholic priesthood. Poorly paid and marginalised, priests represent for Jed embodiments of an altruism, moral virtue, and spirituality that have no place in a godless, individualistic, and basely mercantile contemporary France; for those who do not share their faith, they therefore represent 'a disorientating and inaccessible subject' that frustrates Jed's attempts to capture them in paint (97–98).

As Bernard Maris (2014:38) argues, Jed's 'simple trades' series represents a lament at the passing of a set of professional groups and hence corporatist structures that might serve as 'intermediary bodies' mediating between the atomised individual and the economy, providing a collective identity with its associated forms of morality, social welfare, and cohesion. To quote Maris (103): 'over and above the professions, it is the organisation of work that [Jed] wants to capture. The division of labour in society.' As Maris's choice of language makes clear here ('intermediary bodies', 'the division of labour in society'), he places Houellebecq's work within a republican tradition of corporatism rooted Durkheimian sociology. Yet this appears to be a peculiarly conservative version of that tradition that in its focus on Catholicism, family, and nation surely owes more to Charles Maurras's counter-revolutionary brand of corporatism than it does to Durkheimian republicanism. Indeed, many of Houellebecq's novels are characterised by their laments at the erosion of organised religion, masculinity, family, and nation in a de-industrialised France. Jed will thus end his days childless, unmarried, and alone, having retreated to the French countryside, the *terroir*, to contemplate 'the end of the industrial age in Europe', itself a 'symbol of the generalised annihilation of the human species' (Houellebecq 2010:414). In this, Jed's fate is analogous to that of the anonymous narrator of *Extension du domaine de la lutte* (1994), a disaffected software engineer, whose acerbic critiques of the vapidity of immaterial executive labour are accompanied by laments at absent fathers, family breakdown, and male impotence (Houellebecq 1994). The male protagonists of *Les Particules élémentaires* (1998), meanwhile, are haunted by 'the disappearance of [...] family relations, of the notion of paternity and of filiation' in a French society in which feminism and economic liberalism have apparently destroyed the basis of national community and morality (Houellebecq 1998:156). The extent to which Houellebecq sees marriage, the patriarchal family, religion, and authentic labour as the combined bedrocks of a cohesive national community is emphasised by the contrasting destiny of the male protagonist of the later novel, *Soumission* (2015). Here Houellebecq imagines a France ruled over by an Islamic regime that mandates both arranged marriage and a return to artisanal modes of production. This enables France's moral and social order to be restored and *Soumission*'s central protagonist to end the novel happily contemplating marriage and potential fatherhood.

Through the career of Jed, then, Houellebecq sketches a profoundly conservative account of the decline of French society, a decline he attributes in equal measure to France's loss of its industrial and economic prowess in a now globalised economy, the decline in religious faith, the disappearance of masculine productive labour, and its replacement by what are figured as more feminised, immaterial professions. Houellebecq offers a highly pessimistic vision of the ultimate effects of this decline on France, a vision in which the loss of masculinity and the end of the nuclear family play a central role.

Performing Professionalism

La Carte et le territoire thus posits a straightforward causal relationship between deindustrialisation and the rise of immaterial labour, on the one hand, and a crisis in masculinity, the nuclear family, and the French nation, on the other. At first glance, it might appear that Cantet's film, *L'Emploi du temps*, rehearses these tropes, insofar as it combines a critique of contemporary forms of employment with an apparent lament at the inability of its central protagonist, Vincent, to perform his roles as husband and father. However, Cantet figures the patriarchal nuclear family not as a possible antidote to contemporary capitalism,

114   Republican Citizens, Precarious Subjects

a wholesome natural social institution threatened by the proliferation of immaterial forms of labour. On the contrary, Vincent's family is presented as entirely complementary to capitalism in its current form; it is the locus, as much as the contemporary firm, of the injunctions placed on Vincent to fulfil his role as dynamic, committed, professional financial consultant. Hence while, at a personal level, Vincent clearly cares deeply about the individual members of his family, he nonetheless seeks to escape that family in its role as the social institution that generates the obligations that constrain him. By exploring this dilemma, Cantet offers a series of insights into the contribution made by the bourgeois family to generating the dispositions and behaviours expected of someone of Vincent's social class, education, and professional status.

As we have mentioned, the film centres on the experiences of Vincent, a middle-aged financial consultant who lives in Eastern France, close to the Swiss border. Vincent has recently been sacked but is hiding this fact from his friends and family by pretending he has secured a new job in development aid, working just over the French–Swiss border at the UN in Geneva. Vincent exploits three sources of income to finance this pretence. First, he borrows a significant sum of money from his father, supposedly to buy a flat in Geneva but actually just to fund his family's living expenses. Second, he runs a Ponzi scheme, pretending to former colleagues and classmates from the elite business school he attended that a colleague at the UN has access to illicit investment schemes in Russia that deliver very high rates of return. Third, he gets involved in a scheme to smuggle counterfeit branded goods manufactured in Eastern Europe into Western Europe.

All of Vincent's activities, both real and faked, are thus clearly situated in a newly globalised economy characterised by increased flows of capital and goods between the developed West and the developing world. This is the case as much for the African nations he claims to be helping through his job at the UN, as for the former Soviet bloc countries whose economic liberalisation in the wake of the fall of the Berlin Wall provides both the pretext for his Ponzi scheme and the actual source of the counterfeit goods he smuggles. This is also reflected in Vincent's constant mobility, even rootlessness, as he moves between anonymous car parks, service stations, picnic places, and the lobbies of chain hotels, whether killing time while supposedly on business trips or meeting his friends and former colleagues in connection with his fraudulent scheme.

Modulated Masculinities 115

This sense of rootless mobility also chimes with Vincent's persona, for everything he does relies on lies, counterfeit, and the performances through which he feigns his fictive professional identity. As Martin O'Shaughnessy (2015:84) has pointed out, Vincent is like an actor performing a role and in several scenes we see him learning his lines, repeating to himself phrases culled from a brochure about development aid he picked up from the offices of a non-governmental organisation (NGO) in Geneva. As we have noted in earlier chapters, one of the characteristic features of contemporary management practice is the pressure placed on employees to, as Valérie Brunel puts it, transform their emotions into 'objects to be managed' (2008:88), performing versions of their professional selves that demonstrate their 'capacity for adaptation, transformation, [and] personal motivation' (37). There is a tragic irony here, for Vincent is seeking precisely to escape the pressures involved in performing his role as a confident, efficient financial consultant. Yet his attempts to escape those pressures paradoxically demand that he engage in ever more elaborate performances of the social and professional roles from which he is so visibly alienated, that he expend ever more energy in maintaining the fiction that he is a dynamic financial consultant, chief breadwinner, good husband and father, and dutiful son to his own father, himself a retired wealthy professional man. Vincent's pretence thus allegorises the inescapable nature of the imperative placed on contemporary workers to deliver convincing performances of their own professionalism.

As Cantet has pointed out, *L'Emploi du temps* is a film that 'can be seen as one huge escape attempt' in which Vincent seeks to 'free himself from all form of economic and social capture' (quoted in Marks 2011:490). Vincent's car is one space in which, albeit momentarily, the social, professional, and familial obligations that constrain him are suspended and, in a number of scenes, we see him enjoying the sense of freedom he derives from simply speeding along roads and motorways. In the course of a conversation with his partner in the smuggling enterprise, Jean-Michel (Serge Livrozet), Vincent explains that the only part of his former job he really enjoyed were the car journeys to business meetings. Apparently, he would often extend these journeys, missing his motorway exit just to prolong the pleasure and sense of freedom secured by driving. Vincent further implies that he lost his job precisely because this meant he kept missing important meetings. However, as O'Shaughnessy (2015:76–77) points out, the

116   *Republican Citizens, Precarious Subjects*

freedom that Vincent experiences while driving will prove short-lived as the mobile phone calls he receives in his car, from family members and participants in his Ponzi scheme, drag him back to the network of social and professional obligations that constrain him.

As we have noted, this sense of the impossibility of any escape is mirrored in Vincent's pretence he is employed by the UN in Geneva, a pretence that merely exacerbates the pressures on him to perform a certain professional role. In this way, Cantet depicts Vincent's social and familial obligations as being inseparable from the professional imperatives to which he is subjected. This much is made clear in an early scene in which Vincent attends a school fête in the company of his parents, his wife, and his three children. It is clear that prior to the fête, rather than admit his unemployed status, Vincent has hinted to his wife that he may be about to move jobs. His wife has subsequently told Vincent's mother who has, in turn, passed the news on to his father. At the school fête, assuming the new job is in the bag, Vincent's father boasts to assembled friends and family of his son's professional achievements, insisting they celebrate what he presents as a successful new career move for Vincent. Vincent is thus caught in his own lie by the social and familial networks that define his role as son, husband, father, and chief breadwinner and it is this that forces him to engage in the elaborate charade regarding his supposed job at the UN. Cantet's cinematography emphasises this point. A close-up on Vincent's face reveals his sense of dread, fear, and discomfiture as off-screen the voices of his mother, father, and friends express their admiration at and expectations for Vincent's new career. This sense of dread is reinforced by the accompanying musical soundtrack of foreboding strings in a minor key. It is significant that it should be Vincent's father who is the prime mover in provoking his son's discomfiture here. For the father acts throughout the film as a kind of super-ego, articulating the social, moral, and professional injunctions that constrain Vincent, admonishing his son for his failings and praising him for his supposed achievements. The patriarchal family is hence depicted as being as much the source of Vincent's difficulties as are the injunctions to which he is subjected in his professional life.

By depicting Vincent's entrapment in a network of both familial and professional obligations in this way, Cantet avoids any temptation to figure the family as an antidote to the destructive logics of contemporary labour, the natural basis for an organic social order. Nor does

Cantet figure the kind of immaterial financial labour inherent to Vincent's profession, the performance of efficient professionalism in which he must engage, as a threat to either his masculinity or his role as head of his nuclear family. On the contrary, Cantet shows the audience that immaterial financial labour represents precisely the form in which a man of Vincent's class and education is expected to perform his masculinity and hence fulfil his role as head of his bourgeois family, becoming a fitting successor to his own father in that respect. As we have seen, in *La Carte et le territoire* male workers are depicted as being somehow feminised, and their roles as heads of family threatened, by engaging in immaterial labour. In *L'Emploi du temps*, by contrast, it is because of Vincent's refusal to engage in such labour that his patriarchal role is threatened; it is this refusal that infantilises him, making him financially dependent on his father and losing him the respect of his teenage son, Julien, when the latter uncovers the truth behind Vincent's elaborate charade (Lebtahi and Roussel-Gillet 2005:102).

In this sense, *L'Emploi du temps* depicts the demands of financial immaterial labour as being not antagonistic to masculinity and the bourgeois family, but wholly imbricated with those two phenomena. Indeed, the film relates those three phenomena to issues of class, education, and the evolution of the global economy so as to situate Vincent as a member of a French bourgeoisie that, far from being threatened by financialised globalisation, positively benefits from it. The audience learns that Vincent attended one of France's elite and highly selective *grandes écoles*, a business school whose yearbook we see him leafing through to locate the former classmates he invites to invest in his Ponzi scheme. Cantet alludes here to certain changes in the role played by French higher education in the reproduction and 'reconversion' of those forms of symbolic and economic capital that define the class identity of the French bourgeoisie. These are the changes that determined the emergence of what, in his classic study *La Distinction* (1979), Pierre Bourdieu (1979:360) terms 'the new bourgeoisie', a 'new ethical avant-garde' with its own specific ethos and lifestyle quite different from France's traditional haute bourgeoisie.

Bourdieu argues that with the emergence of the multinational corporation, the offspring of the bourgeoisie could no longer count on simply inheriting a position in the family firm as the means of reproducing their wealth and status. Rather, they had now to 'reconvert' their inherited advantages by acquiring the kinds of

118   *Republican Citizens, Precarious Subjects*

financial-managerial skill inculcated in one of France's growing number of selective business schools. Over the course of the 1960s, 1970s, and beyond, the sons of France's traditional, paternalistic, and nationalistic bourgeoisie thus acquired the professional skills and the more modern, dynamic, cosmopolitan dispositions that would secure them employment in an increasingly globalised corporate sector (Bourdieu 1979:338–61).

The contrast in deportment and values that distinguishes Vincent from his father exemplifies these shifts in the education, culture, and identity of two successive generations of the French bourgeoisie. Vincent's father is an embodiment of the traditional disciplinary bourgeois *paterfamilias*; the décor of his house, his dress, speech, and mannerisms are all formal in a very classical sense. Vincent, by contrast, affects a much more relaxed, modern demeanour; his relations with his own children are far less disciplinary; his family home is characterised by its modernist style; his wife pursues her own career, enjoying a level of autonomy within her marriage that contrasts with Vincent's mother, who repeatedly defers to her husband's authority. Finally, in a conversation with his father about his supposed new job in development aid, Vincent defends a kind of liberal humanitarianism that contrasts strikingly with his father's cursory dismissal of such policies given what he claims to be African governments' inherent financial incompetence. Vincent's openness and liberal cosmopolitanism thus contrast with his father's disciplinary admonitions and implicit racism. He embodies a more modulated form of masculinity and patriarchy, whose symbiotic relationship to globalised financialised capitalism Cantet's film precisely illustrates. Further, through his depiction of the tense interactions between father and son, Cantet highlights a shift in the nature of the bourgeois family itself, from a disciplinary towards a post-disciplinary institution.

L'Emploi du temps thus anatomises the culture, dispositions, ethical and political values of someone of Vincent's class, education, and age with great precision. It is important to remember that when Vincent defends the values of liberal humanitarianism he is involved in a deception, pretending to occupy a professional position he in fact does not. Cantet is surely pointing to a fundamental hypocrisy in the values endorsed by Vincent here. Earlier in the film, the audience sees Vincent flick through a brochure he has picked up in the Geneva offices of a development NGO. A series of close-ups enable us to read such headings as 'Aid Invested in Africa', 'International Financing of African Firms', 'The Economic Integration of Developing Countries', and 'Privatisation and Management'. These headings reveal the extent to which development aid, in its current form, is entirely complicit with neo-liberal policies of privatisation and financial deregulation. Indeed, from the mid-1980s onwards institutions such as the World Bank and the International Monetary Fund (IMF) made development loans to the emerging nations contingent on their adoption of 'structural adjustment' programmes, removing protectionist tariffs, privatising their public utilities, and reducing their public expenditure, according to the terms of the so-called 'Washington Consensus' (Ellwood 2002:47). These policies were also at the core of the so-called 'shock treatment' applied to the former command economies of the ex-Soviet bloc in the 1990s, initiating a wave of privatisations, asset stripping, and the exploitation of natural resources in Russia, in particular (Stiglitz 2002).

This articulation of aid with the neo-liberal deregulation of the developing world is, of course, what provides the pretext for Vincent's Ponzi scheme, his claim to be able to offer his friends and former colleagues high rates of return on investments in the ex-Soviet bloc through contacts he has made in his development work. The friends, former classmates and colleagues Vincent contacts to this end all form part of a network of privileged graduates of the *grandes écoles*. None of those whom Vincent contacts seems at all surprised by the nature of his investment scheme. Vincent is, after all, someone whom they believe to be involved in the supposedly benevolent activity of development aid. Yet the investment opportunities he describes to them involve him profiting from his position by engaging in an illegal scheme that exploits the resources of the former communist bloc. The equanimity with which Vincent's friends react to his supposed involvement in an immoral investment scheme in a developing nation emphasises the fact that they are perfectly at ease with this kind of behaviour. Vincent, his friends, and colleagues are thus shown to be representatives of a class whose material interests are served by this form of globalisation. It is surely significant that the smuggling of counterfeit goods Vincent subsequently engages in, an activity that, unlike his fictive investment scheme, generates real profits, also involves the former communist bloc and the exploitation of a new pool of cheap labour opened up by the fall of the Berlin Wall. As Jean-Michel explains to Vincent it costs him just

120   Republican Citizens, Precarious Subjects

200 francs to manufacture a watch in Poland that he can then sell for 15,000 francs in France. That mark-up, of course, relates directly to the immaterial value of the authentic branded goods of which Jean-Michel sells counterfeited versions.

Through the experiences of Vincent, then, *L'Emploi du temps* plots a very precise cartography of early twenty-first-century global capitalism. This is a capitalism characterised by that 'uneven geography' described by Mouhoud and Plihon (2009:63), by a 'hybridisation' of the international division of labour in which poles of highly profitable financial-cognitive labour, exemplified in the film by the area around Geneva, co-exist with a Taylorised periphery, whose wealth remains dependent on low wage costs and economies of scale, as represented here by Eastern Europe. Cantet's film highlights the ways in which these shifts in global political economy interact with changes in education, class identity, and the institution of the bourgeois family in the particular national setting of France. Cantet rejects any temptation to present either family or nation as bulwarks against these global economic phenomena. Rather, he focuses on the ways in which the French bourgeoisie, its familial institutions, educational trajectories, and socio-cultural identities, have evolved so as to profit from those phenomena.

Insofar as he seeks to 'free himself from all form of economic and social capture', to quote Cantet once more, Vincent's actions represent a refusal to perform his allotted role within this nexus of social and economic forces, a kind of mute, inchoate critique of its exploitative nature. However, that refusal and implicit critique will ultimately come to nothing. At the end of the film, Vincent's deception has been uncovered and his father has intervened to secure him an interview for a new job as a financial consultant. Once again, the role of Vincent's father as super-ego, bringing his wayward son to order, compelling him to accept his responsibilities as both head of family and agent of globalised capital is emphasised here.

In the final scene we see Vincent being interviewed by the Human Resources director of his potential new employers. Asked to explain the gap of several months in his employment history, Vincent confesses that he had lost his 'enthusiasm' for his former job and had been seeking a new challenge in which he could really 'invest' his personal energies. The Human Resources director sympathises, agreeing that 'ambition is an important motor in the development of one's career' before going on to detail the scope of Vincent's future position. This is 'a role that carries great responsibilities' in a 'new domain' and so represents 'an adventure, a financial adventure you understand, of strategic importance to our group but also, above all, to our eyes at least, a human adventure' that will demand 'an immense personal investment' on Vincent's part. As the Human Resources director begins to speak, the camera cuts to a medium close-up of the seated Vincent, slowly tracking into a close-up on his expression, his weak smile belied by the sense of dread, fear, and mute resignation communicated via his eyes. The same musical motif as accompanied the earlier scene at the school fête cuts in, adding to the sense of foreboding. When Vincent responds to the interviewer's remark that his new employers expect 'an immense personal investment' on his part by insisting 'that doesn't scare me at all', the audience knows the opposite is true. As the Human Resources director drones on, the screen turns to black and, after a couple of seconds, the credits roll. As Cantet puts it, at this point Vincent 'may as well be dead' since the new job that awaits him is 'akin to slavery' (quoted in Higbee 2004:247).

By the end of the film, then, Vincent has been restored to his allotted professional, social, and familial roles. Yet this restoration corresponds to a profound personal defeat; he has been dragged back by all the obligations he had sought to escape and will be subjected once more to the obligation to feign his 'immense personal investment' in the new 'human adventure' that his new job, found by his father, will demand. Indeed, the interviewer's overblown language, its evocations of the intense affective labour that will be expected of Vincent in his new role, stands in stark contrast to what the audience has learned about the latter's true feelings towards his professional responsibilities, feelings of profound alienation and disaffection.

From the Workshop to the Call Centre

L'Emploi du temps thus offers an incisive critique of the role of class, education, and the family in the production of a younger generation of bourgeois executives whose attitudes and values complement the demands of global financialised capitalism. Thierry Beinstingel's (2010) novel *Retour aux mots sauvages*, by contrast, focuses on the difficulties faced by a representative of the skilled working class, an unnamed

122   *Republican Citizens, Precarious Subjects*

worker in his early 50s, a former telecoms technician who is forced to modulate his professional and personal sense of self as he takes on a new role in one of his firm's call centres. Beinstingel's account of the difficulties faced by this worker in adapting to his new role is interspersed with references both to the growing number of suicides at his firm and to senior management's clumsy efforts to respond to this situation. The novel's protagonist will not himself commit suicide. Nonetheless he will have to engage in a profoundly alienating performance of his new professional self as an open, convivial, deeply committed service-sector worker. The pseudonym he is told to adopt when dealing with customers on the telephone serves as a tangible marker of the 'fabricated' nature of his new professional identity and of the fundamental betrayal of his true self this involves (Beinstingel 2010:244). The protagonist of *Retour aux mots sauvages* chooses the name 'Eric'; the reader will never learn what his real name is.

The novel thus highlights the alienating nature of call-centre work, while offering a series of insights into the effects of the shift from manual-technical to affective-relational labour, from discipline to more modulated forms of control, on Eric's sense of self, his subjectivity. In his account of the functioning of discipline, Foucault highlights the way in which disciplinary techniques were employed to shape workers' minds and bodies so as to transform them into efficient units of labour in a factory setting. He argues that the goal of these techniques was to produce a particular 'articulation between a body and an object' by defining 'each of the relations that the body must maintain with the object it manipulates'; disciplinary power thus inserted itself 'between the body and the object it manipulates' to produce a new 'body-instrument, body-machine complex' (Foucault 1975:179–80). *Retour aux mots sauvages* depicts Eric being forced to unlearn all of this, to undo the nexus of knowledge and embodied skill that was at the core of his earlier job as a telecoms technician, acquiring the new oral, communicative, and affective-relational skills of a call-centre operative. As one of Eric's colleagues remarks, this will involve a process of re-training his mind and body:

> He's also like all of us. He worked in a trade in which only physical actions counted, tightening bolts, using a screwdriver. Like all of us, he arrived here after dozens of years of silence. Like all of us, an old man who's a newcomer in this call centre.

Modulated Masculinities 123

He found it difficult to begin with: swapping words for silence, his mouth for his hand.

(Beinstingel 2010:14–15)

One of the novel's leitmotifs is Eric's recurrent sense that his hand is becoming atrophied, even amputated and replaced by his mouth (36,59,63,280). The Foucauldian 'body-instrument, body-machine complex' that had previously conjoined his body and mind to his tools and technical-manual labours is being replaced by a new body-machine complex based around the telephone, the mouse, and the computer screen. Eric's mind, body, and subjectivity are thus re-shaped by this new 'agencement', the new set-up, arrangement or disposition of bodies, affects and machines in the call centre:

Thus, everything has been thought out in this comfortable set-up [*agencement*], including the ease with which your hands are getting softer, the right one moulding itself like a jellyfish to the animal called a mouse, the left one positioned beside the keyboard, one or two fingers seeming to type randomly on one or two keys, as though the entirety of your physical actions was independent of your gaze fixed on the screen, when in fact those actions are driven, decided by the light emanating from it.

(Beinstingel 2010:31–2)

This re-shaping of his mind and embodied affects is experienced by Eric as a kind of *feminisation*, hence exemplifying Morini's (2007:42) claim that the immaterial skills demanded of the likes of call-centre workers, 'capacities for relationships, emotional aspects, linguistic aspects', are widely coded as being inherently feminine. Eric thus concludes that his 'new job' will necessitate him mimicking the behaviour of his colleague Maryse, 'becoming a Maryse with the voice of a hostess' (Beinstingel 2010:10). As one of Eric's colleagues explains to him: 'Women have an advantage over us: they never stop talking' (15).

Eric's response to the feminisation he sees as inherent to immaterial, communicative labour is to lament the loss of the combination of masculine camaraderie and concrete technical-manual labour he associates with his former trade (11). Taking his car to be repaired at his local garage, Eric is confronted with a reminder of the lost certainties of skilled masculine manual labour. Once again, the

124 *Republican Citizens, Precarious Subjects*

physical transformation of Eric's hand serves as the tangible manifestation of his feminisation and contrasts with the brute physicality of the garage mechanic: 'But he notices the difference between his now white hand, its delicate skin and the greasy, solid, tendinous paw that is opening the bonnet' (223). Unlike the vapid sales talk Eric must employ at the call centre, the technical vocabulary employed by the mechanic communicates 'something reassuring, logical and concrete' (224). The garage represents a world of materials, whose solidity Eric contrasts with the immateriality and insincerity that characterise communicative work in the call centre: 'Here, materials are in charge, sheet metal, plastic, Teflon, carbon: there's no call for negotiating, persuading, slipping into the false democracy of sales talk. Here, it's a dictatorship of materials' (225).

This re-shaping of Eric's mind and affects is the product of a specific set of management techniques, a mode of governmentality that corresponds precisely to the mixed model of discipline and control that, as we saw in the last chapter, Philippe Zarifian (2009) has identified in his fieldwork among France Télécom call-centre operatives. Eric is, on the one hand, subjected to exacerbated kinds of discipline, in the form of the intensive digital surveillance exercised over his work and the demanding sales targets he must meet. On the other hand, he is enjoined to embody a kind of false conviviality in his interactions with both his clients and managers, who insist on addressing all their employees in the informal 'tu' form. Further, in an effort to elicit their staff's commitment and initiative, Eric's managers employ precisely the kinds of sales challenges and teambuilding exercises that Deleuze (2003:242) sees as characteristic of techniques of control. These departures from more traditional disciplinary hierarchies, this adoption of apparently more relaxed, modulated styles of management are experienced by Eric and his colleagues as profoundly intrusive and coercive, working to undermine the very sense of cohesion they ostensibly seek to generate. As one of Eric's colleagues recounts: 'They made me dance the lambada at one meeting, supposedly to reinforce our team spirit. Result: we all avoided each other for the next three weeks' (241).

For Eric himself, it is management's insistence on addressing all employees in the informal 'tu' form that epitomises the hypocrisy of their supposedly more modulated, less disciplinary style of management. For, he argues, this false conviviality masks the reality of a workplace characterised by unattainable sales targets, intrusive appraisals, and the consequent personal rivalries that undermine any sense of a cohesive community: 'We're sick to death of a firm that's elevated the use of the "tu" form to a rule of conviviality. How many of us have been stabbed in the back by a domineering boss, an envious colleague, a bullying director, only too happy to use the rule of "tu" to play at being our friend' (152). This erosion of any genuine conviviality is not limited to the workplace; it seeps out into broader society to threaten the social bond itself. Eric notes that the computerised call system employed in the call centre greets each customer automatically, relieving the operators of the necessity to do this (20). He contrasts this with his childhood memory of being taught by his mother the importance of formally greeting the baker's wife before placing his order for the family's bread (42). Waiting to be served on his next visit to the bakery, he falls into a reverie, imagining an exchange with the baker's wife that has, as it were, been contaminated by the clichéd script he has to follow at the call centre. Awakened from his reverie, he collects his bread only to notice 'as he was leaving that he has again forgotten to greet the baker's wife' (69). Given the roles of bread as an emblem of French identity and of the baker's shop as the core of local community, this apparently minor lapse functions as a powerful synecdoche for the undermining of all the social rituals, niceties, and formalities that served to cement France's social bond. Everyday sociability, genuine human interactions have been corroded by the 'mots sauvages', the primitive words, of contemporary management discourse and a clichéd call-centre script.

The novel's critique of contemporary management practices thus manifests a certain nostalgia, even conservatism in its laments at the loss of the supposed certainties of masculinity, concrete manual labour, and traditional French national identity. Nonetheless, it does offer a series of insights into the nature of the shift from disciplinary to post-disciplinary modes of governmentality and subjectivity. Indeed, one of the novel's most persuasive aspects is its ability to highlight the relationships between these post-disciplinary techniques, the spate of workplace suicides at the call centre, and the inadequacy of official responses to that tragic phenomenon. The narrative suggests that the suicides reflect the erosion of any collective ethos in the workplace, combined with the pressures inherent to displaying one's autonomy and initiative, while following the prescribed sales scripts to the letter,

126   *Republican Citizens, Precarious Subjects*

keeping to the defined time limits for each call and meeting demanding sales targets.

Beinstingel is himself employed as an executive at France Télécom and his fictional account of the suicides at Eric's workplace clearly alludes to the spate of such suicides he witnessed at his own firm in the first decade of the new century. Indeed, in his age and professional profile Eric corresponds closely to the typical suicide victims at France Télécom. As Ivan du Roy (2009:24) has shown, the majority of these were male technicians in their 50s who had started their careers when France Télécom was still a nationalised public utility and had hence been steeped in a public service ethos now subsumed under more nakedly financial imperatives in the wake of their firm's privatisation. As Eric remarks of the suicide cases at his fictional call centre:

> It is no coincidence that the majority of victims are more than fifty years old. Their work ethic was forged by the ideas of the past: building a better, more egalitarian and collective world. The young workers, who have only known unbridled individualism, are less vulnerable. (Beinstingel 2010:184)

Eric proceeds to describe the erosion of those progressive ideas in the face of successive economic downturns, restructurings, and waves of redundancies (184–85).

Eric thus serves as a personification of a generation initiated into Fordism but now struggling to adapt to the changed imperatives of post-Fordism. His evident nostalgia for the certainties of Fordism is also a nostalgia for its unrealised political promises, for the progressive ideals that inspired his early working life. In this sense, Beinstingel's sometimes nostalgic evocations of Fordist manual-technical labour are very different from and more politically progressive than Houellebecq's nostalgia for order and morality underpinned by patriarchy, family, and nation.

Eric's sense that the progressive, collectivist ideals of the 1960s are now dead seems to be confirmed both by the spate of suicides at the call centre and the inadequate nature of management's proposed solutions to such tragically individualised expressions of employee discontent. Spurred into action by negative media reporting of the suicides, the senior management of Eric's firm intervenes: the managing director visits the call centre and talks to the employees (208–9); a statement released to the press declares his intention to 'put the human element' back at the centre of what they do (210); and questionnaires are distributed to all staff in order to elicit their views on their working conditions and record any instances of workplace suffering (231). There is a terrible irony in these measures, however, an irony by no means lost on Eric's colleagues. Maryse is 'frightened' by the proposal to 'put the human element at the centre' of their working lives, noting that it means 'they won't leave us in peace for a moment' and amounts to the imposition of 'compulsory happiness'. Robert adds that this apparently solicitous slogan in fact rests on a conception of the workers' humanity as a resource to be exploited, 'something transferable […] a substance like skin or bones' (251–52). What Eric's colleagues have grasped is that management's response to the suicides relies on the same psychologising assumptions as did the management methods that provoked so much stress in the first place, the same intrusive mobilisation of its employees' human capital, their affects, personal attributes, and emotions.

The use of a questionnaire to measure levels of stress and workplace suffering is instructive here, as such questionnaires epitomise the shift from the hierarchical commands characteristic of discipline to the more modulated forms of Deleuzean control. Questionnaires might appear to reflect a genuine interest on management's part in what their employees think and feel. Yet, in reality, the demand that employees articulate their feelings and opinions in this way is fundamentally intrusive; it interpellates employees as atomised individuals, not as members of a collective of equivalently qualified professionals whose objectively delimited skills and responsibilities endow them with certain rights and protections. In this respect, the questionnaire and the promise to 'put the human element' at the centre of work in the call centre exemplify Danièle Linhart's notion of 'la surhumanisation managériale', an excessive humanisation of work that is frequently experienced as atomising and intrusive insofar as it erodes any distinction between workers' professional and private selves, abolishing any possibility of 'a demarcation between what those individuals invest in their work and what they are' (2015:11).

The solutions senior management offer to workplace suicide in *Retour aux mots sauvages* are thus symptoms of the very problems they aim to resolve. Beinstingel's novel chimes here with the criticisms of official responses to the phenomenon of workplace suicide articulated by both Anne Flottes (2013) and Yves Clot (2010). As Flottes (2013:9) argues, the response of the French government to workplace suicides

128   *Republican Citizens, Precarious Subjects*

has been to emphasise their psychological motivations, writing into the Labour Code an obligation for employers to protect the mental, as well as physical health of their employees, and stipulating that employers initiate extensive programmes of 'risk prevention'. Hence the 'generally expected response' to suicides in any given workplace has become 'a statistical measurement of malaise, by means of questionnaires or interviews' in just the way that *Retour aux mots sauvages* depicts (50). Clot (2010:133–34) gives the example of employers who now offer their employees 'tickets psy' or therapy vouchers that the latter can redeem at the therapist of their choice in case of any work-related stress. In this way, problems arising from the contemporary organisation of work are radically psychologised and individualised, while their actual political and economic determinants are occluded and ignored.

Eric's senior managers thus offer responses to workplace suicide that partake of the psychologising logic that provoked those suicides in the first place. Hence, there appears to be no escape for Eric and his co-workers. By the end of the novel, although he has not given in to suicide, Eric is nonetheless defeated by the mixed logics of disciplinary surveillance and modulated control to which he is subjected at work. He has found a purely personal antidote in the physical pleasure and sense of communal solidarity he derives from competing in half-marathons. As for the broader 'world', he resigns himself in the novel's final line 'to live with it, work around it, give himself up to the primitive words' (Beinstingel 2010:295). The inescapable nature of Eric's predicament and his quiet resignation at the novel's end suggest close parallels with the fate of Vincent at the close of *L'Emploi du temps*. Both Vincent and Eric represent middle-aged men who are resigned to and have in a sense been defeated by the changed nature of work in the current socio-economic conjuncture.

Slimane's 'Human Adventure'

The hero of Abdellatif Kechiche's 2007 film, *La Graine et le mulet*, appears to suffer a similar fate. A 61-year-old immigrant of North African origin, Slimane finds himself divorced, redundant, and facing the indifference of his adult sons to his paternal authority. Having lost his job as a shipyard worker, he will struggle in vain to forge a new career for himself in the tertiary sector as a restaurant owner. By the

Modulated Masculinities   129

film's final scene, Slimane has been defeated and possibly even killed by the intense efforts he has expended to adopt a new professional identity and hence regain his social and familial roles as breadwinner and *paterfamilias*. In this sense, *La Graine et le mulet* offers a series of evident parallels with both *L'Emploi du temps* and *Retour aux mots sauvages*. Yet the film also offers a series of insights into the specific problems faced by someone of Slimane's age, sex, class, and ethnicity in adapting to the demands of France's post-Fordist economy. Kechiche is thus careful to situate Slimane's dilemma in its particular socio-economic context, showing how that dilemma is at once analogous to that faced by many men of his class and age yet exacerbated by the particular problems that middle-aged ethnic minority men face in contemporary France.

The film's opening scene is set on board a tourist boat taking a group of holiday-makers around the fishing port of Sète, on the French mediterranean coast. A young man of North African heritage, who is later revealed to be Slimane's son Majid (Sami Zitouni), is delivering a commentary to the tourists. He points out the place from which, at one time, could be heard the cries of the merchants in the fishmarket but 'now, it's all done by by computers'. Passing a pile of scrap metal on the docks, Majid remarks wryly that 'previously, we used to have furnaces in France' to melt the scrap down but now 'apparently, they've lost the matches'. These allusions to deindustrialisation, to the replacement of industry by tourism will be reiterated in a subsequent scene when Slimane visits his daughter, son-in-law, and grandchildren in their family home. The son-in-law laments his employer's unwillingness to offer him a permanent contract, before remarking bitterly that there are 'two times fewer fishing boats than ten years ago, so obviously there's less work'. Soon, he notes, 'there'll be no more fishing boats […], only the marina […], no more shipyard […], only tourists'. His wife, Slimane's daughter, explains that the management at her workplace, the local cannery, tried to remove the workers' right to bonus payments, arguing they had no option in the face of increased competition from America. She says that through strikes and protests they got the management to back down. Her husband is sceptical, remarking, wearily, 'They can do whatever they like. They can offshore their production, They go where they can pay just 50 euros a week.'

Further evidence of the decline of local industry and the consequent loss of jobs in the face of offshoring and increased global competition is provided by Slimane's own situation as a worker in the local shipyard,

130   *Republican Citizens, Precarious Subjects*

repairing fishing trawlers. He is called in by his foreman to be told that he will have to reduce his hours in what is 'a rather slow period', that he must 'accept flexible hours if you want to continue working, otherwise, well ...' Indeed, Slimane has already been offered early retirement on the basis that, as his foreman cruelly remarks, he is too old and slow: 'So you're no longer profitable. You're tired out and you're tiring us out. That's the truth of it.' If Slimane has refused early retirement this is, he explains, because although he has worked at the yard for 35 years, only the last 15 of those were recognised in the redundancy package he was offered. The foreman denies any responsibility for this situation, arguing the current owners have no record of Slimane's employment prior to their purchasing the shipyard 15 years earlier. Slimane's status as a North African immigrant is thus shown to have rendered him particularly vulnerable to exploitation. The boatyard's first owners exploited this status by not declaring his presence on their payroll, hence avoiding paying into the pension to which he was entitled. The current owners treat him as a disposable resource, the first on whom to impose flexible working conditions now that the economic conjuncture has turned unfavourable. Slimane's refusal to accept these new flexible terms means he has effectively been made redundant.

The dismissive way Slimane is treated at work, the disrespect shown by his employers for his 35 years of hard work is shown to have a direct effect on his masculine self-esteem. In a short scene, we see Slimane sitting, visibly embarrassed, on the edge of the bed of his partner, Latifa (Hatifa Karaoui), the proprietor of the bar and boarding house in which he has been living since his divorce. Humiliated at his sexual impotence, he scuttles back to his room. Latifa follows him to ask what is wrong, to which he replies: 'I'm only a tenant. [...] Me, I've achieved nothing. I've nothing here, neither for you, nor for my children.' Confirmation of this seems to be offered in a subsequent scene in which his two grown-up sons come to visit him in his room and try to persuade him to return to Algeria on the basis that, since he is both divorced and redundant, 'there is nothing here to hold you back'.

As the sociologist Abdelmalek Sayad (1999:260) has argued, the identities of first-generation North African immigrants to France like Slimane were defined by salaried employment; leaving their homeland and migrating to France only made sense insofar as they could find work there: 'the identity of the immigrant only makes sense, in his own eyes and in those of his entourage, through work and [...] he only exists through work'. Permament loss of work, through illness or long-term unemployment, thus 'cannot fail to be experienced as the negation of the immigrant'. This, then, is the dilemma faced by Slimane, the negation of his very raison d'être, his socio-economic and familial identity as breadwinner and head of family. In this, Slimane exemplifies a situation faced by many immigrant workers of his generation and ethnic origin.

The first generation of North African immigrants were actively recruited by the French State in the post-war decades typically to fill unskilled positions on assembly lines or construction sites. French recruiters favoured illiterate peasants with little or no formal education, precisely because this would render them better suited to such roles, more 'malleable', and easily exploitable (Benguigui 1997:16–17). The industrial sectors in which they were predominantly employed were precisely those that, in the wake of the crisis of Fordism, shed labour or closed down. The low levels of education they had received in their native countries, combined with widespread discrimination in recruitment, made it especially hard for them to find alternative employment in France's rapidly tertiarising economy. These economic shifts challenged middle-aged North African men's established roles as chief breadwinners and heads of family. Such challenges were exacerbated by cultural and ethnic factors that were specific to the immigrant condition. Living in what was effectively a foreign country, this first generation of immigrants from North Africa found themselves bringing up sons and daughters who had been educated in French schools, who were completely at home not only with written and spoken French but also with French social and cultural mores more generally, in a manner that gave them more self-assurance, more linguistic, cultural, and social capital than their fathers.

It is this dual threat to his role as both breadwinner and head of his family that Slimane faces. In this he typifies that more general phenomenon described by Azouz Begag and Christian Delorme (1994:100) as the 'effacement of fathers and the collapse of the traditional family' in France's communities of North African origin. Indeed, in the course of their fieldwork in the wake of outbursts of rioting in the deprived *banlieues* of cities such as Lyon, Paris, and Lille, Begag and Delorme were struck by the 'absence of fathers', something they attribute to precisely these cultural phenomena and socio-economic changes:

132   Republican Citizens, Precarious Subjects

> Marginalised in the social arena, [the fathers] have withdrawn
> themselves from their children's upbringing, leaving these
> responsibilities to institutional representatives such as teachers,
> community workers, the police, magistrates, and social workers.
> Their wives are working to earn money on the side. And, just
> to 'close the trap', any prospect of returning to their countries of
> origin has been abandoned as hopelessly unrealistic.
>
> (Begag and Delorme 1994:99–100)

At the level of cultural representation, the absence of the North
African father and the dysfunctional ethnic minority family have become
leitmotifs of the *banlieue* film, frequently offered as an explanation for
the delinquency of male ethnic minority youth (Tarr 2005). In the most
extreme cases, these phenomena are then essentialised. For example, in
the wake of the nationwide rioting in the *banlieues* in 2005, a number
of high-ranking figures on the mainstream French right argued that
the violence was attributable to the inherently dysfunctional nature
of 'African families' and the absence of paternal authority caused by
the supposedly widespread practice of polygamy among such families
(Arnold 2005).

One of the great strengths of Kechiche's *La Graine et le mulet* is thus
the manner in which it eschews those kinds of culturalist or essentialist
account, clearly situating the effacement of Slimane as breadwinner and
paterfamilias in its specific socio-economic context. As Sayad (1999:260)
points out, faced with the possible 'negation' of his very identity and
raison d'être, 'the search for work' represents 'an act which rehabilitates
and restores the immigrant in his function as immigrant'. This, then,
is how Slimane responds to his situation, seeking to find alternative
employment in the service sector by converting a disused coaster into
a restaurant he will moor on the Quai de la République. This location
is surely not coincidental, suggesting as it does that Slimane's rehabili-
tation as an active economic agent will not merely restore him to his
role as head of family, but will also secure his integration into the
French Republic itself. *La Graine et le mulet* thus recasts the questions
of employment, masculinity, family, and nation that, as we have seen,
are so often raised in fictional accounts of middle-aged male workers.
The film examines the specific ways in which such questions affect a
man of Slimane's age, class, and ethnicity, so as to render his attempted
conversion into a successful service-sector worker all the more difficult.

Modulated Masculinities   133

Just as he converts the disused coaster into a restaurant, so Slimane will attempt to convert himself from unskilled manual worker into a welcome, open, hospitable restaurant proprietor. In doing so, he must become a kind of 'entrepreneur of the self', marketing and selling aspects of his ethnic identity to his new customers. The success of his restaurant will rely on the mullet couscous prepared by his ex-wife and the North African music played by his friends, the other late middle-aged Maghrebi men who live in Latifa's boarding house. As the bank executive who approves the loan that enables Slimane to launch his restaurant explains, he has embarked on 'a truly remarkable human adventure'. There is a striking resonance here with the 'human adventure' on which, according to his new employers, Vincent is about to embark at the end of *L'Emploi du temps* and the 'human element' Éric's senior management seek to inject into the call-centre operatives' working lives. In all three cases, what is highlighted is the exploitation of human capital in service-sector employment, the 'excessive humanisation' of work, to use Linhart's term, that compels our three protagonists to perform more modulated versions of their professional selves.

In *La Graine et le mulet* it rapidly becomes evident that Slimane's education and former occupation have left him lacking both the personal attributes and the objective knowledge necessary to succeed in his new enterprise. Slimane's Algerian origins and his past as an unskilled manual worker have made him taciturn, socially awkward, a man of few words who visibly struggles to adopt the role of genial host on his restaurant's opening night. He also lacks the command of written and spoken French to overcome the multiple bureaucratic hurdles he must negotiate to be able to open a new restaurant. Slimane will therefore have to rely on a network of female friends and family to help him out. Latifa's teenage daughter Rym (Hafsia Herzi), a representative of a younger generation, brought up and educated in France, helps him in his dealings with the bank and town hall. Not only does his ex-wife provide the culinary expertise but, on the opening night, it is his daughters and daughters-in-law who are able to act as friendly hosts to his customers. In this sense, Slimane is obliged to defer to the women in his life, undergoing a kind of feminisation analogous to that undergone by Eric in *Retour aux mots sauvages* or lamented by Houellebecq in *La Carte et le territoire*.

If the women in Slimane's life rally round to help him, his project will be fatally undermined by the actions of his son, a representative

134   *Republican Citizens, Precarious Subjects*

of a younger generation of men of North African heritage. Just as the restaurant's opening night is getting going, Majid notices, among the customers, the wife of the deputy mayor, an attractive young woman with whom he has been conducting an affair. Not wanting this illicit affair to be discovered, he flees the restaurant, driving off without realising that the key ingredient for that evening's couscous is in the boot of his car. Once more the women rally round, Slimane's daughters and daughters-in-law plying the customers with aperitifs, while Rym takes to the stage and begins a belly dance, distracting the predominantly white clientele by pandering to their orientalist fantasies. Slimane, meanwhile, takes to his moped to drive to his ex-wife's flat to try to persuade her to prepare a replacement couscous.

The film's final sequence thus cuts between Rym's attempts to distract the restaurant's customers and Slimane's efforts to track down his ex-wife. However, the ex-wife has left her apartment to distribute left-over couscous to the area's homeless, in accordance with Islamic traditions of charity. Further, Slimane is distracted by Majid's wife who, furious and upset at her husband's serial infidelities, accuses her father-in-law of failing to bring his son up correctly. While Slimane tries to calm his daughter-in-law, three teenage boys of North African heritage steal his moped from outside the block of flats. When Slimane discovers the theft, he tries to chase the boys, who taunt and jeer at him, leading him on a fruitless pursuit through the housing estate. Panting and exhausted, Slimane eventually collapses. The film's final frame is a long shot of Slimane's unconscious body, lying alone on the ground, in front of a block of flats. The screen turns black before the director's dedication, 'To my father', appears.

The ending of *La Graine et le mulet* thus offers an even more extreme image of the defeat of a middle-aged worker than does either *L'Emploi du temps* or *Retour aux mots sauvages*. Slimane's defeat is, like the defeats of Vincent and Eric, directly linked to deindustrialisation and the proliferation of immaterial labour in contemporary France. Insofar as Kechiche laments these developments, this lament does not seem to be motivated by a conservative desire to restore the patriarchal family in its traditional form. Nor does his film communicate any nostalgia for the supposed certainities of industrial labour, alluding as it does to the racism and exploitation Slimane suffered at the boatyard. Rather, Kechiche seeks, first, to pay homage to the sacrifices of men of Slimane's generation and ethnicity. Second, his film implicitly admonishes a

Modulated Masculinities   135

younger generation of French Maghrebi men who, Kechiche suggests, risk betraying those sacrifices. As the musician Hamid (Abdelhamid Aktouche) explains to Rym, Slimane is not setting up a restaurant to make himself richer but rather to provide for his children. As Hamid puts it:

> When we see you all happy and everything, it's brilliant. For guys like us, it's a way of living again ... The solitude, the exile, the humiliation; we forget all that. We say to ourselves that at least we're not here for nothing. We haven't been immigrants for nothing. We haven't .... Do you get it?

Through these themes of sacrifice and betrayal, *La Graine et le mulet* re-inflects the recurrent themes of deindustrialisation, feminisation, and family breakdown to offer a moving account of the situation of first-generation North African male immigrants in France today.

As we have noted, Slimane's ultimate defeat offers a series of parallels with the depictions of defeated male workers we have identified in all of the other films and novels we have discussed above. As we suggested at the beginning of this chapter, this trope of the defeated middle-aged male worker reflects, at the most general level, the challenges posed to traditional conceptions of masculinity by the contemporary labour market. For the combination of deindustrialisation and the rise of immaterial service-sector labour has obliged such men to modulate their personal and professional identities in ways that have apparently challenged their masculinity and undermined their roles as heads of their families. These narrative tropes could risk a certain conservatism, particularly if they produce a series of nostalgic laments at a perceived crisis in masculinity and hence in the patriarchal nuclear family, itself figured as an essential bedrock of a properly functioning society. However, as this chapter has attempted to show, these recurrent tropes have been inflected in various ways by different novelists and film-makers in works that thus generate divergent political meanings.

In the work of Houellebecq, deindustrialisation, the feminisation of immaterial labour, and family breakdown are all lamented as symptoms of a decline in national prestige and social and moral order. Cantet's *L'Emploi du temps*, by contrast, offers an incisive critique of the role of the bourgeois family not as an antidote to globalisation and post-Fordism but as an institution that fosters the forms of economic, cultural, and educational capital that enable the French bourgeoisie to

136 *Republican Citizens, Precarious Subjects*

manage and profit from the workings of financialised global capital. Beinstingel's *Retour aux mots sauvages* is, in places, nostalgic for the supposedly wholesome forms of skilled masculine manual labour and the specifically French forms of sociability it apparently secured. Nonetheless, his novel provides a series of important insights both into what Linhart has termed 'the excessive humanisation' of work and into the self-defeating techniques French employers typically implement in response to the phenomenon of workplace suicide. Slimane's 'human adventure' in *La Graine et le mulet* offers another example of Linhart's 'excessive humanisation', of the pressures inherent to the imperative that this taciturn unskilled manual worker modulate his social and professional identity to become an entrepreneur of the self. Slimane's family plays an ambiguous role in his struggles. At once a source of symbolic and material support, notably through the actions of its womenfolk, his family will ultimately prove the source of Slimane's downfall, through the selfishness of his wayward son, Majid. Hence, as we have argued, Kechiche's film is not so much a conservative lament at the decline of the patriarchal family, as a moving account of the particular dilemmas faced by men of Slimane's age, class, and ethnicity in a deindustrialised France.

Our chosen texts thus offer a range of different depictions of the modulation of masculinity in the wake of the crisis of Fordism, the proliferation of immaterial forms of labour, and the widespread adoption of management techniques designed to solicit, capture, and exploit workers' human capital. Between them, our various films and novels also trace the uneven economic geography characteristic of this post-Fordist conjuncture, depicting that 'hybridisation' of the national and international division of labour identified by Mouhoud and Plihon (2009). Hence *L'Emploi du temps* takes us from the pole of financial-cognitive power in Geneva to the low-wage, low-skill factories of Eastern Europe that produce the counterfeit goods Vincent smuggles. *La Graine et mulet*, meanwhile, depicts the deprived deindustrialised periphery of France itself, in the form of the declining port of Sète. For all its conservatism, *La Carte et le territoire* captures something of the shift in economic power between France and the emerging economies of China and Russia.

Whether more or less conservative in their implications, most of our chosen texts also depict those men engaged in immaterial forms of labour as being feminised as a result. This immediately raises a number of related questions. To what extent is the recurrent depiction of feminised male workers a reflection of anxieties generated by the increasing numbers of women entering salaried employment? How does that literal feminisation of the workforce relate to post-Fordism? To what degree does this pose a further challenge to the highly gendered terms of the French post-war compromise? How have such developments impacted on cultural representations of working women? The next chapter will turn to consider these questions, arguing that the profusion of depictions of feminised, marginalised, or defeated middle-aged male workers has gone hand-in-hand with the emergence of a new stereotype in the form of the figure of the 'femme forte', the strong working woman.

Notes

1 For a detailed statistical account of the extent of what they term 'the crisis of the institution of the [French] family', see Korkoreff and Rodriguez (2012:122–46).
2 For a more detailed analysis of the range of economic, political, and socio-cultural determinants behind this characteristically post-Fordist 'end of patriarchalism', see Castells (2007:192–302).

Chapter 4

Femmes Fortes

Nathalie Kuperman's 2010 novel *Nous étions des êtres vivants* is set in the Paris offices of a children's publisher that has just been bought out by an aggressive French executive, Paul Cathéter. Cathéter is planning to restructure and modernise the business by shifting to electronic publishing and reducing headcount. He appoints an existing employee, Muriel Dupont-Delvich, as his general director, tasking her with identifying candidates for redundancy. Unsurprisingly, Muriel becomes highly sensitive to the way in which her colleagues now look at her, bridling at the possibility they are stereotyping her as a 'femme forte' or 'strong woman' who has renounced those conventional markers of femininity – marriage and children – in pursuit of career advancement and material gain:

> If only I could be spared the looks of my underlings that reduce me to my status as a strong woman [*me renvoient à ma condition de femme forte*]. I was ground down by my mother and father, destined to be nothing but the wife of a rich and powerful husband. I preferred to be my own powerful husband, my own wife, home, holidays and children. Jewellery, power, branded clothes, my Prada glasses, my Dolce & Gabbana jeans, my Mini, the meetings with the neighbourhood conservation committee, the rugs purchased in Morocco, my solid oak Habitat kitchen […]. In short, all those things […] I got them through my own hard graft, without relying on anyone else. Well, yes, I was married once, for a short while. Georges Delvich was my husband, someone I very often used to forget and who in no way corresponded to what I look for in a man. He remained at my

140   *Republican Citizens, Precarious Subjects*

side for almost a year before noticing that I lacked the courage to leave him, so he left me instead.

(Kuperman 2010:62)

Muriel's embittered internal monologue is highly ambiguous. Ostensibly a rejection of the label of 'femme forte', it nonetheless reveals Muriel to conform to certain of that stereotype's defining characteristics – her stated preference for branded goods over children; her coldly dismissive attitude to her ex-husband. At all events, this passage clearly relies on the assumption that the contemporary French reader will immediately recognise the stereotype of the *femme forte* as a powerful professional woman, who has abjured her traditional roles as wife and mother in favour of the ruthless pursuit of professional success and the material benefits this secures.

There is, of course, nothing new in the suggestion that women must renounce elements of their femininity in order to occupy positions of power. In the English-speaking context, we might think of Lady Macbeth, a woman who famously had to be 'unsexed' in order to achieve her ambitions, even as she continued to exploit her supposedly typically feminine wiles to seduce her husband into first sharing, then realising those ambitions. In the French-speaking context, an alternative archetype might be the Marquise de Meurteuil, the central female protagonist of Choderlos de Laclos's eighteenth-century novel, *Les Liaisons dangereuses* (1782), who renounces her expected roles as wife and mother to manipulate, seduce, and destroy her victims, even as she exploits her feminine attributes to assert her power. The *femmes fatales* of classic Hollywood *films noirs* represent more recent iterations of this trope of the powerful woman as a disturbing hybrid of masculine ruthlessness and manipulative feminine guile.

Numerous recent depictions of female executives in French film and fiction draw on such tropes to figure these powerful professional women, these *femmes fortes*, as different kinds of *femme fatale*. In his novel *Marge brute* (2006), Laurent Quintreau depicts a board meeting at KLF, a PR and advertising agency run by the ruthless chief executive Jean-François Rorty. French but educated at Harvard Business School, Rorty has 'been parachuted in' by the agency's American owners to increase the dividends it pays out to shareholders, notably by reducing wage costs through a programme of redundancies and outsourcing (Quintreau 2006:18–19). He is aided in this task by Sophie Castaglione,

Femmes Fortes 141

his Human Resources director, an unmarried, childless, and sexually alluring woman who elicits in Rorty equal measures of fear and desire (76). Castaglione is described by her colleagues as, variously, 'a true Marquise de Meurteuil' (53), 'voracious' (63), and 'a man-eater' (106). She describes herself as 'a true sorceress' (76), a 'Gorgon' (79), who, it appears, is set on exacting a terrible revenge on all men for her own romantic disappointments, most notably by manipulating, seducing, eating up, and spitting out her boss Rorty (74–83).

A similarly disparaging depiction of a female executive as *femme forte* is offered by Philippe Vasset in his novel *Journal intime d'une prédatrice* (2010). The 'prédatrice' or female predator in question is the head of an investment fund that is planning to exploit the natural resources opened up by the melting of the Arctic ice cap. Known simply as 'She' throughout the narrative, or occasionally by her media nickname of 'the Ice Queen', she represents a veritable compendium of misogynistic stereotypes of female power: vain, deceitful, manipulative, jealous, and vindictive, her overvaulting ambition will ultimately prove the source of her downfall and death at the novel's end. Both Éric Reinhardt's novel *Le Système Victoria* (2011) and Alain Corneau's film *Crime d'amour* (2010) turn on the behaviour of powerful foreign female executives, who are at once sexually perverse and the bearers of what are coded as 'Anglo-Saxon' business practices that threaten to destroy the bases of the French family and, through that, of the national community itself. Marie-Castille Mention-Schaar's film *Bowling* (2012) offers a less sexualised depiction of a powerful female employee in the form of a childless Parisian Human Resources director, Catherine (Catherine Frot), who is sent to close down the maternity unit in a town in rural Brittany for reasons of budgetary efficiency. Catherine is thus initially figured as a *femme forte* whose powerful and childless status threatens traditional notions of motherhood and rooted community. Thanks to her salutary exposure to this local community, Catherine reconnects with her maternal instinct, saving the maternity unit by having it reclassified as a 'Maison des bébés', a mark of quality that, her secretary explains, is equivalent to an 'appellation contrôlée'. Motherhood, family, community, and *terroir*, then, finally win out against the nakedly capitalist logic initially personified by a *femme forte*. As we have noted, Kuperman's novel *Nous étions des êtres vivants* also draws on the stereotype of the *femme forte*, albeit in a manner that implies a greater

142   *Republican Citizens, Precarious Subjects*

measure of critical distance than seems evident in the other films and novels cited above.

With the possible exception of Kuperman's novel, these recurrent depictions of female executives as ruthless, manipulative *femmes fortes* would seem to reflect considerable anxiety at the accession of an increasing number of women to positions of power within contemporary French businesses. However, these disparaging depictions of powerful female executives have coincided with the emergence of another, very different category of *femme forte* in French film, novel, and reportage over the same period. This is a category composed of working-class women who are portrayed in a much more flattering light, shown bravely struggling to keep their families and communities together, the guardians of a now-threatened tradition of working-class activism in a context marked by the loss of stable male industrial employment and the consequent waning of the power of their menfolk, as of the workers' movement.

An early example of this is provided by the character of Danielle Arnoux (Danielle Mélador) in Laurent Cantet's film *Ressources humaines* (1999). A middle-aged, working-class woman, Danielle is the representative of the Communist-affiliated trade union, the CGT, at a provincial factory that is in the process of implementing the 35-hour working-week legislation. At the beginning of the film, she stands alone in her determined and vocal opposition to the management's plans, correctly understanding that these involve exploiting the 35-hour legislation to increase workload while reducing headcount. In this, she stands opposed to Jean-Claude (Jean-Claude Vallod), a middle-aged, semi-skilled worker and family man, who embodies a sense of passivity and male working-class defeat throughout much of the film. The eponymous heroine of Medhi Charef's film, *Marie-Line* (2000), is another equally pugnacious and determined working-class woman, who struggles to keep family and community together while working as a cleaner in a supermarket situated in a Parisian *banlieue* from which all male industrial jobs have seemingly disappeared. In Robert Guédiguian's *La Ville est tranquille* (2000), Michèle (Ariane Ascaride) works night shifts in Marseilles' fish market to support her drug-addicted daughter and neglected granddaughter, while her unemployed husband stays at home drinking. François Bon's novel *Daewoo* (2004) and Florence Aubenas's reportage *Le Quai de Ouistreham* (2010) similarly focus on working-class women determined to keep family, community, and the memory of past working-class struggles alive in regions of northern and north-eastern France ravaged by deindustrialisation and mass male unemployment.

These various working-class *femmes fortes* are thus all depicted as being admirable in their resourcefulness and uncompromising determination; all seem to represent variations on the Mother Courage figure and, as such, appear to be diametrically opposed to the much less flattering portrayals of powerful female executives we have identified. Nonetheless, these two apparently opposed variants of the *femme forte* figure do share one significant feature insofar as each involves undermining the centrality previously enjoyed by male workers, as chief breadwinners, husbands, and fathers. The emergence of the figure of the *femme forte*, in both its variants, is thus a corollary of the numerous depictions of men being feminised by the nature of contemporary forms of work that we examined in the preceding chapter.

At the simplest level, the figure of the *femme forte* is clearly a response to fundamental shifts in the nature and extent of French women's involvement in the labour market, shifts that are themselves symptomatic of the erosion of the terms of the Fordist–Republican post-war compromise. French women's massively increased access to higher education from the 1960s onwards, combined with their demands for greater autonomy and the consequent reshaping of the nuclear family have led to significantly improved career opportunities for middle-class women particularly. Hence, the percentage of women in executive or managerial roles has increased significantly, rising from 24 per cent of the total in 1981 to 40 per cent in 2012 (Flocco 2015:15). At the same time, the erosion of the Fordist model of stable male industrial employment has seen a profusion in more flexible, often part-time and relatively poorly paid service-sector employment. As Margaret Maurani and Monique Meron (2012) have argued, the continued expectation that French women should perform the lion's share of domestic labour and childcare duties means that they represent a readily exploitable pool of labour, well-suited to meeting the demand for part-time workers in supposedly inherently feminine service-sector roles. Thus, women's overall levels of participation in the French labour market have increased: in 1975 just 51 per cent of women aged 15–64 were in salaried employment in France, compared to 66 per cent by 2013. French women are now less likely to be unemployed than their male counterparts by a factor of 0.96 (DARES 2015). Nonetheless,

144 Republican Citizens, Precarious Subjects

women remain overrepresented in the areas of part-time and unskilled work. In 2013 women were 2.2 times more likely to occupy unskilled jobs than their male counterparts, 5.7 times more likely to be in part-time work, and 2.9 times more likely to declare themselves underemployed (DARES 2015).

The figure of the *femme forte*, in both its executive and working-class variants, is clearly an attempt to make sense of these phenomena, an attempt that involves greater or lesser degrees of ideological distortion depending on the particular texts or authors concerned. As we have suggested, the figure of the powerful female executive as a kind of destructive *femme fatale* seems to express considerable anxiety in the face of French women's greater access to executive and managerial roles. These anxieties seem all the more exaggerated and misplaced given that, for all their advances in this area, women remain significantly underrepresented among French senior management: in 2013 just 14 per cent of positions on French company boards were occupied by women, an increase of just 1.2 percentage points since 2003 (De Rauglaudre 2015). Misplaced anxieties in the face of women's relatively modest advances in the realm of executive labour are surely not unique to the French context. Nonetheless, as we have argued on a number of occasions, the particular form taken by the Fordist–Republican compromise in post-war France did mean that women's roles as mothers and housewives were given a particular emphasis. Indeed, it might be argued that the noticeable tendency to represent powerful female executives as threats not simply to traditional gender hierarchies but also to the national community reflects the centrality of the figure of the housewife and mother to established conceptions of a functioning French Republic.

The figure of the *femme forte* as assertive working-class woman might seem considerably less conservative in its implications. Yet, however laudably assertive and determined these *femmes fortes* may appear, working-class women portrayed as struggling to keep family and community together are still engaging in reassuringly feminine, maternal, and care-giving roles. Further, given the low-paid, precarious jobs these working-class women typically occupy, they lack the forms of economic, social, or political power enjoyed by powerful female executives and hence represent far less threatening figures.

The figure of the *femme forte*, whether working-class or middle-class executive, thus raises a series of questions regarding both the changing place of women in the contemporary French labour market and the ways in which such changes have been represented in recent films, novels, and documentary sources. This chapter will therefore examine a representative sample of films and texts in which both powerful female executives and strong-willed working-class women play a central role. In the first instance, Reinhardt's novel *Le Système Victoria* and Corneau's film *Crime d'amour* will be examined as epitomising the disparaging depiction of powerful executive women as unnatural hybrids who threaten established institutions of family and national community. Turning to the novel *Nous étions des êtres vivants* will then allow us to consider to what extent Kuperman is able to achieve a measure of critical distance on the stereotype of executive women as ruthless *femmes fortes*. Second, the chapter will analyse the apparently more flattering representation of strong working-class women in Bon's novel *Daewoo* and Aubenas's work of journalistic reportage, *Le Quai de Ouistreham*. In both cases, we will examine the more precarious forms of subjectivity that are depicted as being produced by the literal and figurative feminisation of the French workplace, whether the precarity of the female executive who abjures motherhood and marriage for her career, the precarity of the men whose centrality she has thus displaced, or the precarity of the working-class mother struggling to keep family and community together through low-paid service-sector work. Each of these forms of precarity challenges the highly gendered division of labour at the core of French republicanism and hence of the form taken by the post-war compromise in France. The threat posed to the French Republic itself by these challenges to conventional gender hierarchies is nowhere better exemplified than in the figure of the powerful *foreign* female executive, the *femme forte* who embodies the destructive forces of globalised capitalism in Reinhardt's *Le Système Victoria*.

Femmes Fortes, Femmes Fatales

Reinhardt's 2011 novel tells the tale of the adulterous, passionate love affair between its narrator, David Kolski, and the elegant, powerful business executive, Victoria de Winter. David is a frustrated architect turned project manager, responsible for the construction of a new tower block in La Défense. Married with a young daughter, he is the son of a working-class Polish immigrant father and a French mother

146   *Republican Citizens, Precarious Subjects*

and remains ostensibly committed to left-wing ideals. Victoria, an advocate for globalised capitalism, is much richer and more powerful than David. The Human Resources director of a company that was, originally, 'a jewel in the crown of British industry' but is now 'a group present in twenty or so countries, owned by international, essentially American investors', she spends her working life jetting between Paris, London, and a host of other exotic locations (Reinhardt 2011:33). This mobility not only reflects Victoria's professional role, it also confirms her status as what David terms 'fundamentally expatriate', a woman born in Barcelona to an English mother and a German father, before being brought up in France and then taking up jobs 'in China, Singapore, Germany and nowadays in London' (106). Despite his immigrant origins on his father's side, David is identified as being more rooted in rural France through his mother and grandmother. When his affair with Victoria ends tragically in a murder for which David is the principal suspect, he is pursued by the media and banned from any contact with his wife and daughter. He seeks refuge in an isolated country hotel, close to what he describes to its proprietor as 'my family's village, [the] village where my father met my mother. I spent all my holidays there, from my birth until I was eighteen. My grandmother still lives there today; today she's... wait ... she was born in 1919...' (410).

David's doomed affair with Victoria thus allegorises the fatal attraction felt by elements of the French left, and by the French nation more generally, for the alluring but ultimately destructive promises of neo-liberal globalisation. Victoria is a very particular kind of *femme fatale*; sexually rapacious, temperamental, devious, and enigmatic, she exerts a strong hold over David. On learning that he is merely the last in a long line of men with whom Victoria has betrayed her husband, David marvels at what he figures as her essentially feminine capacity for lying: 'Victoria possesses the ability to transcend any truths that get in her way, inventing other, higher truths that allow her to act, metamorphosed, like a goddess endowed with unlimited powers.' This divinely protean aptitude for mendacity elicits in him equal amounts of desire and fear: 'this fascination did not fail to produce in my imagination, at the same moment, an accompanying sense of terror' (321).

If Victoria's mendacity seems to conform to conventional gender stereotypes regarding women's supposed essential inconstancy and duplicity, her elevated professional role clearly upsets traditional gender hierarchies. We learn that she earns more than her husband and, as she explains to David: 'It's me who pays for almost everything but no-one is allowed to mention it; the subject is taboo and my husband represses it constantly [...] [I]n the eyes of my in-laws [...] I've been so vulgar as to have sought to supplant my husband both symbolically and materially' (341). Victoria also earns much more than David and this, in turn, undermines any possibility of his adopting the dominant role in their relationship. Indeed, it is hard not to interpret David's determination successfully to manage the building of the 'biggest tower block in France' in La Défense as a kind of symbolic compensation for a whole series of challenges to his masculinity (86–87). Even before embarking on his affair with Victoria, David had felt feminised by first studying architecture and then by what he describes as 'the compromise of working in the tertiary sector'. He contrasts his chosen profession to 'the rawness of my father's identity as a worker', lamenting the 'decay' or 'degeneration of the virile ideal that accompanied the development of the service sector' (127). David bitterly recalls early encounters with his future father-in-law, a high-ranking military officer, who mocked 'the *eminently feminine* opinions' he had expressed as a young architecture student (151). Later, Victoria will confess to having assumed David was gay when she first encountered him in the street (109) and, later still, she will express the desire to 'sodomise' him (264).

Victoria is thus depicted as an unnatural hybrid, combining feminine allure and duplicity, on the one hand, with masculine economic and sexual power, on the other. This disturbing mix of conventionally opposing attributes is reflected in her professional life. As she explains to David, to operate effectively at work, she is obliged to 'make concessions to the male beast, show myself to be conciliatory. [...] So I'm not too fussy about the quality of conversations. Sometimes I'm as dull and clumsy as they are. I've even found myself going to matches at old football grounds in Poland. It reassures them to see me as one of them' (73–74). Yet, the novel implies, Victoria's feigning masculinity for the purposes of work is merely one further expression of a predisposition to mendacity that is figured as essentially feminine. Throughout the novel her primary professional task is to negotiate with the trades unions in order to manage the closure of a steel factory in the Lorraine with the loss of several hundred jobs. Her firm's shareholders view heavy industry as an anachronistic, unprofitable burden. So, the factory must be closed, and the jobs sacrificed to enable the firm to move

148   *Republican Citizens, Precarious Subjects*

into 'new technologies' and so boost its share price (520). Here, too, Victoria's ruthless, stereotypically masculine determination to pursue profit despite the human costs is allied with her supposedly feminine aptitude for duplicity, as she convinces the unions they should welcome their factory's re-categorisation as a 'subsidiary', while all the while knowing this is merely a precursor to its outright sale to a Brazilian asset-stripper (527). As David remarks of her negotiating strategy, 'you are wooing them, you are bewitching them ...' (522). Like Lady Macbeth before her, then, Victoria has been unsexed. Yet, again like Lady Macbeth, the cruelty this allows her to exercise, in both her professional and personal dealings with men, continues to be combined with the canny exploitation of some stereotypically feminine wiles.

As the novel progresses, its narrator David becomes increasingly aware that there is no distinction between Victoria's ruthless pursuit of her desires in her private life and her behaviour in the professional domain. Thus, she becomes not simply an incarnation of male fears at both female sexual potency and women's increasing autonomy through salaried labour. She simultaneously serves as a personification of neo-liberal globalisation itself, of its amorality, its rootlessness, its mobility, its insatiable desire for new returns whatever the human costs. Indeed, it is this parallel between the ruthless insatiability of her sexual desires and the insatiability of the globalised capitalism she advocates that lies at the core of the 'système Victoria' that gives the novel its title:

> Such was the system at the basis of Victoria's existence: never stay in the same place, divide oneself up into a large number of activities and projects so as never to be confined in any single truth, all the while finding one's own truth in movement itself. Victoria didn't feel any pity, any remorse, any sadness or anxiety, for she dissolved such feelings through movement and fragmentation. Speed constitutes the truth of our world and not the local situations that such speed enables the powerful to transcend, skate over or glimpse from on high. Victoria felt at home everywhere; she never felt constrained anywhere, having an escape route in place in all circumstances. Only sex could interrupt her headlong rush forward.

The daughter of an English mother and a father from Berlin, brought up for the most part in a country, France, that was not her own, Victoria prided herself on being an international woman, with no ties to anywhere in particular. (Reinhardt 2011:529)

Insatiable, polymorphous, rootless, constantly in movement, and inherently destructive, Victoria's sexual desire is thus directly analogous to the forms taken by contemporary globalised capitalism. Further, it is surely significant that although David engages in marathon sex sessions with Victoria, on several occasions we learn that he never reaches orgasm (221, 346). This, of course, contrasts with David's sexual relations with his wife, Sylvie, that have borne fruit in the form of his young daughter. A wholesome, productive form of sexuality within the nuclear family is thus implicitly opposed to a perverse, unproductive form of illicit sexuality with Victoria and allegorises an analogous opposition between the productive forms of capitalism exemplified by the factory in Lorraine, on the one hand, and Victoria's destructive, insatiable pursuit of financial, immaterial profits, on the other.

Ultimately, Victoria's insatiable sexual desires will be the cause of both her and David's downfall. Having been taken by David to a Parisian porn cinema to engage their mutual desire for group sex, she agrees, despite his protestations, to accompany two unknown men in their van to continue the orgy elsewhere. She is found murdered the next morning by the police, who subsequently arrest David in his family home, ruining his career and family life in the process, leaving him to seek a solitary refuge in *la France profonde*, close to the village of his mother's and grandmother's birth. As he puts it on the novel's final page: 'I wanted […] to immerse myself as deeply as possible in the interior of France' (611). A national identity rooted in the French countryside and in the fixed gender roles of the patriarchal nuclear family has thus been destroyed by a rootless, cosmopolitan, sexually and professionally insatiable foreign female executive. Victoria's violent end serves both as punishment for her temerity in rejecting her traditional role as wife and mother and as an allegory for the self-destructive tendencies of the global capitalism she embodies. This is a peculiarly overdetermined allegory that, although focalised through the experiences of an avowedly left-wing narrator, relies on some profoundly conservative assumptions about gender, family, and rootedness in local community, all figured as keys to the preservation of the integrity of the French national polity.

150   *Republican Citizens, Precarious Subjects*

This figuration of the foreign female executive as a disruptive *femme fatale*, who must be punished for the immoderate nature of her professional and sexual desires, is mirrored in Alain Corneau's 2010 thriller, *Crime d'amour*. The film centres on the murderous professional rivalry between two female executives who work in the La Défense offices of an American consultancy firm. One of these women is a young French junior executive, Isabelle (Ludivine Sagnier), whose blonde hair and youth make of her an embodiment of French innocence threatened by her induction into the immoral world of Anglo-Saxon capitalism. That immoral world is personified by her boss, the ruthless, manipulative, unmarried, childless, and sexually perverse Christine. Christine is played by Kristin Scott Thomas, whose recognisable star persona, combined with her British accent when speaking French and unaccented fluency in English, clearly communicate her 'Anglo-Saxon' origins.

In the film's opening scene, we see Isabelle and Christine working late together in the drawing room of the latter's luxurious home. This is a scene of seduction in which the dark-haired older Christine attempts to seduce the blonde-haired young Isabelle both sexually, by sniffing her perfume and kissing her neck, and ideologically, by initiating her into the sharp practices of the Anglo-Saxon business world. This attempted seduction allegorises, of course, the seduction of good by evil, of youth by experience, and of the honour and integrity of France itself by a cynically exploitative foreign model of socio-economic organisation. Halfway through the scene, Philippe arrives, another of Christine's professional juniors and also her lover. As Christine stretches out on the couch, caressing Philippe's thigh with her foot, she stares into Isabelle's eyes, a wicked smile tacitly inviting her to join them in a *ménage à trois*.

At this point Isabelle makes her excuses and leaves, explaining she will finish her work at home. We cut to a scene in a dimly lit interior, the camera first holding on a stylish but empty dining-room table and chairs, before tracking back across this deserted scene and panning right to reveal Isabelle seated at a polished steel kitchen work surface, working on her laptop and talking to a work colleague on her mobile. The empty table and chairs emphasise what Isabelle has had to give up to become an executive – the husband and children who are conspicuous by their absence. What should, then, have been a scene of feminine domesticity and familial conviviality has been contaminated by the demands of the Anglo-Saxon workplace. This contamination is also represented visually, as the shiny surfaces of Isabelle's immaculate and unused kitchen mirror the glass and steel of the American consultancy firm's offices in La Défense. In two subsequent short scenes, we see Isabelle eating a rushed breakfast before work, standing alone, surrounded by those same shiny surfaces, as if to reinforce this point about the shocking absence of familial conviviality. Indeed, Isabelle's house itself, a modern suburban *pavillon*, whose exterior styling attempts to evoke rustic domesticity, yet whose fashionable interior appears cold and sanitised, represents a kind of degraded simulacrum of a genuine family home.

Later in the film, distraught at her treatment at the hands of the ruthless Christine, Isabelle leaves Paris, seeking refuge and solace at her sister's home in the provinces, the same family home in which Isabelle herself grew up. This house's ivy-covered façade, its provincial location and considerable age connote its rootedness in a *terroir* that is strikingly contrasted to both the anonymity of the Parisian suburb in which Isabelle lives and the cold modernism of her workplace in La Défense. Where Isabelle works, is childless, and unmarried, her sister stays at home, preparing meals for her working husband and looking after their angelic daughter. As Isabelle laments to her sister, she too might have enjoyed this happy domestic life, had she not been seduced by the lure of Anglo-Saxon business into abandoning her maternal role and hence, the film implies, threatening the institutions of family, community, and nation. To quote Isabelle: 'A nice little husband, a nice little daughter, a nice little life, apparently, it's not really my thing.' Marriage, family, and the French *terroir* are thus figured as the antidotes to a destructive model of socio-economic organisation personified by a powerful foreign female executive.

A number of complex plot twists follow, in the course of which Isabelle succeeds in escaping from Christine's grasp by getting away with her murder. As result, Isabelle replaces Christine at the top of the French office of her American employers. However, this moment of professional triumph corresponds to a profound personal defeat. Not only has Isabelle's initiation into the Anglo-Saxon business world led her to commit murder, in the film's final sequence Isabelle also realises there is now no escape for her from the vicious rivalries and ruthless business practices that characterise that world. Thus, *Crime d'amour* depicts Isabelle, a personification of youthful French

152   *Republican Citizens, Precarious Subjects*

innocence, being diverted from her natural role as wife and mother by her involvement with a sexually perverse, unmarried, and childless *femme forte*, who is herself a personification of ruthless Anglo-Saxon business practices.

Reinhardt's Victoria and Corneau's Christine thus both epitomise the disparaging stereotype of powerful female executives as ruthless women who have turned their backs on their feminine and maternal instincts in pursuit of professional power and material gain. It is this stereotype of the *femme forte* that Muriel Dupont-Delvich bridles against in *Nous étions des êtres vivants*, suggesting that Kuperman's novel may thus encompass a critique of that stereotype's conservative assumptions. Yet, as we will show, although Kuperman's novel does offer an apparently more sympathetic portrayal of powerful female executives, it will ultimately attribute what it depicts as their irrationally vindictive behaviour to their lack of a husband and/or children.

Criticising or Rehearsing the Stereotype?

As we have already mentioned, *Nous étions des êtres vivants* focuses on a restructuring programme and a wave of redundancies that sweep through a Parisian children's publisher that has just been bought out by the aggressive businessman Paul Cathéter. Once he has rendered the business more profitable, Cathéter intends to sell it on at a higher price than he paid, pocketing the difference. Although this personification of a nakedly capitalist logic is French, the novel nonetheless manages to imply that the real source of this threat is America. As the publishing house's employees collectively explain: 'We've been bought out by a man who loves North America and who's going to manage us in the American style. Suddenly, America frightens us. We'd never imagined that danger could come from so far away' (Kuperman 2010:18–19).

One of the novel's central concerns is to portray the destructive effects of Cathéter's ruthless management style on the sense of collegiality and professional conviviality that had thus far reigned in the publishing house. The novel takes the form of a series of internal monologues in which each employee expresses their reactions to their firm's restructuring, interspersed with a Chorus, through which the employees' collective hopes and fears are voiced. The Chorus thus represents a collective identity undermined by fears, rumours, and the backbiting and unseemly juggling for the favours of Paul Cathéter that the spectre of redundancy unleashes. This working community at threat serves as a microcosm of French society as a whole, itself threatened by the forces of globalised capitalism. Having been worried by rumours that Cathéter intends to relocate the business from central Paris to some distant, anonymous suburban trading estate, the Chorus is delighted to learn that in fact they are moving to the quarter around the Place de la République: 'République, République, République … A metro station that is lucky for most of us. [...] It's right in the centre of Paris [...]. République, what a relief!' (41). This almost incantatory repetition of the word 'République' suggests that the employees are relieved not simply because they will avoid a lengthy daily commute but also on account of the symbolic relief that the Place de la République offers as emblem and guarantor of French republican values of community and social solidarity in the face of Cathéter's American style of management.

Not only does Kuperman's novel thus rehearse the now familiar trope that sets a good French republicanism against its malevolent Anglo-Saxon nemesis, that dichotomy is also overdetermined by the question of gender. For gender is explicitly placed at the core of the novel's concerns. Publishing is a commercial sector with a high proportion of female employees, something often interpreted as a reflection of women's supposedly innate facility for linguistic and communicative skills. The fact that this is a children's publisher means that work is doubly feminised here, since both those feminine 'soft skills' and the female employees' presumed maternal instincts apparently predispose them to the production of children's magazines and games. As one of the employees remarks: 'We are, principally, women and the few men who work amongst us have taken on effeminate airs' (40).

This process of feminisation does not, of course, affect the businessman Paul Cathéter; he personifies what are figured as a set of inherently masculine, ruthless, commercial values that threaten to shatter the firm's older commitment to feminine solidarity between its employees and maternal concern for its young customers. Caught at the centre of this struggle between masculine and feminine values is Muriel Dupont-Delvich, whom Cathéter promotes to the post of *Directeur général* to help him identify suitable candidates for redundancy. Thus, as Muriel herself explains, she will have to supplement her stereotypically feminine aptitude for personal relationships and personnel management

154   *Republican Citizens, Precarious Subjects*

with Cathéter's more masculine commitment to the rational calculation of future profit, regardless of the human cost:

> I acknowledge that for someone like me who likes people, who takes pleasure in listening to their problems, who participates in their lives, dispensing advice and consolations, it will be difficult to distance myself from my staff. I will struggle to force myself to consider their complaints as unjustified petulance, to navigate between my memories of the relationship we used to enjoy and the reality of our current relations. Because, Paul Cathéter has warned me, I'll have to change my style of management: 'Do you want to play a role in turning this business around, or hold onto values that will lead to its going bust?' (Kuperman 2010:44)

Muriel must, therefore, become a kind of unnatural hybrid; masculine, through her commitment to Cathéter's goals, she will nonetheless continue to rely on what she herself figures as an inherently feminine gift for achieving those goals by devious means: 'that gift for organising things in a way that suits me without anyone realising that I'm pulling the strings' (34). It is in tacit recognition of her new hybrid identity that she refuses the feminised job title of *Directrice générale*, opting for *la Directeur général* instead, in a coining that juxtaposes the feminine article 'la' with the masculine forms of both 'directeur' and 'général'.

Rather than condemning Muriel for adopting this unnatural, hybrid identity, Kuperman invites the reader to sympathise with her, presenting it as evidence of the extent to which women are forced to alienate their true identities in order to succeed in a commercial world dominated by aggressive masculine values. However, this critique is highly ambiguous in its implications. On the one hand, Kuperman clearly intends to criticise the particular pressures working women face. Yet, on the other, in positing femininity and ruthlessness as inherently opposed, she risks reasserting that stereotype according to which women are fundamentally gentle, caring, compassionate, hence maternal beings for whom ruthlessness represents a fundamental alienation of their essential identities. At this point, Kuperman risks no longer grasping characteristics gendered as feminine as being socially constructed but positing them as inherent, essential, even biologically determined by women's supposed maternal function. This slippage between the social and the biological is also evident in the novel's account of the process whereby Muriel selects from among her colleagues the names of those she will put forward as candidates for redundancy. Here Muriel will be seen to act from a mix of jealousy and vindictiveness that is attributed to her divorced and childless status in a highly problematic way.

One of the colleagues Muriel nominates for redundancy is her former personal assistant, Ariane Stein. Muriel and Ariane had initially enjoyed a very close working relationship. However, this ended abruptly the day Ariane announced her pregnancy and imminent marriage. As Ariane explains: '[Muriel's] wrath descended on me when I announced to her that I was pregnant, four years after we first met, four years during which we had lived in a kind of idyll. [...] She liked me young and unmarried, she liked me when I was completely dependent on my work' (80–81). Muriel's 'wrath' does not only reflect her annoyance that her assistant will be distracted from her work by marriage and children, however; it is also rooted in her frustrated maternal instincts and the jealousy she consequently feels when Ariane gives birth to a son named Antonin, the very name Muriel had intended to give her own child. For we learn that, as a much younger woman, Muriel had fallen pregnant, passionately wanting to keep the child, her future son. Her then partner, however, forced her to have an abortion and she is now tormented by this 'high treason' and by memories of what might have been: 'I retain the image of a sort of female saint destined to a filial love that was frustrated on a whim' (150). Muriel feels that her co-workers, the vast majority of whom are mothers, mistrust her on account of her unmarried and childless status: 'Everyone in this firm knows I haven't got any children' (63). Motivated by what Ariane describes as an 'infantile jealousy', Muriel hoards all the free toy samples the company is sent to prevent her co-employees taking them home as presents for their own children. On finding this hidden cache of toys in Muriel's office, Ariane remarks: 'Muriel Dupont-Delvich *is* the children that she hasn't had' (111). Muriel's decision to nominate Ariane for redundancy is thus an expression of her pathological jealousy at her colleague's motherhood and an act of displaced vengeance for her ex-partner's 'high treason'.

These allusions to Muriel's frustrated desire for children contain a surely legitimate criticism of male partners who pressure women into unwanted abortions. However, that point could have been made without depicting the victim of such pressure as being so pathologised by her experiences as to exact revenge on a former friend and

156 *Republican Citizens, Precarious Subjects*

colleague, who played no role whatsoever in the original offence. Here Kuperman seems to have slipped from attributing Muriel's behaviour to the malign influence of Paul Cathéter to attributing it to pathologies inherent to a woman prevented from realising her biological destiny and becoming a mother. Thus, while Cathéter's planned restructuring provides the pretext for Muriel's actions, their true cause lies elsewhere, in the pathologies attendant on her frustrated desire to have children of her own.

Towards the end of the novel Muriel resigns her position, angry at Cathéter's insistence she place the interests of the firm above caring for her elderly father. Once again, Kuperman articulates here an entirely pertinent critique of the pressures faced by working women who struggle to reconcile their professional responsibilities with the domestic and caring duties they are still expected to perform. However, her account of what happens following Muriel's resignation sees her slip away from this focus on the injustices inherent to the social construction of gender roles and back towards more conservative assumptions about motherhood, marriage, and the nuclear family. Muriel is replaced as general director by Ariane Stein. Ariane's motivations in selecting candidates for redundancy seem as problematic as were Muriel's. One of the names she puts forward is that of Dominique Beccaria, whom Ariane has chosen purely because Dominique shares the same first name as her ex-husband's new partner. Ariane is both profoundly jealous of her ex-husband's new partner (137–39) and tormented by 'nostalgia for family life and […] the feeling my life is a failure' (140). Thus, where Muriel's ruthless professional decisions are ultimately determined by her lack of children, Ariane's actions express her nostalgia for a husband and conventional family. Both Muriel and Ariane are hence depicted as behaving in an irrational and vindictive fashion in the professional domain and this pathological behaviour is directly attributed to their inability to fulfil their traditional roles as wives and/or mothers.

On one level, then, Kuperman seeks to criticise the particular pressures faced by women in executive positions and hence encourages the reader to sympathise with, rather than condemn, Muriel and Ariane's behaviour. Ultimately, however, the ruthless decisions taken by these women are depicted as being determined not by the exigencies of their professional roles but by a mixture of irrational jealousy and petty vindictiveness rooted in their lack of children or husbands. Similarly, Kuperman tends to naturalise the predominance of women in the publishing industry, rather than interrogating those cultural, socio-economic, and institutional forces that condition young women to study 'softer' humanities subjects, hence predisposing them to employment in low-paid sectors like publishing. Indeed, this naturalising of publishing as inherently feminine is key to the whole narrative, which hinges on a fundamental opposition between the benevolent, caring, feminine qualities of the publishing firm, in its original form, and the malevolent, destructive, masculine commercial values personified by Cathéter. Thus, despite its greater sympathy for powerful female executives, Kuperman's novel relies on the same essentialised oppositions as structure both *Le Système Victoria* and *Crime d'amour*, oppositions between a destructive foreign socio-economic model, on the one hand, and national community, guaranteed by femininity, marriage, and motherhood, on the other.

As we have argued, on one level the emergence of the figure of the powerful female executive as *femme forte* reflects certain observable changes in the French labour market characteristic of post-Fordism. Indeed, the corpus of novels and films we have identified offers some insights into the manner in which these changes have been mediated through older assumptions about women's supposedly inherent aptitudes and strengths. Thus, Kuperman's focus on the publishing industry, alongside the profusion of depictions of female directors of Human Resources – Reinhardt's Victoria, Sophie Castiglione in *Marge brute*, Christine in *Bowling* – reflects the extent to which women's accession to executive roles has tended to be concentrated in those areas where supposedly feminine communicative and interpersonal skills are valued. The frequency with which these powerful professional women are figured as threats to marriage, family, and national community, meanwhile, reflects something specific about the centrality of marriage and motherhood to the French post-war model. As we demonstrated in the last chapter, male workers were given a central role in the French post-war model as primary breadwinners and heads of the patriarchal nuclear family. One corollary of the centrality of the male breadwinner was the emphasis placed on women's roles as homemakers and child-bearers, something institutionalised in the generous system of child benefits inherent to the French model (Palier 2005:3). This, in turn, reflected the importance of 'natalism' in French government circles, the emphasis placed on maintaining the birth-rate in order to safeguard the strength and vitality of the French nation (Le Bras 1991). Through

158 Republican Citizens, Precarious Subjects

the later decades of the twentieth century, of course, women gained increased control over their bodies through birth control and greater access to salaried employment. The French authorities sought to ensure they would not wholly abandon their childbearing responsibilities by increasing the provision of crèches (Windebank 1997) and institution-alising forms of part-time work that encouraged working women to continue to take primary responsibility for more traditional domestic and maternal tasks (Maurani and Meron 2012). As Jan Windebank (1997:67) argues, 'the ideology of motherhood in the sense of women feeling the need to have children in order to be "fulfilled", even if not in the sense of staying at home to look after them' hence 'still holds strongly in France'.

The emergence of the figure of the female executive as *femme forte* thus reflects these various socio-economic and political shifts, as well as the contradictory fashion in which they have interacted with older assumptions about women's appropriate roles as wives and mothers. The depiction of female executives as *femmes fortes*, unnatural beings who threaten not merely marriage and family but the very Republic itself, represents a striking expression of those contradictions. The other variant of *femme forte*, the strong working-class woman, is a similarly ambiguous figure: ostensibly depicted in more flattering terms and clearly reflecting the decline in stable male industrial employment, this figure is nonetheless bound up with notions of gender, family, and nation in very particular ways. In turning to the representation of working-class *femmes fortes* in François Bon's novel *Daewoo* and Florence Aubenas's book of reportage *Le Quai de Ouistreham*, we will examine the insights these two texts offer into both the interrelationships between class, gender, and employment and the ideological frames through which those interrelationships have been mediated.

Gender, Space, and Class

The most obvious distinction between the working-class women who feature in Bon and Aubenas's respective accounts and the powerful female executives we have discussed so far reflects the immense disparity of wealth and power between these two categories of *femme forte*. As *Daewoo* and *Le Quai de Ouistreham* make clear, this disparity is spatialised in particular ways. One of the characteristics shared by the powerful professional women whose depictions we have thus far analysed is their rootless mobility. As we saw, Reinhardt's Victoria was described as being 'fundamentally an expatriate'; the 'predatress' in Vasset's *Journal intime d'une prédatrice* is depicted moving effortlessly between New York, Paris, Scandinavia, and the Arctic; in *Crime d'amour*, Isabelle's working life takes her from Paris to Cairo and Washington, DC. At one level, this mobility is simply an accurate reflection of the uneven economic geography identified by Mouhoud and Plihon (2009), the stark division between metropolitan centres, in which cognitive, economic, and political resources are ever more concentrated, on the one hand, and an impoverished periphery, on the other. In *Le Système Victoria*, this is exemplified by Victoria's restless movement between metropolitan poles of power – Paris, London, New York, Singapore – and the deindustrialised periphery represented by the factory in Lorraine whose closure she is plotting. Of course, as we have noted, this polarity is frequently interpreted in a fundamentally conservative ideological manner, so that mobility and rootlessness are themselves uncritically posited as unhealthy and destructive.

The working-class women in our sample of texts are, by contrast, characterised by their stasis; their lack of economic power and the nature of their low-skilled employment preclude any such international mobility; the regions in which they were born and live are those that have been left behind by deindustrialisation and the consequent increasing concentration of economic power in metropolitan centres. Nonetheless, these regions and the women who inhabit them are shown to be caught up in different ways in global movements of capital and labour. These interrelationships between gender, social class, marginalised regions within a given nation state, and newly deregulated flows of international capital are exemplified by the situation in which the women in *Daewoo* find themselves. Indeed, the story of Daewoo's establishment in France, its exploitation of a ready pool of predominantly female workers in the deindustrialised Lorraine, its subsequent bankruptcy, leaving those women to compete for a small stock of precarious service-sector jobs, all exemplify phenomena we have previously identified as symptoms of the crisis of Fordism both within France and globally.

Daewoo is the product of Bon's extensive fieldwork among the predominantly female ex-employees of three factories set up in the Lorraine region of North Eastern France by the giant Korean corporation

160   Republican Citizens, Precarious Subjects

Daewoo in the late 1980s and early 1990s. Although it draws heavily on documentary evidence and transcriptions of interviews with Daewoo's former female employees, Bon describes it as a 'novel' in recognition of the significant amount of reconstruction and remodelling he carried out on this factual material (Altes 2008:82–83). Daewoo's factories, producing electronic goods such as microwave ovens and televisions, had been lured to the Lorraine by extensive French and EU subsidies. Yet as early as 1999 Daewoo had begun a programme of downsizing the workforce, before closing all the factories during 2002 and 2003, leaving around 1,200 workers redundant and significant unpaid bills for corporation tax and contributions to workers' social insurance funds (Gilbert 2011:316–17).

Daewoo had been a massive conglomerate whose activities ranged from shipbuilding and steel production to electronics and automobile manufacturing. It was one of South Korea's *chaebols*, the major industrial corporations set up in the wake of the Korean War as part of the government's economic and social reconstruction project that channelled investments into strategically important industries to meet goals set in successive five-year plans. By the 1980s, however, and particularly after the financial liberalisation measures initiated in 1993, what Jang-Sup Shin and Ha-Joon Chang (2003:77) refer to as 'the developmental state' began to recede, as the Korean government pursued a neo-liberal programme of deregulation in both the industrial and financial sectors. Import protections were abolished and the *chaebols*, with the Daewoo Group leading the way, began to pursue 'aggressive investment strategies', seeking to become 'fully fledged multinational corporations by investing overseas to capture new market opportunities'. These expansion plans were financed by raising short-term loans, often from foreign creditors, in a manner that 'stretched their management resources […] and increased their financial risks'.

In 1997 the high level of indebtedness of *chaebols* like Daewoo combined with the Asian financial crisis of that year to force the Korean government to ask the International Monetary Fund (IMF) for a loan. The loan was contingent on Korea agreeing to a structural adjustment programme that included reducing the debt-to-equity ratios of *chaebols* like Daewoo, forcing them to sell off assets and peripheral concerns to concentrate on their core activities (Shin and Chang 2003:56). As a result, Daewoo, which had been declared bankrupt in 1999, sold its automotive arm to General Motors at 'distress prices', while Daewoo

Electronics was taken over by its creditors and its activities radically scaled down (89–105). Its French production facilities in the Lorraine were hence closed and off-shored to Turkey and Eastern Europe in search of lower wage costs.

The Daewoo debacle exemplifies a cycle David Harvey argues is characteristic of globalised financialised capital operating under a neo-liberal regime of governance. In a deregulated global financial market major financial institutions recycle their surpluses by extending loans to emerging economies with insufficient care or scrutiny. When those loans turn bad, the IMF and World Bank step in to provide bail-outs that are contingent on so-called 'structural adjustment' programmes that amount to little more than fire sales of that emerging nation's assets and enable the financial sector to recover their money, while leaving workers and citizens to carry the real costs. Harvey (2006:46–48) calls this process 'accumulation by dispossession' since it involves global financial institutions accumulating profit by dispossessing ordinary citizens of formerly collectively owned assets.

In the case of Daewoo, this process of 'accumulation by dispossession' was exacerbated by the corrupt practices of the company's senior management and enabled by the French government's own abandonment of the kind of economic interventionism for which it had once been famous. In France, the iron and steel industries that had provided the basis of Lorraine's regional economy had been in decline since the mid-1970s. The French authorities were thus eager to encourage new industries and employers to take the place of the declining steel furnaces and mills. Rather than channelling strategic investments into domestic industries, as had been the case in the immediate post-war decades, the government sought to encourage forms of foreign direct investment, in accordance with neo-liberal doctrine. Hence, it gave significant grant aid to Daewoo to encourage them to set up shop in the Lorraine and was able to supplement this with EU funding, since the region was at the heart of a 'New European Development Area'. This area extended into Belgium and Luxembourg and sought to exploit this central location, with its good transport infrastructure and ready pool of labour lying idle because of the deindustrialisation of all three countries. The French government were also keen to curry favour with Daewoo's Chief Executive, Kim Woo-Chong, in return for his help in winning a contract to build a new high-speed train in Korea against stiff German and Japanese competition (Bon 2004:205). Woo-Chong, for his part,

162   *Republican Citizens, Precarious Subjects*

was happy to accept the honours the French government awarded him, in the form of French citizenship and a *Légion d'honneur* (Legon of Honour), since this would help him escape corruption charges pending in his native Korea.

The story of Daewoo in the Lorraine exemplifies the kind of uneven economic geography, the rapid flows of international capital and the polarity between financial-cognitive centre and neo-Taylorist periphery that Plihon and Mouhoud argue characterise the current economic conjuncture. Daewoo's decision to set up factories in the Lorraine reflects the shift from a nationally based, essentially Fordist economic strategy to a globalised kind of post-Fordism, as evident in Daewoo's shift from *chaebol* to multinational corporation. The French authorities' attempts, first, to find a global export market for their TGV, itself originally a product of the French model of investment in strategic national industries, and second to compensate for the decline of the national heavy industries by encouraging foreign direct investment reflects analogous shifts in the governance of the French economy. What the Lorraine offered Daewoo corresponds to precisely those resources Mouhoud argues all 'flexibile Taylorist firms' seek, namely 'rich pools of labour, high quality transport and telecommunication infrastructures, and a strategic position in relation to international business hubs' (in Vercellone, ed. 2003:133). If the Lorraine's pool of *female* labour proved particularly attractive to Daewoo, this presumably reflected a range of different factors. First, the kind of work involved in the production of electronic commodities in their so-called 'screwdriver factories' required none of the hard physical labour of the former steel and iron production plants, labour often assumed to be the preserve of men. Second, female employees were preferable to male former steel workers, given the latter were associated with a long history of labour militancy. Third, in a region stricken by high male unemployment, women would be so desperate for work as to constitute a cheap pool of flexible labour.

Yet, as Mouhoud has pointed out, investments in the 'neo-Taylorist' pole of the current international division of labour are highly volatile and often short-term. Investments in metropolitan poles of cognitive resources tend to be long-term, as the educational, cultural, and social bases of accumulated cognitive power take many years to build up. Pools of low or semi-skilled Taylorised or neo-Taylorised labour, by contrast, require much less long-term investment. As Mouhoud puts it, in terms that apply precisely to the Daewoo situation: "'Flexible

Taylorist" firms manifest a strong propensity to the volatility of their productive units. The state subsidies they are granted can play a role in attracting them to a given region but cannot in any way guarantee they will stay there over the long term' (in Vercellone, ed. 2003:133).

The unemployed women Bon depicts in *Daewoo*, these former Daewoo employees, are thus situated at the nexus of these developments in national and global political economy, the primary victims of those processes of 'accumulation by dispossession' identified by Harvey. The women Aubenas encounters in the course of researching *Le Quai de Ouistreham* are subject to analogous forces, albeit on a smaller, more strictly national scale. Aubenas is a journalist and her book a reportage of the almost six months she spent in 2009 employed in low-skilled jobs in the formerly industrialised region around Caen, in Normandy. Aubenas works primarily as a cleaner and the majority of her co-workers are women. One of the companies she works for is run by a 30-something couple, who five years earlier invested the money they had made as well-paid advertising executives in Paris to buy a cleaning business in Normandy. The couple, Monsieur and Madame Mathieu, are adherents of the kind of can-do, small-scale entrepreneurialism that successive French governments have sought to foster among the population in an effort to boost growth and employment. They describe their business as an 'adventure', asserting that anyone who has 'the courage and the will' can avoid unemployment (Aubenas 2010:114). What this kind of voluntarism ignores, of course, is that the capital they have invested in their new business was accumulated on the basis of the concentration of economic and cultural power in Paris. The success of their business in Normandy, meanwhile, relies on the existence of a pool of desperate working-class women, obliged to accept flexible, poorly paid, degrading work to keep body and soul together. The Mathieus thus exemplify the increased inequalities between Paris and the provinces, professional and working classes provoked by deindustrialisation and further exacerbated in the wake of the Global Financial Crisis (GFC) of 2008. It scarcely needs to be pointed out that the GFC conforms precisely to Harvey's model of 'accumulation by dispossession' – a profusion of risky loans turned bad followed by the imposition of austerity programmes that hit the poorest hardest while ensuring major financial institutions got their money back (Turner 2008).

164   *Republican Citizens, Precarious Subjects*

Femme Forte, Mother Courage

The fact that Bon and Aubenas should both focus on the experiences of working-class women thus reflects an observable economic reality related to the ways in which post-Fordist deindustrialisation and deregulated global finance interact with gender, class, and geographical space. Further, it is noticeable that both authors represent these phenomena in a very similar manner, depicting these working-class women as figures of patient, but determined resistance. The unemployed men in these deindustrialised communities, meanwhile, are either simply absent or, at best, portrayed as weakened, marginal figures. As one of the redundant Daewoo women puts it: 'Women are less likely than men to react by doing something stupid. Keeping going for the kids, doing what's necessary to get from one day to the next: the cycle of shopping, washing, what the weather's like' (Bon 2004:31). In *Le Quai de Ouistreham*, Aubenas encounters 20-something Marilou and her unemployed boyfriend, who accompanies Marilou on her cleaning jobs because 'without her he does not know what to do with himself. He gets bored. In their couple, Marilou is the woman in charge' (Aubenas 2010:86). Another co-worker, Françoise, leaves for work at 4 a.m. returning at 8 p.m., while her husband, on long-term sick leave, stays at home doing the cooking, housework, and childcare (122).

Sociologists Stéphane Beaud and Michel Pialoux (2003:154–55) have argued that this displacement of men by women as primary breadwinners and heads of household is a general phenomenon in French working-class communities. Drawing on their extensive fieldwork in a *banlieue* of Montbeliard, whose inhabitants had traditionally found employment in the local automotive industry, they note the emergence of what they term 'these "bizarre" kinds of couple, in which women attempt, employing whatever resources fall to hand, either to make up for the absence of working-class men (in the case of single-parent families in which the mother has custody of the children) or to compensate, as far as possible, for the social disqualification of such men, who find themselves selling their unskilled labour on a labour market that has no use for it'. If Beaud and Pialoux provide a useful sociological context for understanding the recurrence of the figure of the working-class *femme forte*, their terms of analysis are by no means neutral, betraying a certain anxiety at the shifts in gender roles they document.

As we will demonstrate, such anxiety is also evident in the way in which Bon and Aubenas represent the marginalisation of male workers in the face of the rise of more feminised forms of work typical of post-Fordism, whether the cleaning jobs Aubenas undertakes on the camp sites and cross-channel ferries of deindustrialised Normandy or the work in Daewoo's screwdriver factories that employed 'the most precarious and least qualified workforce' (Bon 2004:215). In both instances working women are subject to the kind of mixed model of both Deleuzean control and Foucauldian discipline we have identified in earlier chapters, exhorted to manifest their commitment, autonomy, and initiative in rigidly prescribed forms. In Chapter 1 we mentioned the imperative to which Aubenas (2010:164) is subjected to prove her 'personal passion' and 'motivation' for the job of part-time cleaner. The women working on Daewoo production lines are subjected to analogous exhortations designed to capture and exploit their human capital, their most individual affects and aptitudes. One of the former Daewoo workers, Barbara, tells Bon of the slogan, 'Challenge, Sacrifice, Creativity', that the company posted on the wall at the entrance to the women's changing rooms: 'They couldn't understand that, here, those kinds of words didn't work. The girls would scribble over the slogan in marker pen and management kept repainting it until they had enough and took it down' (Bon 2004:106). Another ex-Daewoo worker, Géraldine, has kept an archive of company literature exhorting their employees to view the restructurings, changed working patterns, and intensification of workload that preceded the factory closures as opportunities to overcome their resistance to change, demonstrate their adaptability and initiative, and face the new economic realities head-on (90–98). This attempt to render individual employees responsible for economic developments over which they have no real control will subsequently be echoed in the discourses to which the women are subjected after they have been made redundant, both in their employability training sessions and in interviews for precarious service-sector work. Whether applying for jobs promoting local produce at a supermarket dressed in traditional Alsatian costume, working as a host at the Smurf World theme park, a security guard for a pet chainstore, or as a call-centre operative, the women will be compelled to perform the role of committed, motivated, enthusiastic employees.

As in the instance of the women scribbling over the company slogan, the ex-Daewoo workers are depicted opposing a no-nonsense,

166   *Republican Citizens, Precarious Subjects*

straight-talking resistance to this kind of inflated, hypocritical management discourse. In addition to recording the testimonies of the former Daewoo workers, Bon transcribes excerpts from a play, also entitled *Daewoo*, that he produced in 2004 at the Théâtre de la Manufacture in Nancy. In one of these excerpts, 'The Great Farce of Retraining and Employability', four former female Daewoo workers mercilessly parody the discourses of managerialism, cutting through its characteristic euphemisms and circumlocutions, mocking its use of English-language jargon to connote modernity and openness to international commerce. In so doing, they reveal the brute economic realities these stylistic traits seek to conceal:

> SARAÏ: And what if I said: 'Due to changing market conditions the firm has recorded some poor results. It's only appropriate to react by securing improvements to productivity by means of redundancies that will be painful but vital to the firm's survival'?
> NAAMA: That means: We're all sacked. [...]
> SARAÏ: *Je check le downsizing.*
> NAAMA: Come again?
> SARAÏ: [...] *Je check le downsizing.* That also means I'm sacking people, except it's more polite. You really should've understood.
> (Bon 2004:176)

The absurdity of the discourse of employability, which assumes combatting mass unemployment is simply a matter of personal commitment, is given similarly short shrift:

> TSILLA: Everyone their own boss, live out your passion. Create your own business, construct your own job; it's very quick and easy. Give it a try! Any defeatists will be struck off the lists; it improves the unemployment statistics. (178)

In common with many French commentators, Bon characterises this kind of discourse as a sort of Orwellian 'novlange' or 'newspeak' (128). This allusion to the regime of Big Brother reflects not simply the occlusion of truth in managerial discourse, it also points to the totalitarian logic that lies concealed behind the apparently gentle appeals to the workers' personal, human characteristics. The label 'newspeak' thus identifies this discourse as one tangible expression of the contradictory mix of elements of modulated control and hierarchical discipline that is characteristic of contemporary management.

A more systematic form of resistance to this vapid managerialism is embodied in the figure of Géraldine, who keeps a detailed archive documenting the statements of the firm's management and the French authorities, as well as a record of the protests against the closures. As she explains to Bon, she started to accumulate this data while the factory was still operative, posting excerpts from company documents and statements by politicians and government advisors on the staff noticeboard. She then began to track down the authors of these statements, writing to them individually to ask for explanations for their vapid declarations regarding the necessity of restructuring and job losses. She took to posting the scrupulously polite but vacuous responses she received on the same staff noticeboard (90–98). In this way, as she explains, she sought to challenge the monopoly of knowledge and understanding claimed by these so-called experts and to subvert the assumption that workers like herself were characterised by their ignorance of economic reality and illogical resistance to necessary change:

> 'It's quite simple, really. There are all those words that they present as representing self-evident truths, reason itself, those gentlemen called "experts": tons of words. And if we, if we say that perhaps there's a different way of looking at the issues, well that means we've understood nothing, we're behind the times, we're refusing to get out of the way. Female workers only know how to whinge; they're not able to see the bigger picture, from the perspective of the market. So, if I talk about our troubles, it's "no thanks", and then we have to listen to them telling us: "Oh, it's the same old story, we've understood, we read about it every morning in the paper …"' (Bon 2004:90)

Géraldine's actions thus challenge the conventional distribution of places and social roles that confines workers like herself to the domain of emotional but inarticulate complaint, while assuming reasoned argument to be the preserve of an enlightened elite of managers, experts, politicians, and government advisors.

Bon's Géraldine has a very close equivalent in *Le Quai de Ouistreham* in the figure of Victoria, a 70-year-old former cleaner and trade union activist whom Aubenas meets after attending a demonstration in Caen to protest at the redundancies sweeping through Normandy in the wake of the 2008 financial crisis. According to Aubenas (2010:66), Victoria 'has something about her of those pretty pioneers, smiling at the radiant

168   Republican Citizens, Precarious Subjects

future, on posters of female workers in the 1960s'. Since Victoria was born and brought up on a farm, only moving to Caen to seek work in 1959, she serves as an embodiment not only of a lost era of trade union militancy but also of the optimism and social mobility secured by France's post-war boom. She tells Aubenas of her union activities with her friend Fanfan, a supermarket cashier, setting up a section to represent the increasing number of 'precarious' workers, in the face of the hostility of male trade unionists, before both were made redundant in the late 1980s (127–30). Later, Victoria invites Aubenas to a picnic organised by former female factory workers, whose protests against the closure of the local Moulinex factory in 2001 received widespread media coverage throughout France and won them reputations as trouble-makers among local employers (189–94). In a context in which male workers are marginalised, even effaced, Victoria and the Moulinex women represent the living traces of a history of struggle and resistance. Yet their figuration as embodiments of working-class militancy is overlaid with a sense of melancholy. Victoria is haunted by a sense of loss, of lost jobs, lost conviviality with co-workers, lost hopes (263). Hoping to distract her, Aubenas takes her new friend to see the offices in which she, Aubenas, works as a cleaner, unaware they have been built on the old site of the Société Métallurgique de Normandie, that former 'working class fortress' at whose furnaces Victoria's own husband had worked until the day in 1993 when they closed and he 'fell gravely ill, that very evening, like so many other ex-workers' (264).

Thus, even as Aubenas lauds the resilience and determination of a woman like Victoria, her account is infused with melancholy at the loss of a tradition of male working-class labour and militancy whose absence Victoria both signals and supplements. A similar dynamic, an analogous sense of melancholy and defeat infuses Bon's *Daewoo* also. At its simplest, this is a melancholy born of the failure of the women, for all their courageous resistance, to prevent the closure of Daewoo's factories and is epitomised by the figure of Sylvia. Sylvia was a trade union activist and close friend of Géraldine, who committed suicide in the wake of the factory closures. Bon recounts his visit to Sylvia's apartment, empty except for the boxes of her books in the hall, and juxtaposes this with reports from the local paper about the Celtic artefacts recently uncovered by the excavations for a new TGV line (151–52). As this juxtaposition makes clear, Bon understands his task as a novelist to be an act of socio-economic archaeology.

Femmes Fortes   169

A first layer of excavation involves Bon digging beneath the current reality of the Daewoo women, their redundancy, their struggles to secure even precarious service-sector employment, to uncover the truth about the Daewoo closures, the details of the financial and political corruption behind Daewoo's establishment in the Lorraine, the huge subsidies the company received, its unpaid taxes, and so on. Bon also engages in a second, deeper level of archaeological excavation to uncover the remnants of a lost world of more stable, predominantly male employment in the iron and steel industry that Daewoo was supposed to have replaced. In this sense, even as these strong Daewoo women embody their own proud struggles, they also mark an absence, the disappearance of more traditional male embodiments of working-class pride and identity. These once proud male workers haunt the pages of *Daewoo*, largely represented by their very absence, although sporadically evoked when Bon remembers the months he spent during his university vacations working as a temp in the steel works at Longwy.

At one point, Bon interviews Barbara, a worker who had been much involved in protesting against the Daewoo closures but who now works in one of the few remaining steel works in the region. Barbara recounts the exhausting nature of the struggle to keep the Daewoo factories open: "'You're knackered, you stay up all night talking. You show yourself to be strong, right to the end. You don't have the right to break down'" (111–12). 'Her words' manifest a 'nobility of attitude', Bon remarks, implicitly contrasting them with the management's degraded 'newspeak', before concluding, 'it's not every day you come across someone so admirable' (112). Barbara describes her current job at the steel plant as 'pontier', 'a bridgeman', as if, Bon notes, 'the word could not have a feminine form' (109). The word 'pontier' sparks a memory of another bridgeman, Fred, whom Bon remembers from his time working at the Longwy plant as a student back in 1974, at a time when the steel industry employed tens of thousands of men in the region.

Having described the noise and heat of working in a foundry, Bon is struck by the delicacy of Barbara's hands: 'and I gazed at her hands with their slender fingers, at the three rings, one of which had a tiny blue stone – a contrast with the way Barbara had used the word "pontier"...' (111). While he clearly admires Barbara's strength and tenacity, Bon appears nonetheless uneasy at what he takes to be the contradiction between her delicate feminine hands and her current occupation, a

170   Republican Citizens, Precarious Subjects

contradiction also expressed in Barbara's use of a masculine noun, *'pontier'*, to describe her professional role. Bon's portrayal of Barbara is far less censorious than the depictions of powerful professional women as unnatural hybrids we identified in Reinhardt's and Kuperman's novels. Yet he is clearly uneasy at a world in which women with delicate hands engage in hard manual labour and occupy professional roles gendered as masculine.

Our sense that Bon remains wedded to a highly traditional notion of the appropriate division of labour between the sexes would seem confirmed towards the very end of his novel, when his work of socio-economic excavation reaches its final layer. Here Bon visits a limestone plant that represents the 'old realm of men' in which 'only a handful of women work'. Having enumerated the multiple uses for lime in the modern economy, he asks whether 'this is what Daewoo's electronics plants were missing'. His answer to this question slips between, on the one hand, suggesting what the Daewoo plants were missing was equivalent demand for its products and, on the other, implying that what they lacked were the virtues of hard but honest masculine toil, what he terms 'the elementary idea of work':

> Here work retains its eternal attributes, of danger to the body, physical effort and the struggle of man to submit himself to matter. [...] In the huge scale of everything here, the purification process, the 1,200 degree oven working in the frozen air of the Meuse, against a monochrome landscape, yes, we should anchor ourselves in the elementary idea of work: tearing resources from the earth, grinding and crushing them, transforming them. The dust that covered us would go into our towns, our trains, the steel of our cars and even the pages of this book.
>
> And the great effort expended by these men as they laboured day and night, replacing each other at the controls of fork-lift trucks, of plant, of the electronic surveillance systems, that effort was saving them from what had been forced on their sisters at Daewoo: tomorrow there would still be demand for lime. (Bon 2004:240–41)

This paean to 'the elementary idea of work' appeals to very traditional notions of gender and *terroir* to posit male industrial labour, rooted in the very soil of France, as the antidote to the precarious, feminised service-sector employment that now predominates in the Lorraine.

Bon's excavations have thus hit bottom, uncovering a primary layer of wholesome masculine extractive labour. One layer above that, Bon uncovers the traces of skilled labour in the Lorraine's steel foundries, figured as equally masculine and equally wholesome. One layer further up he finds the feminised, flexible, unskilled work in Daewoo's now closed screwdriver factories. The top layer, more feminised and inauthentic still, is the present of a jobs market characterised by low-paid service-sector work. Bon's work of socio-economic archaeology thus traces in reverse a narrative of fall from inauthentic feminised service-sector employment back to honest productive masculine industrial labour. For all his sensitivity to the Daewoo women's plight and admiration for their resilience, it is clear that ultimately, for Bon, their situation is to be lamented insofar as the feminised labour they perform is a degraded simulacrum of true labour, that 'elementary idea of work', the hard physical labour performed by men.

As we noted at the opening to this chapter, the French labour market has become significantly feminised since the 1970s. There are many more women in executive positions than was once the case and women, overall, are more likely to be in paid employment than are French men. The different iterations of the figure of the *femme forte* are symptoms of these changes as well as of the anxieties they have generated. This is particularly true as regards the representation of powerful female executives, who, as we have shown, are repeatedly portrayed as unnatural hybrids threatening the institutions of family and national community by flouting traditional gender roles. The typical depiction of this category of professional, wealthy career women contrasts strongly with that of their working-class counterparts, who tend to be shown in much more admiring terms, figured as courageous defenders of family and community in the context of the loss of male working-class power. Nonetheless, the depiction of these working-class *femmes fortes* in both Bon's *Daewoo* and Aubenas's *Le Quai de Ouistreham* is by no means devoid of conservatism and nostalgia, as they remain defined in terms of what they are not, namely the absent heroic male worker.

As we have argued, the emergence of the two variants of *femme forte* over recent decades reflects the highly gendered nature of the French post-war compromise. For that compromise institutionalised women's roles as wives and mothers while according men the role of chief

172   *Republican Citizens, Precarious Subjects*

breadwinner and paterfamilias. The recurrent depiction of powerful executive women as unnatural hybrids thus reflects the extent to which the presence of women in executive roles challenges their former enclosure in the realms of domesticity and motherhood. Working-class *femmes fortes* are, as we have noted, typically depicted in much less censorious, even in flattering terms, presumably because their roles in struggling to keep family and community together can be reconciled with more traditional notions of femininity and care-giving. Further, as our reading of Bon's *Daewoo* suggested, these paeans to working-class women's resilience can remain haunted by the absence of their once heroic male counterparts. Here too, this surely reflects something quite specific about the French post-war compromise and the way in which a certain myth of the heroic male worker was promoted right across the political spectrum. This myth was personified in a variety of figures: the miners, whose struggles to secure the energy source for France's post-war reconstruction had been lionised during the so-called 'Battle for Coal' (Diamond 2011); the railway workers, famed for their Resistance activities during the war and their role in getting France moving again after the Liberation; the 'métallos de chez Renault', who embodied the values of State-sponsored industrial progress in the post-war decades. These icons of industrious working-class masculinity were 'mobilised as symbols of progress not just by the labour movement but by the state and the *patronat*', in accordance with the 'productivist ideology' that defined the French post-war model (Clarke 2011:447). If *Daewoo* and *Le Quai de Ouistreham* pay homage to the courageous resilience of working-class *femmes fortes*, they simultaneously lament the passing of those icons of industrious working-class masculinity, the miner, the 'cheminot', and the 'métallo'.

In short, the recurring figure of the *femme forte*, whether executive or working class, betrays a persistent form of Fordist nostalgia, which means that legitimate criticisms of labour market precarity are vitiated by laments at the transformation of traditional gender roles and identities. The feminisation of the workplace, which might have been interpreted as an opportunity for French republican–corporatism to become more inclusive and less rigidly gendered, seems largely to be understood as a threat and an occasion for nostalgia. This kind of Fordist nostalgia is exemplified by the sociologists Stéphane Beaud and Gérard Mauger, who remark wistfully, at the opening of their book *Une Génération sacrifiée?* (2017), that 'in mass media imagery, the masculine figure of the "métallo", which for a long time symbolised the working class, is giving way to that of the female supermarket checkout assistant' (7). As the title of their edited collection indicates, their interest is in the manner in which the loss of stable industrial employment has produced a 'sacrificed generation' of working-class French youth. Over the preceding two chapters we have examined the effects of France's transition from a Fordist to a post-Fordist regime of accumulation on adult men and women, respectively. As Beaud and Mauger suggest, alongside the figures of the *femme forte* and the middle-aged man, forced to modulate his masculinity to adapt to the new jobs market, recent years have seen the emergence of the figure of the *doomed youth*, whose career options and opportunities to find a stable place in French society have been 'sacrificed' to the demands of the current economic conjuncture. This figure of the doomed youth also poses a fundamental challenge to the terms of the Fordist–Republican post-war compromise. For that compromise promised to integrate all of the nation's young citizens, regardless of their ethnic, regional, or class origins, into the Republic. This it was to achieve through the interrelationships between the egalitarian Republican School and a labour market that would endow everyone with a secure professional identity, in accordance with the corporatist Durkheimian 'division of labour in society'. Recent film and literature offers a profusion of figurations of young French citizens for whom this system has conspicuously failed, whether on account of inherited disadvantages of class and ethnicity, by dint of profound shifts in the nature of the educational field, or because of fundamental changes in the structure of the labour market. The next chapter thus turns to consider the nature and significance of the various iterations of the figure of the doomed youth, showing how, in this domain also, socio-economic shifts have produced more precarious forms of subjectivity that challenge established conceptions of French republican citizenship.

Chapter 5

Doomed Youth

Jean-Marc Moutout's 2003 film, *Violence des échanges en milieu tempéré*, focuses on the experiences of Philippe Seignier (Jérémie Renier), a young man of provincial origins and a recent graduate of a Parisian business school, an elite *grande école*. Philippe is just starting his career in the La Défense offices of the American management consultancy, Macgregor. He is sent to the provincial factory of Janson Metal Industries, near Chartres, to implement a system of *kanban* or total quality production. Philippe is initially an enthusiastic advocate of these new management techniques, believing they will give the workers greater control over their working lives. Gradually, however, he becomes disillusioned as he realises that the skills audit he is tasked with carrying out among the factory's workers will in fact be used to identify candidates for redundancy, hence reducing headcount, boosting productivity, and rendering Janson Industries more attractive to foreign buyers. As Philippe wrestles with his conscience, his burgeoning relationship with single-mother Eva (Cylia Malki) falls apart under the strain. Ultimately, he decides not to speak out and this betrayal of his youthful ideals is communicated in the three consecutive scenes that make up the film's final sequence.

In the first of these scenes, we see Philippe attend an end-of-year office party to celebrate Macgregor's continuing economic successes. The Chief Executive of Macgregor's French office addresses the assembled employees, prefacing his pep talk by explaining wryly that he has been chosen for the task because, before his business career, 'I had the misfortune to take a Masters in Philosophy. No-one's perfect!' Having delivered a paean to his company's values of competitive entrepreneurialism, the chief executive leads Philippe

176   *Republican Citizens, Precarious Subjects*

and his assembled co-workers in chanting, in English, the company's slogan 'Work hard, play hard! Work hard, play hard!' We then cut to two young men fishing on the banks of the River Eure on the outskirts of Chartres. Adji (Samir Guesmi), of North African heritage, has just been made redundant from his job in the Janson factory canteen, while his unemployed white French friend Serge (Bernard Sens) has been abandoned by his girlfriend, Adji's sister, who has left Chartres to seek her fortune in Paris. When a luxury river cruiser passes by, Adji struggles to read and pronounce the English name, 'Viking River Cruises', painted on the side of its hull, before jokingly asking Serge whether he is planning to attend his meeting at the local Job Centre or commit suicide. We then cut to the film's final scene, in which we see Philippe and his elegant new girlfriend arriving at a beach in the South of France to enjoy their summer holiday. In fact, this same scene featured at the film's opening, the whole narrative having thus been recounted in flashback.

If this final sequence depicts Philippe's successful integration into the world of powerful business executives, it also strongly implies that this success amounts to an act of profound self-betrayal on his part. This much is emphasised by the vapidity of the slogan he chants, the fact that it is in a foreign language, English, and the audience's knowledge that its underlying philosophy in no way corresponds to Philippe's personal beliefs. This message is reiterated in the final scene by Philippe's choice of an elegant, apparently bourgeois girlfriend over the woman he really loves, the working-class Eva. The technique of flashback, meanwhile, emphasises the inevitability of Philippe's entrapment in this mercenary world of globalised financialised capitalism. Philippe, then, is a young man whose education and exposure to the world of Anglo-Saxon financialised capitalism has *doomed* him to betraying his national identity, his political beliefs, and his most authentic personal desires. Adji and Serge are similarly doomed but in a more brutally economic way. Provincial working-class and/or ethnic minority young men, they have been left behind by the economic forces personified by Philippe.

The importance of education to these phenomena is clearly indicated in two ways in this final sequence. First, the chief executive's disparaging remark about his Masters in Philosophy points to the abandonment of older, humanistic, arguably specifically French intellectual values in favour of more naked commercial 'Anglo-Saxon' ones. Second, the contrast between the ease with which Philippe chants the English slogan 'Work hard, play hard' and the difficulties Adji experiences in pronouncing 'Viking River Cruises' highlights the disparity in educational capital that separates the two: Adji's education has clearly left him ill-equipped to cope in the world of global commerce into which Philippe has just been integrated.

Moutout's *Violence des échanges en milieu tempéré* thus paints a dispiriting picture of the prospects awaiting French youth in the current educational and economic conjuncture, whether those young people find themselves, like Philippe, at the summit of the academic and professional hierarchy, or whether, like Adji and Serge, they languish at the bottom of that hierarchy. The fates suffered by all three of these protagonists strike at the core of established notions about the proper role of French education, in its close interrelationship with the labour market, in ensuring the integration of all France's citizens into a cohesive society and polity. Someone like Philippe would be expected to form part of a so-called 'republican elite' of highly trained executives, selected and promoted through the meritocratic structures of the republican education system to work in the general interest of the French republic as a whole. Working-class and ethnic minority citizens, such as Adji and Serge, should have been integrated into the Republic through their education, equipped with the skills necessary to find the stable employment and professional status that would guarantee their social rights and identity within France's republican–corporatist system. However, in both cases the opposite appears to be true. The elite education Philippe has received in his *grande école* leads him to undertake actions that are profoundly detrimental to his fellow citizens and corrosive of any sense of social solidarity. Serge and Adji's education, meanwhile, has conspicuously failed to equip them with the skills they need to prosper in the current economic conjuncture.

Moutout's portrayal of these two categories of doomed youth is by no means an isolated case. Since the 1980s, young, unemployed, working-class and/or ethnic minority inhabitants of France's deprived *banlieues* have formed the subject of almost obsessive representation, whether in the sub-genre of the *banlieue* film, of which Mathieu Kassovitz's *La Haine* (1995) remains the best-known example, in often sensationalist media reporting (Berthaut 2013), or in more sympathetic sociological studies, exemplified by the patient, detailed analyses of Stéphane Beaud and Michel Pialoux (1999, 2003).

178   *Republican Citizens, Precarious Subjects*

More recently, young executives and recent graduates of elite *grandes écoles*, doomed to self-betrayal and disillusionment by the demands of the contemporary workplace, have also become recurrent figures in both fictional representations and testimonial accounts. Moutout's Philippe has an important predecessor in the form of Frank (Jalil Lespert), the young protagonist of Cantet's *Ressources humaines* (1999), a working-class student at an elite Parisian business school who is sent to work as an intern in the same provincial factory on whose assembly line his own father still works. Frank is employed to help implement the 35-hour working-week legislation. Like Philippe, he is initially enthusiastic about his role but gradually realises that the factory's management is exploiting the 35-hour law to introduce more flexible working patterns and increase workload while implementing a wave of redundancies. Having revealed these redundancy plans to the factory's workers, Frank provokes a strike in which he plays an active role. At the end of the film, as the strike continues, Frank's future seems radically uncertain: he has lost his place on the internship that formed a compulsory element of his business studies degree; the offer of a permanent management job at the factory after his graduation has been rescinded; he is now thoroughly alienated from the management class his studies were preparing him to join.

In his 2014 film, *La Crème de la crème*, Kim Chapiron offers a poignant allegory of the corruption of France's academic elite by the mercenary logic of contemporary capitalism in his tale of a group of students at an elite Parisian business school, who set up a prostitution ring to service the desires of their fellow students. Alongside these fictional representations, personal testimonies of recent *grande école* graduates have further contributed to this trope of disillusionment. Sophie Talneau's *On vous rappellera* (2004) and Jonathan Curiel's *Génération CV* (2012) recount their respective authors' sense of surprise and disappointment at struggling to find employment despite their elite education. Alexandre des Isnards and Thomas Zuber's *L'Open Space m'a tuer* (2008) is an acerbic account of the disjuncture between their aspirations, as graduates of an elite *grande école*, and the exploitative realities and meaningless routines of the executive positions they in fact occupy.

This chapter will thus focus on these two recurrent figurations of doomed French youth, the disillusioned young graduates of France's elite *grandes écoles* and those working-class young men and women from the *banlieue* apparently locked out of the republican polity altogether. To focus on these two groups is inevitably to overlook all those young people situated in between those two extremes who have also struggled to find a place in French society in recent decades, compelled to accept precarious terms and conditions of work on poorly paid internships, temporary contracts, agency work, and so forth. Nonetheless, as Robert Castel (2009:382–83) has pointed out, the problems experienced by *banlieue* youth should not be seen as reflecting the latter's 'exotic' or exceptional characteristics. Rather, these problems merely represent the most extreme form of a more general 'dynamic of living in precarity' affecting 'society as a whole'. Similarly, if even the most academically successful of French graduates are shown to be struggling and disillusioned then this says much about the extent of the problems facing French youth as a whole. In this sense, our two chosen categories of doomed youth can be understood to represent extreme examples of much more general phenomena. Examining the ways in which these two categories have been represented in film and sociological literature will allow us to extend our focus to consider how the changes in the French labour market we have discussed thus far have interacted with changes in education to produce particular forms of precarity among French young people, forms of precarity that challenge their ability to become fully fledged citizens of the French Republic.

As we have noted in earlier chapters, the republican, corporatist nature of the French post-war compromise assumed that a meritocratic system of public education would equip all young citizens with the skills necessary to take up the stable employment that would guarantee access to a social identity and welfare benefits. The Republican School would thus feed into a corporatist system of work and welfare ensuring social solidarity between all France's citizens. The figures of both disillusioned *grande école* graduates and unemployed *banlieue* youth provide further evidence of the contemporary crisis in that corporatist system. In previous chapters we have focused on the role played by new management techniques in this crisis of French republican corporatism, showing how the emphasis on 'skills' over 'qualifications' and the consequent formation of workers as 'entrepreneurs of the self' cultivating their personal stocks of 'human capital' undermined older collective social identities based on trades or professional groups. This chapter will extend our focus to consider the role of education in these processes, showing how an equivalent emphasis on post-disciplinary

180   *Republican Citizens, Precarious Subjects*

techniques as the means to develop the 'human capital' of every student has impacted the French educational field also.

In education as in the labour market, then, established notions of republican citizenship are being challenged, as students and recent graduates are enjoined to adopt the more modulated, precarious subject position of the 'entrepreneur of the self'. Of course, the typically upper-middle-class graduates of a *grande école* are much better equipped to adapt to this new role than are *banlieue* youth. That this disparity in educational, social, and economic capital is *spatialised* in particular ways is evident in the polarities between the elite spaces of the Parisian business school or the La Défense headquarters of a management consultancy, on the one hand, and the provincial factory facing closure or the deindustrialised *banlieue* with its underfunded schools, on the other. Examining a sample of recent depictions of disillusioned *grande école* graduates and doomed *banlieue* youth will thus allow us to clarify the interrelationships between youth, education, social class, ethnicity, and the uneven economic geographies that characterise contemporary France. Indeed, the educational and career trajectories followed by our various representatives of doomed youth map these geographical and socio-economic polarities in ways that both rehearse and re-inflect well-established dichotomies between Paris and the provinces, wealthy centre and marginalised periphery.

From the Provinces to Paris and Back Again

As we have already noted, the two films *Ressources humaines* and *Violence des échanges en milieu tempéré* feature young working-class protagonists who have left their provincial birthplaces to travel to Paris to pursue their education and career. These two young protagonists then return to the provinces, equipped with all they have learned in the capital, eager to apply their newly acquired knowledge to the benefit of their fellow provincial citizens. There is nothing new in fictional narratives that centre on a brilliant young man of modest provincial origins who makes his way to Paris to pursue his education and seek his fortune. Indeed narratives with such trajectories at their heart have a central place in French culture, being exemplified in classic nineteenth-century novels such as Honoré de Balzac's *Illusions perdues* (1837–43), or Gustave Flaubert's *L'Éducation sentimentale* (1869), to name but two. There is, moreover, nothing new in these trajectories ending in disillusionment. Thus, in *L'Éducation sentimentale*, having arrived in Paris, Frédéric Moreau drifts between the worlds of art, the law, and commerce without ever managing to commit himself to any of these, in a kind of proto-modernist renunciation of the will. The disillusionment experienced by Lucien de Rubempré, the protagonist of *Illusions perdues*, is rather more political in its implications, reflecting his disgust at the commercialisation of art and literature in the wake of the fall of the *ancien régime* and its replacement by a socio-political order whose liberal values the royalist Balzac is eager to criticise.

The narratives of *Ressources humaines* and *Violence des échanges en milieu tempéré* at one level rehearse these well-established narrative tropes. Indeed, *Violence des échanges en milieu tempéré* could be interpreted as a replaying of Balzac's critique of nineteenth-century liberalism updated for the contemporary era of financialised capitalism. The scene in *Illusions perdues* in which the journalist Étienne Lousteau enlightens De Rubempré as to the degraded commercial values that actually dominate the Parisian literary field has a direct equivalent in Moutout's film. The role of Lousteau falls here to Philippe's immediate superior, the ironically named Hugo Paradis (Laurent Lucas), a man whose dark hair, goatee beard, and ruthlessly manipulative character make of him an embodiment not of heaven (Paradis) but of hell. Paradis is a truly diabolical or Mephistophelean character, who initiates his young charge into the dark practices of corporate takeovers and mass redundancies. It is Paradis who first reveals to Philippe that the apparently more collaborative modes of work inherent to the Japanese management techniques they are implementing in Janson's provincial factory are in fact merely pretexts to intensify workload, get workers to reveal their colleagues' failings, and pave the way for mass redundancies.

However, there is at least one important way in which *Violence des échanges en milieu tempéré* departs from these established narrative tropes and this reflects the manner in which recent shifts in the division of cognitive and financial power have been mediated through space in and around the French capital. As Franco Moretti has shown, the trajectory of the brilliant young provincial always brought them first and foremost to the Quartier Latin: 'a precocious product of the urban division of labour, this space of high learning, established in the late middle ages and unchanged ever since, is also, and in Balzac first of all, *the world of youth*: converging from all over from France towards

182   *Republican Citizens, Precarious Subjects*

this square mile set on making their fortune' (Moretti 1998:95). These young protagonists then swiftly move on, seeking 'the objects of their desire', women and money, in other central Parisian *quartiers* in which economic and social capital is concentrated, 'in the Faubourg Saint-Germain and Saint Honoré, in the Chaussée d'Antin, in the *demi-monde* of the Boulevards' (ibid.).

One of the most striking features of the trajectory followed by Philippe in *Violence des échanges en milieu tempéré* is that it bypasses central Paris; he is drawn neither to the Quartier Latin, the traditional seat of French culture and learning, nor to the central Parisian *quartiers* that have historically been the locus of French economic and social power. He gravitates rather to La Défense, a space on the margins of Paris whose starkly modernist tower blocks of forbidding glass and steel lack any of the specifically French historical or cultural resonances associated with the central Parisian *quartiers* over which they loom and whose power they have now displaced. The inhumanity of La Défense is emphasised both visually and verbally from the very beginning of *Violence des échanges en milieu tempéré*. In the film's opening sequence we see Philippe arriving on the metro in the morning, lost in a mass of anonymous worker drones. A montage of shots highlights the inhumanity of La Défense, the camera panning up the glass and steel facades of towering office buildings, for example, to emphasise their intimidating size. In his first exchange with his girlfriend Eva, Philippe laments the alienating working conditions in La Défense, offering her advice on how best to survive in what he describes variously as an 'ant heap' and a 'goldfish bowl'. There is a very strong sense in which the film figures La Défense as being *in* France yet not really being *of* France, a non-French space located on the margins of the nation's capital, the locus of global financial forces that threaten to undermine any specifically French polity or society.

Insofar as central Paris features at all in *Violence des échanges en milieu tempéré* it functions as a space of leisure or of domestic life, spaces of potential escape from the exploitative power dynamics located in La Défense. When Philippe and Eva go on their first date, they meet outside a central Paris metro station, Eva emerging from the metro to find Philippe gazing in admiration at the classical architecture on display there. When the couple go to look at a flat together, this too is in central Paris and they take a trip on a *bateau-mouche*, a tourist boat along the Seine, to discuss whether to take the flat or not. Central Paris thus appears to have been relegated to the status of a dormitory town or museum city. This opposition is reproduced when Philippe goes to work in Chartres. He stays in an anonymous chain hotel situated on a soulless out-of-town trading estate. One evening, as he telephones Eva to complain about his loneliness and disillusionment, Philippe gazes out over the trading estate through his hotel window. A subjective panning shot reveals a landscape of retail sheds, neon signs, and streams of cars on a distant motorway flyover, a landscape as anonymous as the tower blocks of La Défense. This dystopian scene contrasts strikingly with the warmth and conviviality of the bar Philippe frequents in the historic centre of Chartres during his leisure time.

La Défense and the trading estate are thus both new loci of economic power and striking manifestations of the manner in which that power is reshaping national space, eroding any markers of specifically French identity, history, or sociability. These soulless spaces of capital are also contrasted with the French countryside, itself figured as the repository of more authentically French values. At one point in the film, Eva comes to visit Philippe as he works in the provinces. They spend an idyllic weekend together, escaping the pressures of work by cycling through the surrounding countryside, stopping off to taste wine and cheese at local farms. In the course of one such tasting, Philippe jokes to Eva that he may abandon his high-powered executive career, returning to his provincial origins to raise goats. If this allusion to the myth of *terroir* is semi-ironic, the film nonetheless does seem to set up a binary opposition between the destructive forces of global capitalism located in the decidedly non-French space of La Défense, on the one hand, and the apparently more rooted certainties of industrial production in Janson's provincial factory, on the other. Immediately following the opening sequence in which the cold anonymity of La Défense is established, we cut to a shot of the interior of Janson's provincial factory. The camera pans along a line of massive steel presses, whose weighty solidity is emphasised by the 50-something production manager, Roland Manin (Olivier Perrier), as he explains how they work to a group of local schoolchildren he is leading around the factory floor on an educational visit.

Janson's provincial factory is thus not only identified as the embodiment of a certain solidity, safeguarding the livelihoods of its workers, it is also figured as a space of republican education, nurturing the next generation of French citizens. By representing the interests

184 *Republican Citizens, Precarious Subjects*

of his employer, the American management consultancy Macgregor, and of their clients, the Janson factory's foreign buyers, Philippe threatens to destroy all of this and his destructive potential reflects the extent to which his own educational trajectory has deviated from the traditional French republican model in two closely related ways. First, his bypassing of the Quartier Latin in favour of La Défense exemplifies a fundamental shift in economic and cultural topography, the erosion of specifically French values of art and education in favour of the anonymous forces of global capitalism. Second, in common with Frank, the central protagonist of *Ressources humaines*, Philippe's trajectory deviates from that expected of a young member of France's republican elite. This expectation holds that the most academically brilliant among France's youth, no matter how modest their origins, should be able to progress to the summit of the meritocratic republican education system, gaining entry to the highly selective *grandes écoles*. Having been thus initiated into the nation's republican elite, such individuals would then be expected to put the fruits of their education to work for the benefit of all France's citizens. If Philippe and Frank singularly fail to do this, it is because they are the products of a radically changed higher education system, whose graduates are now destined to work in a manner that is detrimental both to themselves and to their fellow citizens.

The Republican Elite Led Astray

As we have already noted, Frank and Philippe are not merely young people of provincial origin who have travelled to Paris to pursue education and career before returning to the provinces again inspired with all they have learnt. They are also, to a French audience at least, immediately recognisable as the products of a peculiarity in that country's higher education system, namely the existence of the elite, highly selective *grande école* sector. Where French university is open to anyone who has passed the *baccalauréat* or school-leaving certificate, entrance to the *grandes écoles* is based on a highly selective examination system. Students typically sit these entrance exams two years after passing the *baccalauréat*, having spent the intervening years following a highly intensive course of study in a so-called *classe préparatoire*, itself typically attached to the most prestigious *lycée*, or high school, in their region. Historically, the most prestigious *grandes écoles* have been located in or around Paris and, particularly in the post-war period, their graduates have come to dominate the realms of culture, education, politics, and business in France.

One way in which the existence of such elite, selective institutions has been reconciled with the French republican commitment to equality and meritocracy has been through the development of the notion of a 'republican elite'. The argument here is that performance in the competitive entrance exams to any *grande école* is assessed on purely objective academic criteria and thus access to such institutions is open to all French students equally, whether they hail from a wealthy Parisian background or have modest provincial origins. Further, having gained entrance to a *grande école* based purely on their inherent academic abilities, students would then be educated to the highest possible level, imbued with knowledge of universal value. On graduating and taking up leading roles in French society, such individuals would then be guided by those universal values such that, in their professional lives, they would form a republican elite dedicated to promoting the so-called 'general interest' of the Republic and all its citizens. For example, graduates trained in the social or human sciences at the *École normale supérieure* (ENS) might spend some years teaching in a provincial *lycée*, sharing the benefits of their elite education with the broader population. Subsequently, they might return to Paris to pursue intellectual careers that contribute to the general interest by boosting France's intellectual and cultural prestige. Meanwhile, graduates of the more technically or scientifically oriented *grandes écoles*, such as *Polytechnique*, *Mines*, or *Ponts et chaussées*, might go out into the provinces to form a cadre of engineer-technocrats whose expert knowledge would improve France's infrastructure and industrial base for the benefit of all French citizens.

This myth of the engineer-technocrat serving the general interest was cultivated throughout the nineteenth century in the social theories of thinkers from Saint Simon to Auguste Comte. In the early twentieth century, think tanks like X-Crise developed this vision further to advocate scientific planning of all aspects of economic, social, and political life, overseen by this technocratic elite, as the key to resolving the problems caused by the depression of the 1930s without recourse to either fascism or bolshevism (Clarke 2013). In the 1950s and 1960s, this figure of engineer-technocrat morphed to merge with that of the

186   *Republican Citizens, Precarious Subjects*

more Americanised *jeune cadre dynamique* or dynamic young executive, tasked with overcoming the shame of military defeat, occupation, and collaboration with the Nazis by leading France's efforts to embrace more modern, rational modes of socio-economic and political organisation. In her study of the post-war modernisation of France, Kristin Ross identifies the character of Daniel in Elsa Triolet's 1959 novel *Roses à crédit* as personifying this new figure. As Ross points out, Daniel has left the provincial rose farm on which he grew up to study at a Parisian *grande école* specialising in horticulture. Here he intends to master the scientific techniques that will enable him to return to his family farm and develop a new kind of rose that will have the perfume of a traditional flower but the form and colour of a modern one. Thus, Daniel will put his elite education to work for the benefit of the citizens of his local community, hence serving the general interest while securing the perfect synthesis of tradition and scientific modernity (Ross 1995:165–76).

What is so striking about the educational and career trajectories of Frank in *Ressources humaines* and Philippe in *Violence des échanges en milieu tempéré* is the extent to which they first rehearse yet ultimately completely invert the trajectory followed by a character like Triolet's Daniel. In this way, Frank and Philippe come to represent the complete perversion or corruption of the notion of a French republican elite. As we have noted, both young men apparently represent shining examples of the meritocratic republican education system at work. Of modest provincial origins, both men have, through their innate intellectual abilities, managed to scale the heights of that system, gaining access to prestigious *grandes écoles*. Both men then return to the French provinces, eager to apply their newly acquired knowledge to the benefit of their fellow citizens. Yet, in the course of both films, each man will learn that the knowledge he has acquired functions not in the general interest of those citizens but acts rather to their detriment, destroying the jobs, livelihoods, and communities of the provincial working class.

Implicit in the fates of Frank and Philippe, then, is a critique of the particular kinds of *grande école* of which they are the products. For these two young provincials have not gone to Paris to study at one of France's State-run *grandes écoles,* such as the ENS, Polytechnique, or Mines, where they might have been imbued with universal truths, with the highest forms of knowledge in the humanities, science, or technology. Rather, they have followed a different trajectory, going to Paris to study at one of the increasing number of business schools and it is here that they have learned the financial and managerial values that prove so detrimental both to themselves and to their fellow citizens. In this sense, our duo's educational trajectories reflect a fundamental shift in the field of French higher education that has taken place from the 1970s onwards, namely the seemingly unstoppable rise in the number, power, and prestige of business schools at the expense of the more properly academic *grandes écoles* that had previously been tasked with producing France's republican elite.

This development was first systematically charted by Pierre Bourdieu in his 1989 study *La Noblesse d'état*. Bourdieu compares the state of French higher education and of the *grandes écoles*, in particular, in the 1960s and the 1980s. In the 1960s, the most prestigious *grandes écoles* were those that enjoyed the greatest autonomy from the realms of politics or business, schools that delivered a rigorously academic training, schools such as the ENS that produced a cadre of researchers in the sciences and the humanities, or such as Polytechnique or Mines that produced highly trained engineers. By the 1980s, however, those institutions had lost power and prestige in the face of the rise of a range of institutions that had closer links to the worlds of politics and business, schools such as the *École nationale d'administration* (ENA), the *Institut d'études politiques*, more commonly known as Sciences-po, and the *École des hautes études commerciales* (HEC). These institutions deliver a less rigorously or autonomously academic curriculum that aims to inculcate more general financial, managerial, and administrative skills in its graduates. Two of them, HEC and Sciences-po, are semi-private and fee-paying. Together, Bourdieu argues, they produce a homogeneous business and political elite that moves seamlessly between high-ranking positions in French government, the civil service, and the management of large French corporations, themselves often wholly or partially State-owned. The rise of institutions such as HEC and Sciences-po has, moreover, been accompanied by an explosion in the number of business schools. These private, fee-paying institutions, often disparagingly dubbed *petites grandes écoles*, promise their graduates access to lucrative business careers.

Bourdieu attributes this shift to a range of factors, such as the fact that in the wake of the events of May 1968, upper-middle-class parents were determined to keep their offspring away from a university sector associated with political radicalism, overcrowding, and underfunding.

188   *Republican Citizens, Precarious Subjects*

At the same time, the increasing concentration and financialisation of French business meant that there was greater demand by major employers for graduates endowed with the newer kinds of managerial-financial qualification delivered by business schools. Shifts in the post-war French economy have thus been mirrored in shifts in the field of higher education in ways that, Bourdieu (1989) laments, are undermining older republican ideals that defined the role an educational elite should play in serving the general or universal interest of all French citizens.

A series of more recent studies has extended and updated Bourdieu's critique of the rise of independent, fee-paying business schools at the expense of more traditional republican institutions. In his 2015 study *School Business*, Arnaud Parienty laments the increasing commercialisation of French education and the consequent dependence of academic and career success on inherited wealth and privilege rather than inherent intellectual ability. Thus, Parienty notes with alarm the rise of private business schools, whose fees range from 10,000 to almost 20,000 euros a year and that are increasingly owned by private equity funds (2015:163, 203). As he points out, in the ten years to 2014, 80 per cent of the overall increase in student numbers in French higher education was accounted for by private institutions (154). This increase in the number of students in private, fee-paying institutions has been accompanied by a threefold rise in the number studying in business schools over the same period. This reflects what Parienty terms a 'shift in the scale of values in France', so that where traditionally business school students were looked down upon by engineering or humanities students, disparagingly dubbed 'grocers', now business schools have become a favoured destination (192–93). It is this shift in the hierarchy of educational values, of course, that Macgregor's chief executive expresses in *Violence des échanges en milieu tempéré* when he apologises to his colleagues for having studied philosophy, before remarking wryly that 'no-one's perfect!'

Further down the educational hierarchy, Parienty documents the rise of private, fee-paying *classes préparatoires*, of private secondary schools, and of the boom in private tutoring encouraged by the decision, in 2005, to make this tax deductible (79–83). As Parienty concludes, the increasing commercialisation of education represents a corruption of fundamental French republican ideals, a betrayal of the mythological status of republican schoolteachers as 'dark-suited Republican hussars' sent out into the French countryside to banish ignorance and religious superstition in the names of universal truth and the freedom, equality, and fraternity guaranteed by a meritocratic education system: 'How can we accept this kind of discrimination based on money? You don't have to be a dark-suited hussar of the Republic to be disgusted by this serious distortion of our educational system' (18).

What Parienty interprets as the corruption of academic values by nakedly commercial imperatives has also had a fundamental impact on the form and content of the education delivered to France's young republican elite. Muriel Darmon draws on two years of fieldwork in the *classes préparatoires* of a prestigious provincial lycée to examine what she terms 'the making of a dominant young elite'. In the course of her fieldwork, Darmon compared the form and content of teaching in two different *classes préparatoires*, an economics stream preparing its pupils to study at a business school and a scientific stream preparing for study at an engineering school. She notes that the scientific stream remains focused on the transmission of a corpus of strictly academic and technical knowledge, alongside more generic critical thinking skills. The scientific stream is thus characterised by the attempt to inculcate in its pupils 'a taste, an outlook and a culture that is specific to the discipline' (Darmon 2013:244). In the economics stream, by contrast, there is much less emphasis on strictly academic knowledge and much greater importance placed on the process of '"working on the self" – a term borrowed from psychology and designating the discovery of oneself [...] – or working on one's whole "personality"' (249). Discipline, understood in its two senses as both a hierarchical mode of governmentality and a body of academic knowledge, is thus significantly modulated in the economics stream. As Darmon notes:

> In the discourse of teachers in the scientific *classe préparatoire*, it is academic progress that forms the major part of the change [they expect of their pupils]. [...] By contrast, in the economics *prépa* this term is considered too weak or is not employed, the term 'metamorphosis' being preferred. [...] The latter term is more radical in its effects and in the areas it covers, being analogous to a genuine conversion. In addition to its intellectual, academic, corporeal, and cultural aspects, it comprises, as we have seen, a personal and psychological dimension, that of 'working on the self', of 'developing one's personality'. This includes the

190   *Republican Citizens, Precarious Subjects*

> techniques and skills involved in the 'management of the self'.
> (Darmon 2013:252–53)

As Darmon shows, in order to succeed in their interviews and oral examinations, candidates for one of France's business schools will have to demonstrate their 'authenticity', 'sincerity', and 'frankness', or, at least, they will have to learn how to perform those attributes by a wholesale process of '*working* on their authenticity' (257). She quotes a teacher explaining to a pupil that oral examinations for a business school 'aren't like a school test in which there are right and wrong answers. It's "Operation Seduction" do you see?' (265). For Darmon, the kind of techniques employed in the economics stream represent a decisive shift away from the role attributed by Foucault to education under a disciplinary mode of governmentality: 'It is no longer a question of fabricating "machines", to use a term Foucault applies to a soldier subjected to discipline, but rather individuals who manage their own selves' (76). As she also notes, this shift towards more modulated, post-disciplinary forms of control in the educational setting 'accompany and anticipate an equivalent development within the firm' (287). Indeed, the kind of 'work on the self' demanded of pupils in the economics stream is directly analogous to the shifts from a 'qualifications model' to a 'skills-based model', from discipline to more modulated forms of control we have detailed in our analyses of contemporary management practices in earlier chapters.

Taken together, the developments in the French educational field identified by Bourdieu, Parienty, and Darmon reflect a number of interrelated shifts, from the rise of multinational corporations and globalised financial institutions demanding general financial-managerial skills of their graduate employees, through the increasingly competitive jobs market that encourages anxious middle-class parents to invest in private education for their offspring, to the reconceptualisation of education itself as a financial investment in accumulating an individualised stock of 'human capital'. As Foucault (2004:235) points out, this is a notion of human capital that extends far beyond the traditional academic demarcation of the knowledge appropriate to a given discipline and embraces the kinds of intangible personal skill that Darmon describes students in the economics stream being enjoined to cultivate. The 'work on the self' depicted by Darmon precisely anticipates the kind of 'management of the emotions' Valérie

Brunel (2008) observes in her fieldwork among French management consultants.

The full significance of the trajectories followed by Frank and Philippe, as of the disillusionments they suffer, reflects the extent to which they both embody these educational shifts. They are aspirant members of Bourdieu's 'new bourgeoisie', that 'ethical avant-garde' to which, we argued in Chapter 3, *L'Emploi du temps*'s Vincent already belongs. Like Vincent, Frank and Philippe are the products of the increasing prestige of business schools over more academic, properly republican *grandes écoles*, and their sense of self closely reflects the post-disciplinary educational regime to which they have been subjected and through which they have been subjectivated. Frank's enthusiasm for the more modulated working patterns imposed by the 35-hour legislation and Philippe's initial advocacy of supposedly more co-operative Japanese production techniques clearly communicate both men's initial commitments to these characteristically post-disciplinary modes of management. Indeed, both *Ressources humaines* and *Violence des échanges en milieu tempéré* highlight the extent to which the post-disciplinary worldview shared by Frank and Philippe conflicts with the values and assumptions of an older generation of workers, whose sense of self was formed under the earlier disciplinary regime.

As part of his efforts to smooth the introduction of the 35-hour week, Frank draws up a questionnaire and distributes it to all the factory workers in an attempt to solicit their preferences regarding the organisation of their working lives. That evening, over dinner, Frank's father, who, as one of the factory workers, himself completed the questionnaire, asks his son: 'So, have you marked my exam yet?' A close-up on Frank's face reveals his reaction of bewilderment and frustration. What Frank imagined to be a post-disciplinary tool of dialogue and participation between equals has been interpreted by his father as a mechanism of management discipline, analogous to an exam script requiring correction and assessment by a hierarchical superior.

In *Violence des échanges en milieu tempéré* Philippe's tense interactions with the middle-aged production engineer Roland Manin represents another aspect of this clash between post-disciplinary and disciplinary logics. In this context, the terms 'disciplinary' and 'post-disciplinary' refer simultaneously to a body of knowledge, a mode of governmentality, and the forms of subjectivity these produce. Manin embodies the specific scientific-technical knowledge of the engineer and his

192   *Republican Citizens, Precarious Subjects*

dedication to the conventions of his metier inculcated through years of work on the factory floor. This he contrasts disparagingly to the more nakedly financial logic embodied by Philippe and the purely theoretical and general knowledge of management he has derived from his elite studies. As Manin remarks angrily to Philippe:

> Nowadays, only cash counts. Your studies at a *grande école* taught you to think like that. As for me, it was my father who got me a job here. I was 16. I've held every position on the factory floor to get to where I am. So, I know the job. That's why the guys respect me. Where do you think your grand theories will take us? And when you leave, it'll be up to us to keep things going. As always. And I'm not sure we'll be better off as a result.

In a later exchange, Manin demands of Philippe: 'Monsieur Seignier, if I asked you make a component with a bore of 10 microns at an angle of 17 degrees, could you do it?' To which Philippe replies, 'No, but I know how to make sure it's delivered to the customer as quickly as possible. That's *kanban*, Monsieur Manin.' These exchanges epitomise what Moulier Boutang (2010:73) has described as the collapse of 'the traditional culture of the engineer and his dominant role' under a Fordist mode of production, in the face of the rise of the logics of finance, marketing, and managerialism embodied by Philippe as a product not of an elite engineering *grande école* but of the increasingly powerful business school sector. As we have seen, these financial and managerial logics will prove profoundly detrimental to Frank and Philippe's fellow citizens, prompting waves of redundancies in both cases.

The full import of the depiction of doomed young executives like Frank and Philippe thus relates not simply to the exploitative realities of the contemporary workplace but reflects also their status as products of an elite education system whose republican and universalistic ideals have been corrupted by the rise of private fee-paying business schools. Initially, both men are committed to ideals of social justice, seeing themselves as members of a republican elite dedicated to improving the lot of the provincial working class. They gradually discover, however, that there is a fundamental contradiction between this self-image and the realities of the ruthless global financial forces whose interests they actually must serve. This is the source of a profound sense of socio-psychological precarity concerning their position in French society, whether they should stake their allegiance to the workers, among whom they grew up, or to the global business elite, into whose ranks they are being inducted. This apparently purely personal crisis has much broader socio-political implications insofar as it embodies a challenge to the very French republican compact, to the notion that all citizens, from the educational elite to the working class, might work together in solidarity to further the general interest. *Ressources humaines* and *Violence des échanges en milieu tempéré* both suggest that compact is now irreparably broken on account of fundamental shifts in both the nature of global capitalism and the structure of French higher education. It is those shifts in higher education that mean that France's brightest and best are now being educated to promote managerial and financial interests that run directly counter to the interests of their fellow citizens.

An Education in Proxenetism

This notion that the rise of France's business schools is leading the nation's young academic elite astray is also at the centre of Kim Chapiron's 2014 film, *La Crème de la crème*. The film is set in an exclusive business school on the outskirts of Paris, a fictional *grande école*, then, that nonetheless corresponds closely to France's oldest and most prestigious business school, HEC. The narrative initially focuses on two second-year roommates, Dan (Thomas Blumenthal) and Jaffar (Karim Ait M'Hand), who struggle to fit in, to gain access to any of the school's exclusive social clubs, and hence to get girlfriends. At a raucous welcome party for first-years, Dan befriends an attractive new blonde student, Kelliah (Alice Isaaz). Although Kelliah rejects Dan's sexual advances, she bonds with him on the basis that she shares his sense of being distanced from the school's exclusive social clubs and cliques. Indeed, as the film progresses we learn that Kelliah comes from a working-class immigrant home in the Parisian *banlieue* and has been accepted into the school '*sur dossier*'. That is to say that rather than having followed the usual route of *classe préparatoire* followed by rigorous examination, she forms one of a small quota of students from disadvantaged backgrounds admitted on the basis of their academic records alone. Kelliah is, then, another example of the myth of republican meritocracy at work, the student of modest socio-economic

194   *Republican Citizens, Precarious Subjects*

origins who, through innate ability and hard work, has gained access to France's academic elite. Yet, as the film develops, it becomes evident that the lessons she learns at business school run directly counter to the republican ideals she might initially seem to embody.

In conversation, Dan and Kelliah work out that his and Jaffar's difficulties with girls reflect the fact that they are caught in a vicious circle – the fewer girlfriends they have, the lower their perceived value on the school's intensely competitive sexual market, hence the less likely they are to get girlfriends. Dan works out that if they invest some money purchasing the sexual services of an attractive girl from outside the school, this will give the impression they are in high demand, hence raising their value on the sexual market and increasing their chances of getting a real girlfriend. Dan thus applies the knowledge of economics and business he has learned at business school, specifically his understanding of so-called 'Veblen goods' that are perceived to be more valuable the higher their price, in order to justify engaging in prostitution. He persuades Kelliah to recruit a beautiful supermarket shelf-stacker as a sexual partner for his friend Jaffar, on the basis that Kelliah shares a form of gender and class affinity with the girl that will smooth over such potentially delicate negotiations. The plan works, Jaffar's sexual value duly increases, and he manages to find a girlfriend from among his fellow students.

Meanwhile, a fourth student, Louis (Jean-Baptiste Lafarge) has been observing events and persuades Dan and Kelliah to extend their plan by setting up a prostitution ring to service the needs of a much broader section of the school's male students. As he explains, the true value of attending such a school lies not in the knowledge one acquires but in the networks and contacts one establishes. Kelliah and Dan are, however, sadly excluded from all the important social networks, the first on account of her working-class origins, the second because of his geekiness.[1] Setting up a prostitution ring is the obvious way of overcoming these obstacles. Kelliah thus sets about recruiting a team of working girls from among the beautiful young women she encounters in her everyday life, relying on her working-class nous to persuade them that prostitution is no more exploitative and much more lucrative than working in their current low-paid precarious jobs as receptionists, shop assistants, leaflet distributors, and so forth. The prostitution scheme proves a runaway success and much of the film is given over to lurid drink- and drug-fuelled nightclub scenes and sex parties.

Perhaps inevitably, the school authorities get wind of the scheme and, in the film's final scene, Kelliah, Dan, and Louis are expelled. Ironically, their brilliant futures are thus potentially ruined by their having applied to the letter the lessons about economics and social networking they learned at the very business school that is now expelling them. The tone of *La Crème de la crème* is highly ambiguous, at once lamenting and revelling in the scenes of immorality and sexual decadence it voyeuristically depicts. Nonetheless, it clearly does offer one further exemplification of the trope of doomed French youth, of aspirant members of a republican elite corrupted by the mercenary values disseminated via the nation's increasingly dominant business schools. The poignancy of Kelliah's ultimate fate, like that of Frank and Philippe before her, is proportionate to the extent to which she might have embodied a shining example of the French Republican School's founding values of egalitarianism and meritocracy, its ability to identify and promote its most talented young citizens, regardless of their minority ethnicity or modest social origins. Kelliah's expulsion from her elite business school, like the disillusionments suffered by Frank and Philippe, signifies the crisis of those French republican ideals in the current educational and economic conjuncture.

Doomed Youth in the *Banlieue*

As we have pointed out, for all the difficulties faced by Kelliah, Frank, and Philippe, they nonetheless remain relatively privileged, belonging to an academic and, in Philippe's case, professional elite. Given this is the case, it might seem perverse to focus on such individuals rather than on social categories whose experiences of educational failure, unemployment, and economic precarity surely make them more deserving of the epithet 'doomed youth'. If there is one group of French youth more frequently depicted as doomed by the current economic conjuncture it is surely the young working class, often ethnic minority inhabitants of the *banlieue*, the large socially deprived housing projects on the deindustrialised outskirts of major French cities. As we pointed out in Chapter 1, these suburban housing estates were often built specifically to house workers employed in nearby factories. They also became home to a disproportionate number of immigrant workers, themselves recruited to perform unskilled labour in those same

196 Republican Citizens, Precarious Subjects

factories. With the loss of those unskilled industrial jobs over the 1980s and 1990s, the *banlieue* became one area in which the socio-economic fallout of Fordism's crisis was felt most early and most acutely. These socio-economic problems became 'ethnicised', as Azouz Begag and Christian Delorme (1994:15) put it, insofar as unskilled immigrant workers, their children and grandchildren have suffered exacerbated levels of unemployment through a combination of poor qualifications and discriminatory recruitment practices. A 2017 national survey revealed that 26 per cent of young *banlieue* inhabitants leave the school system with no formal qualifications, as against the national average of just 14 per cent (Céreq 2017:18). Young *banlieue* inhabitants who *do* have qualifications, meanwhile, suffer significantly higher unemployment levels than similarly qualified candidates not from the *banlieue*. Unemployment rates for those with five years' post-*baccalauréat* education are 11 per cent for young *banlieue* inhabitants versus 9 per cent for non-*banlieue* inhabitants. The rate of unemployment among those with less prestigious vocational qualifications, the CAP or BEP, are 40 per cent for young *banlieue* inhabitants versus 26 per cent for non-*banlieue* inhabitants. Three years after leaving formal education, just 49 per cent of young people with two immigrant parents are in stable long-term employment, compared with an average of 57 per cent for all young people and 73 per cent for those from upper-middle-class families (43).

These kinds of statistic have led sociologists Stéphane Beaud and Gérard Mauger (2017:7–17) to dub these young working-class people 'a sacrificed generation', struggling to find their place in a 'deindustrialised France'. Since the 1980s, extensive media coverage has highlighted the relationship between educational failure, unemployment, criminality, and, more recently, Islamic radicalism in the *banlieue*. Over the same period, the sub-genre of the *banlieue* film has offered a range of fictional representations of these phenomena. As Carrie Tarr (2005) has argued, *banlieue* films made by outsiders, that is by directors of white European ethnicity, tend to be more sensationalist and hence apocalyptic in tone than the more muted, social realist films made by insiders, by ethnic minority directors. Yet, if we take Kassovitz's *La Haine* (1995) and Malik Chibane's *Hexagone* (1994) as representative of each of those categories, both are characterised by an equivalent sense of doom-laden pessimism. In *La Haine*, this is evident in the structuring device of a countdown to the inevitable moment of destructive violence in which the three central young male protagonists find themselves embroiled at the film's end. In the less sensationalist *Hexagone*, the voiceover of its central male protagonist, Slimane (Jalil Naceri), communicates his pessimism throughout the film, from his opening description of the sense of stasis and imprisonment hanging over his unemployed peers to his reaction to the death of his brother from an overdose and the arrest of his friend Karim (Driss El Haddoui) for drug-dealing at the film's close. Philippe Faucon's more recent film, *La Désintégration* (2012), offers an even more pessimistic representation of doomed *banlieue* youth in its depiction of a young man of North African heritage whose disgust at both the exploitative working conditions suffered by his parents and the discrimination he faces in the jobs market leads him to radical Islam and suicidal terrorism.

As Ugo Palheta has pointed out, and as the above examples suggest, 'when people discuss the career difficulties encountered by working class youth, it is almost always a matter of ethnic minority boys […], young men from the *banlieue*'. Too often 'excluded from the field of vision' are thus 'young working class women', whose statistically observable 'higher average level of qualification' is presumed to render their educational and career trajectories less precarious (in Beaud and Mauger, eds. 2017:99). Yet this overlooks the extent to which these young women too suffer from low educational achievement and a consequent relegation to low-prestige vocational streams that typically lead into precarious, low-paid service-sector employment in retail, catering, or social care (103). As we noted, it is from among these categories of young working-class women that Kelliah is able to recruit working girls for the prostitution ring she and her friends set up in their elite business school in *La Crème de la crème*. A more detailed and hence insightful fictional account of these phenomena is offered by Houda Benyamina's 2016 film *Divines*, which focuses on the formal and moral education of 16-year-old Dounia (Oulaya Amamra), a young woman of North African heritage who lives with her unmarried mother in a Roma camp, a shantytown, on the edge of a run-down housing estate in the Parisian *banlieue*.

At the beginning of the film, Dounia is studying for a *BEP Accueil* in the local *collège*, that is to say a vocational qualification taken at age sixteen as training for work as a receptionist. Dounia's school, like the qualification for which she is studying, stands at the antipodes in the French educational hierarchy to the elite business schools attended by

198   *Republican Citizens, Precarious Subjects*

Kelliah, Frank, and Philippe. Nonetheless, the form and content of her education mirrors the kinds of poor disciplinary techniques that Darmon identified in her analysis of the *classes préparatoires* and hence seems to aim at turning Dounia, in her turn, into an entrepreneur of the self.

Banlieue Youth as Entrepreneurs of the Self

Early in *Divines*, we see Dounia at school, being forced to repeat a role play in which she acts as receptionist while one of her peers acts as her customer. The teacher upbraids Dounia for not taking the exercise seriously, insisting she sit up straight and, above all, not forget to smile. As the teacher takes over the role of customer, Dounia begins to mock the exercise, adopting an exaggerated smile and an excessively subservient and solicitous tone. Exasperated, the teacher asks her what she wants from life since she clearly believes a career as a receptionist to be beneath her. Dounia responds by chanting, in English, 'Money, money, money!', encouraging her classmates to join the chant, something they do to accompanying jeers and laughter. The situation rapidly deteriorates as Dounia launches into a tirade directed at her teacher, ridiculing her profession, poor salary, ugly clothes, narrow lifestyle, and lack of ambitions. Declaring she will one day earn more than her teacher has ever dreamed of, Dounia storms out of the classroom.

The education that Dounia so noisily rejects in this way represents the very antithesis of the elite academic education received by the *grande école* graduates whose depictions we examined in the first half of this chapter. A *B.E.P. Accueil* forms part of the low-prestige vocational streams of French secondary education, streams in which students of working-class and ethnic minority origin are significantly overrepresented. As Palheta points out, 'almost 70% of female students in French vocational education' are of working class origin and are 'concentrated in a very narrow range of career specialisms (low grade admin, social care and healthcare, retail, hotel and catering) where job opportunities remain less secure than those associated with male-dominated specialisms' (in Beaud and Mauger, eds. 2017:103). Yet there is at least one very striking similarity between the depiction of education in *Divines* and Muriel Darmon's account of the kind of 'work on the self' that candidates for France's elite business schools are required to undertake in the much more prestigious *classes préparatoires*. Like the privileged students Darmon studies, Dounia is enjoined to engage in a work on her self, an exercise in self-fashioning in the course of which she will acquire the necessary psychological and personal attributes to equip her for a life of doubtless precarious, low-paid, feminised, tertiary-sector employment. Dounia's act of rebellion is thus a refusal to engage in this work of self-fashioning, to perform her allotted role as motivated, passionate, yet servile low-paid service-sector employee.

The depiction of education in *Divines*, then, contains an implicit critique of the failure of the French Republican School to live up to its universalistic, egalitarian ideals, of the ways in which, on the contrary, it tends to produce and reproduce class distinctions between the predominantly middle-class students who follow the more prestigious academic streams and the predominantly working-class students following more vocational paths. This depiction also contains an implicit critique of more recent developments in republican education that, according to the authors of *La Nouvelle École capitaliste* (2012), have made the educational system ever more subservient to the demands of employers and the contemporary labour market.

Christian Laval and his co-authors argue that up until the 1980s, vocational training in French state schools formed an intrinsic part of the republican post-war consensus, exemplifying what we termed in Chapter 2 a 'qualifications model'. According to that 'qualifications model', the vocational training delivered through the Republican School gave access to nationally recognised qualifications that themselves corresponded to specified job functions as laid down in one of the range of 'collective conventions' negotiated between trades unions, employers, and government in each 'branch' of industrial activity. This 'correspondence' between formal qualifications and 'jobs occupied' rested on a shared 'recognition of the value of qualifications in terms of professional and social status' that was characteristic of 'Fordist capitalism' (Laval, et al. 2012:94). This 'overarching apparatus, put in place after 1945' has, however, 'today been radically undermined' as whole sectors of industry have disappeared and vocational training has responded to employers' demands for a more flexible, adaptable, supposedly autonomous workforce. From the 1980s onwards, Laval and his co-authors argue, vocational streams in French state schools have

200   *Republican Citizens, Precarious Subjects*

become focused on the development of more intangible, personalised 'skills', on the need for students to develop their own 'flexibility', on preparing them for 'the permanent recycling of their productive capacities'. Furthermore, they conclude, 'the new models of training' aim at 'the fabrication of a new form of subjectivity', by 'preparing young people mentally for the necessity of becoming the individual managers of their stock of skills, continually readapting to organisational and productive contexts in a state of permanent change' (95–96). In short, the education Dounia receives is directed towards encouraging her to develop her stock of human capital in accordance with the demand for a more modulated, adaptable professional identity that, as we have demonstrated throughout this study, now typifies the French labour market.

Dounia's act of rebellion in the classroom is thus both a rebuke to the founding myth of French republican education and an aggressive rejection of the shift to a post-disciplinary, more modulated form of education focused on producing subjects adapted to contemporary forms of flexible, precarious employment. However, as the plot unfolds, it becomes clear that Dounia's rebellion is self-defeating, that the alternative path she has chosen will ultimately prove fateful.

Having rejected formal education, Dounia persuades local drug-dealer Rebecca (Jisca Kalvanda) to take her on, attracted by the latter's evident financial and sexual autonomy. Once Dounia has proved her worth as a street-level dealer, Rebecca entrusts her with a more dangerous task: she must seduce Rebecca's former drug supplier Reda (Farid Larbi), gaining access to his flat in order to steal his stash of drug money. To achieve this, Dounia will have to exploit her most personal attributes, her physical attractiveness and charm, learning how to carry off a look of glamorous sophistication. In a scene set in Rebecca's flat in the *banlieue*, we thus see Dounia practising walking in high heels with an empty kebab box balanced precariously on her head. As Dounia walks gingerly around the flat, Rebecca expounds her personal philosophy of ruthless entrepreneurialism, apparently gleaned from various self-help manuals. As Rebecca explains:

> Why do you think poor people stay poor? [...] It's because they don't dare to do anything. You have to dare to be rich. You close your eyes, you visualise the cash [*la thune*] and it will come to you

Doomed Youth 201

[…]. Cash [*la thune*] is an energy, it's a flow; you have to call it to you; you have to tell yourself: I dare to be loaded.

Paradoxically, the criminal activities Dounia has adopted in rejection of her formal education apparently require of her an analogous process of self-fashioning, an analogous working on and performance of the self. Where Dounia's teacher exhorted her to sit up straight, smile, and adopt the positive attitude required of an aspirant receptionist, Rebecca enjoins her to undertake an equivalent process of cultivating and exploiting her most personal physical and psychological attributes. We noted how, in *La Crème de la crème*, the protagonists' involvement in a prostitution ring represented not the antithesis of the values inculcated in their elite business school but rather the extension of such values to their logical extreme. Something similar is depicted in *Divines*, as the entrepreneurial values Rebecca applies to drug-dealing, as well as the kind of self-fashioning Dounia engages in to prepare to seduce Reda, are shown to represent merely the extension of more mainstream values, educational and working practices to their logical extreme. Indeed, it is instructive here to recall the *classe préparatoire* teacher cited in Muriel Darmon's study, who enjoined his students to view their oral examinations as a kind of 'Operation Seduction' rather than an objective test of their knowledge. At her school, Dounia was being trained for one form of 'Operation Seduction', encouraged to adopt the submissive role of a receptionist, seducing her clients with a friendly smile. Having rejected that kind of education, she paradoxically finds herself training for another form of 'Operation Seduction' through which she will literally seduce Reda before stealing his money.

Dounia's training as Rebecca's henchwoman thus represents a kind of distorted mirror image of the training on offer to her in the Republican School. Ultimately, the film suggests that her application of that training to the realm of criminality will prove an even greater dead-end than the limited career opportunities her formal education offered her. At the cost of physical assault and attempted rape, Dounia manages to locate and steal Reda's drug money. Rather than return it to Rebecca, however, she gives half of it to her best friend Maimouna (Déborah Lukumuena), keeping the other half to fund her planned escape from the *banlieue*. Before she can escape, Dounia is forced to return to the *banlieue* to free Maimouna from the clutches of a furious Rebecca who is threatening to exert a violent

202 Republican Citizens, Precarious Subjects

revenge on Dounia and her best friend for their betrayal. A violent altercation ensues in Rebecca's hideout in a locked cellar underneath one of the residential tower blocks, in the course of which a fire is started. Dounia and Rebecca are able to escape by squeezing through a narrow opening but Maimouna is too overweight to get out. When the fire brigade arrive, despite Dounia's implorations, they refuse to intervene without police protection, fearing they will be attacked by the local youth as happened during the last such incident. By a terrible irony, it was Dounia herself who had led the earlier attack on the firefighters and so she is forced to watch her best friend die, knowing that it is her involvement in crime and delinquency that is the cause of Maimouna's death. The tenacity, assertiveness, and initiative that Dounia demonstrated in her determination to get rich quick and escape her limited *banlieue* existence have thus proved profoundly self-destructive. Dounia's ultimate fate is surely less a warning against her own hubris than a lament at the limited opportunities open to someone of her class and ethnicity, caught between a future of precarious, low-paid tertiary employment and the embrace of a criminal form of entrepreneurialism that will prove destructive for herself, her friends, and her community.

Uber in the *Banlieue*

One criticism that might be made of *Divines* is that its violently dramatic ending risks a certain sensationalism. The film may thus seem unrepresentative of the surely more mundane reality of life for the majority of *banlieue* inhabitants engaged in daily struggles to find employment, bring up families, and keep body and soul together. However, the detailed fieldwork conducted by sociologists Stéphane Beaud and Michel Pialoux indicates that Dounia's embrace of a criminal variant of entrepreneurialism is by no means as untypical as it might appear. In the 1990s and early 2000s Beaud and Pialoux undertook fieldwork in a *banlieue* of the Eastern city of Montbéliard, a *banlieue* built to house workers from the nearby Peugeot plant, including a significant population of Turkish and Moroccan immigrants. With the economic downturn of the 1970s and 1980s, the Peugeot plant stopped recruiting, leaving the sons and grandsons of both French workers and first-generation immigrants struggling to find work or a place in

French society. As the primary source of local employment dried up, the *banlieue* in question became a site of economic deprivation, characterised by rising criminality, family breakdown, and the erosion of those political structures – the trades unions and the local communist party – that had given a sense of identity and meaning to working-class youth.

What Beaud and Pialoux (2003:381) term 'the destructuring of the working class' over these years was exacerbated by shifts in the educational field and the adoption by Peugeot of so-called Japanese management techniques. Between 1996 and 2001 the company initiated a system of just-in-time (JIT) production within its factory, while outsourcing component manufacture to a host of local subcontractors, themselves subjected to Peugeot's stringent total quality production standards. Work in both the Peugeot factory and its subcontractors thus demanded higher levels of autonomy, initiative, co-operative working and multi-tasking of workers on the factory floor (125–55). Where the company had once been happy to employ unskilled, poorly qualified workers, it increasingly began to demand the *baccalauréat* or even university-level qualifications of new recruits to jobs on the factory floor. Further, the kinds of collaborative, relational, cognitive, and affective skill demanded under the new JIT production regime ran directly counter to the 'street culture' through which working-class young men in the *banlieue* were typically socialised, a culture that emphasised confrontation and virile, even aggressive, self-assertion over the more relaxed co-operative and communicative 'new behavioural norms based on an Americanised model of management' (133). The consequent exclusion of poorly qualified working-class and ethnic minority young men from the labour market, exacerbated by experiences of social and racial discrimination, fuelled the rise of both criminality and Islamic radicalism (Beaud and Pialoux 1999:428–29).

Those young *banlieue* inhabitants who *had* managed to gain employment in Peugeot's modernised factory were, by definition, better qualified than workers of their father's or grandfather's generation had been. One of the results of their greater exposure to formal education was a tendency to reject as old-fashioned and limiting an older social identity rooted in the collective struggles of the labour movement. This new generation of factory workers tended to imagine any future socio-economic advancement in much more individualised, entrepreneurial terms. This generation, 'almost all inhabitants of the impoverished

204   *Republican Citizens, Precarious Subjects*

housing estates of the 1990s and of immigrant heritage', Beaud and Pialoux (1999.451) suggest, 'rejects in its entirety the heritage of the working class and dream of individual success as small businessmen'. The belief in the virtues of small-scale entrepreneurialism as a way out of the problems of unemployment, economic deprivation, and racial discrimination has by no means been limited to the young inhabitants of the *banlieue* themselves. On the contrary, over recent years the French authorities have also embraced this notion, actively promoting entrepreneurialism and, more specifically, entrepreneurialism through the growth of Internet platforms such as Uber as a solution to the problems experienced by *banlieue* youth.

One tangible manifestation of the French government's faith in Internet platforms as the answer to unemployment in the *banlieue* was the so-called *Opération 70000 Entrepreneurs Dans les Quartiers*. Launched in 2016, this initiative brought the State employment agency Pôle Emploi together with private companies such as Uber and Rent-a-Car and a range of NGOs, such as Adie (*Association pour le droit à l'initiative économique*) and *Positive Planet France*. A series of job fairs were held in deprived *banlieues* with the aim of putting the local unemployed who were considering becoming taxi drivers in contact with potential employers (Baumard 2016). In order to understand what was at stake here, it is worth retracing the genesis of this initiative through a brief history of some of its participants.

Positive Planet France is an organisation that aims, according to its website, to 'fight against unemployment in working class *quartiers* by helping people excluded from the jobs market to create their own business'. It was set up by Jacques Attali, a social commentator and economist who acted as advisor to François Mitterrand between 1981 and 1991, before becoming the first head of the European Bank for Reconstruction and Development between 1991 and 1993. During Sarkozy's presidency, Attali chaired a commission looking into ways to boost French economic growth. The Attali Report of 2008, for which the young *Inspecteur des Finances*, Emmanuel Macron, served as *rapporteur*, proposed, among other things, liberalising regulated professions, such as taxi drivers and pharmacists, as a means of promoting small-scale entrepreneurialism among France's unemployed. This led, in 2009, to the legalisation of private minicabs, the so called VTCs (*Voiture de Tourisme avec Chauffeur*), a necessary precondition for Uber's entry into the French taxi market when they first arrived in the country in 2011 (Abdelnour 2017:155–56).

A second precondition for Uber's success in France was the availability of easy credit to enable the unemployed to purchase suitably luxurious cars. This is the role played by Adie, an organisation that provides loans to any recipient of unemployment benefit seeking to set up their own business. Adie takes its inspiration from Bangladesh's famous Grameen Bank, the pioneer of the use of microfinance in the developing world as a means of providing development aid that bypasses the allegedly corrupt and inefficient organisms of local states. In the developing world, microfinance initiatives reflect the belief that where aid can foster dependency, loans will generate a kind of self-reliant entrepreneurialism among the most impoverished. In France, Adie works on the principle that extending loans to the unemployed will similarly reduce unemployment while avoiding the dangers of so-called welfare dependency.

At the time of Sarkozy's presidency, Adie's treasurer was a man called François Hurel. Hurel authored a report for Sarkozy's Minister for Trades, Retail and Small Business, Henri Novelli, in which he proposed the creation of a new legally recognised status for small-scale entrepreneurs. In 2008 Novelli charted a bill through Parliament that recognised this new status of 'auto-entrepreneur' for those running small businesses with annual turnovers below a fairly modest limit, exonerating them from certain fiscal and administrative burdens, while affording them some measure of social insurance (Abdelnour 2017:101–2). This was the final precondition for Uber's establishment in France, enabling Uber drivers to register as auto-entrepreneurs and VTC operators, funded by loans from Adie.

In promoting the new status of 'auto-entrepreneur' to both the general public and his fellow parliamentarians, Novelli repeatedly presented unemployed ethnic minority *banlieue* youth as the prime beneficiaries. As he put it in 2009:

> What better motor of social mobility is there than the firm? But the *auto-entreprise* is better still: requiring neither financial resources, nor qualifications, nor the right connections, it puts a youth from the *banlieue* on the same level as a pensioner from the 16th *arrondissement*. What counts is the initial idea and the

206 *Republican Citizens, Precarious Subjects*

> personal drive [*la niaque*] to get it off the ground. It truly is a
> status that will facilitate social peace.
>
> (quoted in Abdelnour 2017:106)

For Novelli, the new status of auto-entrepreneur offered a way of avoiding what he took to be the rigidities and hierarchies inherent to France's corporatist system of formal qualifications, work, and welfare. In so doing, he insisted, it could unleash the entrepreneurial spirit already present in the *banlieue*, a spirit that only out-dated class warriors would seek to deny:

> Contrary to the old Stalinists hanging on to their dreams of out
> and out collectivisation, the younger generation, even those on
> the left, and notably ethnic minority youth, has nothing against
> business. On the contrary, they dream of setting up their own
> business and earning lots of cash [*de la thune*]. If this wasn't true,
> how come Bernard Tapie was the darling of the *banlieues* for so
> many years?
>
> (quoted in Abdlenour 2017:111)

Novelli's mix of street slang – *la niaque, la thune* – and can-do entrepreneurialism recalls nothing so much as Rebecca's speech vaunting criminal enterprise and 'the cash [*la thune*]' it brings in *Divines*.

As Sarah Abdelnour (2017:71) has pointed out, Novelli's political roots are on the neo-liberal side of the mainstream French right, as evidenced in his role as campaign director to Alain Madelin in the presidential elections of 2002. His support for the status of the 'auto-entrepreneur' thus reflects Novelli's belief in the virtues of the market over welfare or economic interventionism. However, the status also gained the support of French Socialists, remaining in place throughout Hollande's presidency, on account of the social justice gains it could supposedly secure. Macron, of course, had always been in favour. In 2016, in response to complaints about the exploitative terms and conditions suffered by those 'auto-entrepreneurs' who were employed by Uber, he remarked that it was better for *banlieue* youth to work as Uber drivers than 'to hang around on street corners or deal drugs' (quoted in Vouteau 2018:161).

Thus, small-scale entrepreneurialism, in general, and platform capitalism, in particular, are now promoted by politicians from across the political spectrum as a solution to the problems of unemployed ethnic minority *banlieue* youth. Recent reports on the platform economy by both the *Conseil d'État* and IGAS (*Inspection générale des affaires sociales*) repeat the assertion that employers like Uber offer a solution to what the *Conseil d'État* terms 'the social and territorial fracture' (Conseil d'État 2017:21), not least because booking a service via the Internet means customers cannot see in advance that a service provider is of non-European origin and hence there is no possibility of racial discrimination (Amar and Viossat 2016:81).

There is evidence that significant numbers of young men from the *banlieue* have indeed taken up the opportunities offered by employers like Uber. Statistics from 2016 indicate that young men with a history of unemployment are overrepresented among Uber drivers in France (Landier, et al. 2016:5). In Paris, the majority of such drivers come from the northern and south-eastern suburbs of Paris, that is to say from the most economically deprived, deindustrialised working-class suburbs with high ethnic minority populations (Amar and Viossat 2016:81). At a more anecdotal level, in her personal account of working as an 'auto-entrepreneur', Sophie Vouteau (2018:240) claims that every Uber driver she has ever met is an ethnic minority young man from the *banlieue* with a prior history of unemployment. On her visits to both the offices of Adie and the 23rd *Salon des Entrepreneurs* in Paris in 2016, she is struck by 'the incredible diversity of the attendees. […] There are Blacks, Arabs, South-East Asians, and all these "French people of diversity" seem to have been brought here by the wave of entrepreneurialism that is sweeping over our morose and anaemic economy' (18).

The French authorities' attempts to promote small-scale entrepreneurialism and working for Internet platforms as a solution to the problems of the *banlieue* thus seem to be enjoying some success. However, even promoters of such solutions, such as the *Conseil d'État*, have expressed concerns about their potential effects on the social fabric. In its report, the *Conseil* worries that the atomising tendencies inherent to platform work risk eroding 'the forms of social bond and the social solidarity produced in industrial society' in the 'factory/firm', itself defined as 'the centralised space in which human bonds were created and collective organisations defending the interests of workers were formed' (Conseil d'État 2017:90). As the *Conseil*'s vocabulary makes clear, the report is alluding here to the erosion of that characteristically French republican vision of the role of the division of labour in

208   *Republican Citizens, Precarious Subjects*

society, of professional corporations and trades unions in safeguarding social solidarity and the social bond.

This concern is expressed more trenchantly still by the sociologist Sarah Abdelnour in her study of what she sees as the exploitative realities of working as an 'auto-entrepreneur'. She argues that the status of 'auto-entrepreneur' is 'contributing to the disengagement of individuals from collective structures and hence profoundly undermining the French social model' (2017:262). Not only does this risk leaving French citizens atomised and impoverished, it also risks bankrupting the work-based social insurance funds on which the French social model was based, as 'auto-entrepreneurs' contribute so little to them:

> The 'auto-entrepreneur' mechanism undermines the very bases of our social system by inciting us to leave salaried employment, but also by putting social insurance funds in deficit, by promoting the ideology of an atomised, ultra-responsible individual and by transforming each of us into a micro-entrepreneur of our own life, plunged into a world of permanent economic calculation, of work and discipline but also of solitude and uncertainty. (Abdelnour 2017:315)

If Abdelnour emphasises that the status of 'auto-entrepreneur' necessitates workers transforming themselves into Foucauldian 'entrepreneurs of the self', she also highlights the extent to which this represents a fundamental challenge to the very bases of the French post-war republican corporatist compromise. For the very purpose of the kind of corporatism first theorised by Durkheim in his *De la division du travail social* and subsequently integrated into the post-war settlement was to establish forms of salaried labour, professional status, and collective representation that would guard against social atomisation and competitive individualism, hence securing social solidarity. Abdelnour's words here offer further confirmation of the working hypothesis that has guided us over preceding chapters, namely that the more modulated, entrepreneurial modes of subjectivity inherent to post-Fordist forms of work are perceived as profoundly disruptive and precarious insofar as they strike at the very core of the corporatism that underpinned more traditional conceptions of French republican citizenship.

The French authorities' promotion of entrepreneurialism and platform capitalism as solutions to unemployment in the *banlieue* thus epitomises the shift from a disciplinary to a more modulated post-disciplinary mode of governmentality whose effects we have traced over the course of preceding chapters. The solutions to unemployment in the *banlieue* are no longer seen to lie in State intervention and the interests of the young unemployed no longer seen as being best represented by the collective structures of the labour movement. These solutions have been radically individualised, so that it is no longer the State or politicians that are held responsible for securing growth and jobs but rather the unemployed themselves through their own commitment and entrepreneurial drive. Yet, as Vouteau argues (2018:160–61), it is hard to make a living as an Uber driver and so young Uber drivers face a future of continuing impoverishment, now exacerbated by indebtedness. In *Divines* we are offered a fictional representation of a young woman from the *banlieue* whose engagement in a criminal form of entrepreneurialism dooms her future. Abdelnour and Vouteau both suggest that the engagement of ethnic minority *banlieue* youth in the legal entrepreneurialism of platform capitalism may doom them to a similar fate.

As this chapter has sought to demonstrate, the doomed *banlieue* youth finds his or her unlikely analogue in the figure of the disillusioned *grande école* graduate, doomed to entrapment in the destructive networks of financialised global commerce. In one sense, these two figures would seem poles apart since, as we have noted, *grande école* graduates, whatever disillusionments they may suffer, remain hugely socially, culturally, and economically privileged in comparison to their peers in the *banlieue*. Yet, these two character types do share something important in the sense that they are both symptoms of a series of fundamental changes in the fields of education and employment that have posed profound challenges to established assumptions regarding how those two fields should interact to produce an integrated, cohesive Republic. At the top end of the social hierarchy, the rise of the business school and of the financialised multinational corporation is depicted in our sample of films as having challenged fundamental French republican assumptions about the proper role of the nation's academic and professional elite, as a republican elite serving the general interest is transformed into a business class undermining the national interest to the benefit of global financial interests. At the bottom end of the social hierarchy, the promotion of small-scale entrepreneurialism and platform capitalism is portrayed as having fundamentally undermined

210 *Republican Citizens, Precarious Subjects*

older notions about the proper role of the Republican School, salaried employment, and corporatist professional identities in securing the integration of all of France's citizens, regardless of class, sex, or ethnicity, into a cohesive social whole. Doubtless, there is an element of myth-making at work here, in the sense that, in reality, the republican elite could be haughty and self-interested, while the Republican School often reproduced existing class divisions, as much as it worked as a tool of social integration. Nonetheless, even if these institutions often failed to live up to their progressive ideals, those ideals were strongly embedded in public discourse and could hence be appealed to in struggles to mitigate more nakedly economic logics. The depictions of disillusioned *grande école* graduates and doomed *banlieue* youth we have examined in this chapter suggest that those ideals are increasingly disappearing from the French public sphere, being replaced by an emphasis on more entrepreneurial values that risk imposing profoundly precarious kinds of social identity and existence on France's young citizens.

Recent representations of both *grande école* graduates and *banlieue* youth thus turn on the close historical relationship between education, salaried employment, and integration into the Republic. Two of those factors – employment and Republican integration – have also been at the centre of debates and political protests regarding the place of undocumented migrants, the *sans papiers*, in French society and polity. The next chapter turns to consider these questions, arguing that undocumented migration and the *sans papiers* movement need to be understood as intimately related to the shifts in the French labour market whose effects we have been tracking throughout this book.

Notes

1   The film implies, in places, that the marginalisation of its three central protagonists also reflects their ethnic minority status – Ben is Jewish, while both Jaffar and Kelliah are of North African heritage.

Chapter 6

Sans Papiers

On 23 August 1996, more than 1,000 French police, including eight companies of riot police, smashed down the doors of the Saint Bernard Church in the eighteenth arrondissement of Paris, bringing its occupation by about 300 undocumented immigrants, or *sans papiers*, to a violent end. That evening the French film star Emmanuelle Béart appeared on the 8pm news programme of terrestrial channel France 2 to give her eye-witness account of the events. Béart was one of a number of French celebrities and intellectuals who had publicly supported the *sans papiers*' demands that the French authorities recognise their existence and provide them with the papers that would allow them to 'regularise' their status. Visibly upset, Béart described what she had seen:

> First of all, I'd like to say that I'm not here in my capacity as an actress but as a woman and mother of two children. [...] What you showed on TV doesn't come close to the suffering of all the children who I stayed with right to the end. I'd like to add something that's not clear on some of the images you showed, namely that there were several violations, notably of a church whose doors were broken down with axes, whose stained glass windows were smashed ... Children ..., for my part, I had a small child, because the children were clinging on to us, trying to understand in a sort of terror, of tears, of shouts ... a small child on my lap who wet himself he was so frightened, who couldn't find his mother or his father. [...] I want to make it clear that I don't belong to any political party. I turned up through human solidarity with some nappies, some milk. I am myself a mother

212   *Republican Citizens, Precarious Subjects*

of two children. [...] I only met people who have worked in France, who have a family, or who are unmarried — just because you have no children doesn't mean you don't have the same rights as everybody else. I only met people who have tried to form a family, to live here where life is tough but possible. In their countries, people are suffering. I've just come back from Mauritania; people are dying over there. In Mali, people are dying also. [...] What I saw this morning, I'll never forget but that's not important. What the children saw this morning, they won't ever forget either and that's very serious.[1]

On watching Béart's appearance on French TV news it is impossible not to be moved by the anger, passion, and courage of her intervention on behalf of the *sans papiers*. Nonetheless, that intervention does seem to display all of the limitations inherent to what might be termed the stance of apolitical humanitarianism that she adopts. Her insistence that she does not belong to any political party, combined with her appeal to what she figures as her natural human feelings of solidarity as a woman and mother, risks overriding any analysis of the specifically political or economic factors that both 'push' migrants to leave their native countries and 'pull' them into Western Europe. For she implies that the *sans papiers* are to be supported insofar as they are *suffering victims* and this is reinforced by her focus on the all too pathetic image of a crying child wetting himself in fear. The way in which she represents Mali and Mauritania as places of famine and death, meanwhile, plays into media stereotypes of sub-Saharan Africa as an undifferentiated morass of poverty and suffering dependent on benevolent Western aid and intervention for its salvation.

Béart's stance of apolitical humanitarianism stands in stark contrast to the analysis of the *sans papiers'* situation offered by one of the movement's two leading spokespeople, the Senegalese undocumented immigrant, Madiguène Cissé. In an interview published a year after the violent evacuation of the Saint Bernard Church, Cissé situated the *sans papier* movement in France within a series of international political struggles against the deleterious effects of neo-liberal globalisation, in the form of the structural adjustment programmes imposed on indebted developing nations by the International Monetary Fund (IMF) and World Bank from the 1980s onwards. As she put it: 'We believe the struggle, in Senegal and elsewhere, against structural adjustment programmes and our struggle is one and the same struggle.' Campaigning for 'labour rights', Cissé argued, was at the heart of the *sans papiers* movement (quoted in Ticktin 2011:44–46).

Cissé thus emphasises two specific, interrelated political and economic phenomena – the impact of neo-liberal global economic governance on countries in the developing world and the functioning of the labour market in France itself. This dual emphasis has an echo in Didier Fassin's work on the limitations of what he terms 'humanitarian reason'. Fassin argues that, up until at least the 1970s, issues such as immigration were typically interpreted through a political prism that figured immigrants as agents in an economic system that exploited their labour. Nowadays, however, immigrants such as the *sans papiers* tend to be viewed as suffering victims deserving of compassion and support on purely humanitarian grounds. He suggests that one problem with this shift is that the victim deserving of humanitarian aid is necessarily placed in a position of passivity, indebtedness, and hence inequality vis-à-vis their compassionate benefactors:

> Those at the receiving end of humanitarian attention know quite well that they are expected to show the humility of the beholden rather than express demands for rights. [...] When compassion is exercised in the public space, it is therefore always directed from above to below, from the more powerful to the weaker, the more fragile, the more vulnerable – those who can generally be constituted as victims of an overwhelming fate.
>
> (Fassin 2011:3–4)

Béart's emphasis on suffering young children, her depiction of undocumented migrants as victims fleeing famine in Africa represent precisely this constitution of the *sans papiers* as 'victims of an overwhelming fate'. Not only does this risk robbing the *sans papiers* of any agency, it is also misleading in that by no means all of those undocumented migrants who make it into France are fleeing absolute immiseration or imminent death. Indeed, the two spokespeople of the Saint Bernard *sans papiers*, Cissé and Ababacar Diop, were university educated and came from relatively privileged backgrounds in their native Senegal (Blin 2010:93–96). One further problem with Béart's brand of apolitical humanitarianism is thus that it implies that any *sans papiers* who is not immiserated or who cannot be figured as a suffering

214   *Republican Citizens, Precarious Subjects*

victim is deserving neither of rights nor of solidarity. In this sense, humanitarianism can unwittingly facilitate the kind of dismissal of the *sans papiers* movement penned by Thierry Blin, who points to the relatively privileged backgrounds of Cissé and Diop, as well as their career successes after 1996, as evidence of that movement's fundamental illegitimacy (Blin 2010).

Given the inherent limitations of apolitical humanitarianism, this chapter will argue for the necessity of understanding the phenomenon of undocumented migration into France as one further symptom of the kinds of shift in global economic governance and the national labour market whose effects we have examined over preceding chapters. As we noted in Chapter 1, it was the crisis of Fordism that led the French government to 'suspend' all further mass immigration into France in 1974, thus rendering the vast majority of new labour immigration illegal. The proliferation of precarious, low-paid, post-Fordist forms of work in France, however, produced a continuing demand for a pool of flexible immigrant labour. Meanwhile, the dominance of neo-liberal forms of global economic governance significantly contributed to poverty and political instability in the developing world, notably through the structural adjustment programmes of the IMF and World Bank that imposed reductions in social spending, privatisation, and trade liberalisation on developing nations. Understanding undocumented migration requires a grasp of these shifts towards post-Fordism, neo-liberal economics, and post-disciplinary governance. These shifts are often obscured not only by humanitarianism but also by the assumption that the problems faced by immigrants in France are wholly or primarily attributable to racial prejudices and government practices that have their roots in the nation's historical experience of colonialism and imperialism. In this sense, questions of immigration and ethnicity are taken to occupy a separate domain, quite distinct from the problems of employment and precarity we have examined in our preceding chapters.

Returning to Political Economy

Over recent decades, academic discussions of immigration and ethnicity in France have tended to concentrate on tracing contemporary forms of racial discrimination to that imperial past, attributing their persistence to the nation's failure to work through the problematic inheritance of colonialism. This kind of approach, based on the insights of Memory Studies, is typified by Dominic Thomas's *Africa and France* (2013), in which the problems faced by immigrants and ethnic minorities are attributed to what its author characterises as 'glaring failure of decolonisation' in France (Thomas 2013:87). As a result, Thomas repeatedly traces contemporary issues back to their supposed origins in the undigested inheritance of Western colonialism. Hence, he compares today's Mediterranean so-called 'migrant crisis' to the trans-Atlantic slave trade, evoking 'perilous Mediterranean crossings whose recalibration echoes an earlier *middle passage*' (Thomas 2013:70). Similarly, in a discussion of the European Union's (EU's) common immigration policy, which formed the basis for Nicolas Sarkozy's adoption of a 'selective' immigration policy between 2004 and 2012, Thomas argues that these policies have their 'historical antecedents' in the '1884–1885 Berlin Congress' (157).

The problem with these two historical analogies is their lack of any precision or specificity. Undocumented migrants, who struggle to make their way to the North African coast and then pay large sums of money to attempt to cross the Mediterranean, are in a completely different situation to enslaved Africans in the middle passage; their economic status, their political and legal rights, the role they may play in the European labour market are all wholly different from the role and status of enslaved Africans at the time of State-legitimised plantation slavery. Deciding how best to respond to the migrant crisis demands we understand these historical, economic, and political specificities, specificities that hasty analogies with the Atlantic slave trade surely risk occluding. Similarly, the EU's common policies on immigration and integration, like Sarkozy's 'selective' immigration policy, were not based on the philosophy that inspired the carving up of Africa between the imperial powers at the Congress of Berlin. On the contrary, these more recent policies were directly inspired by Gary Becker's (2011) theories of human capital and his emphasis on the beneficial role of labour migration in boosting each nation's stock of such capital: these theories were not elaborated until the 1970s and 1980s. As we will demonstrate in the course of this chapter, the positive value placed on migrant labour in such theories was to prove an important resource for the *sans papiers* themselves in their struggles for residency rights under Sarkozy's presidency.

216   *Republican Citizens, Precarious Subjects*

There is no doubt that the history of French imperialism has exerted a significant influence over current discriminatory government policies. However, as Emmanuelle Saada argues and as our examples from Thomas's book demonstrate, there are real dangers in adopting 'a continuist vision of history that links in too linear a fashion colonial and contemporary examples of discrimination, assuming them all to be the products of an unchanged form of racism' (Saada 2006:78–79). Such racism, rooted in France's history of colonialism, is always mediated through and re-inflected by current issues, not least by questions of contemporary political economy. The theories of human capital that have determined recent French immigration policy are the same theories as have so affected the working experiences of French nationals that we have examined in previous chapters. The liberalisation of global flows of capital that, as we saw in Chapter 3, fuelled the prosperity of executives like *Emploi du temps*'s Vincent has also proved to be one of the primary drivers of undocumented migration from the developing world. Hence, it is important to grasp that the *sans papiers*'s situation represents one further product of the logics of economic de-regulation we have examined in earlier chapters, even as we acknowledge the specific impact of the legacies of colonialism on that situation.

Highlighting the impact of political economy on the *sans papiers* in this way will also help us to avoid some of the pitfalls of an apolitical humanitarianism. Focusing on the role undocumented migrants play within the contemporary labour market makes it much harder to reduce them to the status of passive victims. They become, rather, active agents demanding rights based on their contribution to the economy and society of their host countries. By extension, citizens of those host countries are forced to consider the benefits *they* derive from undocumented migrant labour and hence the debts *they* owe to the *sans papiers*. Any simple hierarchy between the benevolent Western provider of aid and the indebted migrant is thus undermined.

It is, of course, the case that the phenomenon of undocumented migration into a country such as France is not wholly attributable to the French labour market's demand for a cheap, flexible, mobile labour force. The European migrant crisis of the 2010s, for example, has been driven to a significant degree by conflict, insecurity, and political repression in locations such as Libya, Syria, Iraq, Afghanistan, and Eritrea. However, undocumented migration from those locations is rarely driven purely by war, famine, or repression; as Heaven Crawley and her co-authors argue, 'there is often a complex and overlapping relationship between "forced" and "economic" drivers of migration' in such cases (Crawley, et al. 2018:63). Moreover, war, famine, and repression are scarcely purely natural phenomena, often being caused or exacerbated by iniquitous trade regimes, neo-liberal development policies, and debt servicing arrangements, not to mention clumsy political and military interventions by developed nations seeking privileged access to natural resources in the developing world (Bhabha 2018:104). Here again, an exclusively humanitarian approach can obscure these economic and geo-political factors, occluding the extent to which the governments and citizens of developed nations are themselves fully implicated in the processes that drive migration. Highlighting the role of undocumented migrants as workers will not address all of these questions. It may, nonetheless, offer those migrants a position from which to articulate a claim to rights as active agents, rather than merely to assistance as suffering victims. Further, it represents an important first step in the process of considering the full range of political and economic factors driving undocumented migration.

The *sans papiers*' struggles to have their rights acknowledged and their situation regularised has undergone a number of troughs and peaks since the evacuation of the Saint Bernard Church in 1996. The election of a left coalition government in 1997, ostensibly committed to a less repressive immigration policy, removed the issue from the top of the political and media agenda for a number of years. However, the election of a right-wing government in 2002, the two periods during which Nicolas Sarkozy served as Minister of Interior (2002–4, 2005–7), and his presidency (2007–12) brought the issue back to the forefront. From 2003 onward, Sarkozy set quotas for the minimum number of undocumented migrants to be expelled from France each year and this saw the number of expulsions take off once more (Cette France-là 2012a:176–87). The *sans papiers*' struggles have continued throughout the two succeeding presidencies of Hollande (2012–17) and Macron (2017 to date).

One of the by-products of the spike in expulsions under Sarkozy from 2003 on was a proliferation of protest movements and fictional films highlighting the plight of the *sans papiers*. This chapter will analyse a sample of these films and protest movements. It starts by examining two films, Philippe Lioret's *Welcome* (2009) and Olivier Nakache and Éric Toledano's *Samba* (2014), arguing that these

218   *Republican Citizens, Precarious Subjects*

exemplify the limitations of a purely humanitarian approach to these issues. Each film attempts to garner audience sympathy for the *sans papiers* cause by depicting its respective migrant protagonists as fundamentally attractive and admirable individuals. Yet this emphasis on sympathetic *personal* attributes is a precursor to infantilising the two characters in question, reducing them to the means by which their white French benefactors overcome their own emotional and spiritual crises. Indeed, these two films represent two missed opportunities to depict the varied political and economic drivers of undocumented migration, insofar as they gesture towards such drivers before then subsuming them under more sentimental, even ethnocentric plot devices. The chapter then turns to consider Gauz's *Debout-Payé* (2014), a novel that satirises the limitations of precisely this kind of sentimental humanitarianism, before highlighting the *sans papiers'* role within the political economy of post-Fordism to salutary effect. Finally, the chapter examines a series of strikes by the *sans papiers* between 2006 and 2011, in which that role within the contemporary French labour market provided the key point of mobilisation. Those strikes, like Gauz's novel, suggest that it is precisely by emphasising the *sans papiers'* economic function that we can understand the extent to which their situation is intimately related to the changes to the French labour market and the challenges to established notions of French republican citizenship that, we have argued in previous chapters, are inherent to post-Fordism.

Missed Opportunity 1 – *Samba* (2014)

Nakache and Toledano's 2014 film, *Samba,* tells the tale of the relationship between its eponymous hero, a Senegalese *sans papiers* played by Omar Sy, and Alice, a French senior executive suffering from burn-out, played by Charlotte Gainsbourg. At the film's opening, Samba is working as a *plongeur* in a luxury Paris hotel, hoping to progress to the level of trainee chef. These hopes are dashed, however, after Samba is picked up by the police, arrested, and sent to a detention centre. He is then released with an *obligation de quitter le territoire français,* a legal document stipulating its bearer leave France within a month or face immediate expulsion. Having thus lost his job in catering and being forced to rely on poor quality forged papers, Samba is obliged to seek ever more precarious forms of employment, signing on at an agency for temporary jobs in construction, street repair, and picking through household waste at a recycling centre. It is during his spell at the detention centre that Samba first encounters Alice, the high-flying executive who, having burned out, is taking a few weeks' sabbatical to work as a volunteer for a charity helping undocumented migrants and refugees.

That the film offers little explanation of the circumstances behind Alice's burn-out can itself be read as indicative of quite how widely debated the issue of workplace suffering has become in France. It seems that the filmmakers can rely on the fact that the contemporary French audience is familiar with this issue and will immediately recognise and understand the figure of the burned-out executive, with little or no further explanation required. If the issue of workplace suffering is one that has acquired a high cultural and political prominence in France over recent decades, the question of the *sans papiers* has acquired a similarly high profile, as we noted at the opening of this chapter.

Nakache and Toledano's film appears to offer the possibility of thinking these two issues together, of relating concerns about the degradation of the terms and conditions of French workers to the question of the place of the *sans papiers* in France, of the positions occupied by undocumented migrants within the contemporary French labour market. For the range of jobs occupied by the character Samba – in hotel and catering, construction, and waste management – typifies the process that the geographer Emmanuel Terray first defined by means of the oxymoron 'la délocalisation sur place' or 'onshore off-shoring' (in Balibar, et al. 1999:9–34). As Terray argues, multinational corporations can radically reduce their wage costs by off-shoring their manufacturing facilities to low-wage economies in Eastern Europe or the developing world. Certain, primarily service, functions cannot, however, be off-shored in this way: construction, health and care work, security guards, cleaners, workers in hotels and catering cannot be off-shored to the developing world since they need to be present in the developed world to deliver their services direct, in situ. A pool of flexible, insecure, undocumented workers allows employers to enjoy all of the benefits of geographical *off-shoring* but *onshore*, in France itself. Undocumented migrants can be employed to perform tasks in the security, catering, hotel, construction, health and care sectors at very low, sometimes illegally low, rates of pay and under

220   *Republican Citizens, Precarious Subjects*

very insecure terms. Such workers are unlikely to complain to the authorities since to do so would reveal their presence and potentially provoke their expulsion from France.

As Terray points out, it would be wrong to think of this pool of undocumented workers as anomalous or as some kind of archaic hangover from less enlightened, more exploitative times. On the contrary, he argues, the *sans papiers* are 'at the summit of modernity' (18), insofar as the legal and economic precarity they suffer, their radically flexible terms and conditions of employment, represent merely the most extreme case of phenomena affecting the contemporary French labour market in its entirety (34). In *Samba*, those more general phenomena of precarity and labour flexibility are personified by Alice, in her role as the immediately recognisable figure of the burnt-out executive. Thus, the film raises the possibility of linking the *sans papiers* question to the issue of workplace suffering by depicting both as symptoms of precisely those developments in political economy we have examined in preceding chapters. For these are symptoms that affect both relatively privileged French nationals, like Alice, and undocumented migrants, like Samba, whose economic prospects in his native Senegal have been severely damaged by successive structural adjustment programmes from the 1980s on (Dembele 2003). The film might even have imagined some form of solidarity emerging between Samba and Alice based on an awareness of the analogous forms of exploitation from which they suffer.

However, *Samba* never delivers on this promise. On the contrary, it rapidly subsumes these questions of political economy under a romantic plotline that has some troublingly ethnocentric connotations. By the film's dénouement, Samba will be significant primarily insofar as what is represented as his natural *joie de vivre*, humour, spontaneity, and sexual attractiveness help Alice to overcome her feelings of burn-out. Thus, at the film's end, Alice returns to her successful executive career bolstered by the injection of vitality her romantic involvement with Samba has given her. We see her successfully running a high-powered business meeting, her confidence restored thanks to wearing Samba's lucky football shirt under her business suit, itself merely a physical token of the life force with which Samba has literally and figuratively invigorated her in the course of their romantic encounters. Needless to say, this scenario, in which the jaded Westerner turns to the spontaneous vitality of the African Other as a source of spiritual and physical renewal has a long and inglorious history in Western primitivist discourse. Frantz Fanon identifies and parodies this trope in his *Black Skin, White Masks*, in terms that seem eminently applicable to the narrative of *Samba*:

> When the whites feel that they have become too mechanized, they turn to the men of colour and ask them for a little human sustenance. [...] In a society such as ours, industrialized to the highest degree, dominated by scientism [...] now and then when we are worn out by our lives in big buildings, we will turn to you as we do to our children – to the innocent, the ingenuous, the spontaneous. We will turn to you as to the childhood of the world. You are so real in your life – so funny, that is. Let us run away for a little while from our ritualized, polite civilization and let us relax, bend to those heads, those adorably expressive faces. In a way, you reconcile us with ourselves.
>
> (Fanon 1986:98–101)

Ultimately then, rather than being represented as a worker, an active agent playing an identifiable role within the French economy who might make a claim to equal rights based on that role, Samba is reduced to serving as the means by which the white bourgeois liberal comes to feel better about herself, makes herself and, allegorically, French society in its entirety, whole again.

Missed Opportunity 2 – *Welcome* (2009)

This kind of occlusion of political economy, in favour of sentimentalism, the infantilisation and subordination of the *sans papiers* to serving as the means by which the white liberal can feel whole again is also a defining feature of Philippe Lioret's 2009 film *Welcome*. Set in Calais, *Welcome* tells the tale of the relationship between Simon Clamart (Vincent Lindon), a local swimming instructor in the process of being divorced by his wife Marion (Audrey Dana), and the young Kurdish migrant Bilal (Firat Ayverdi). Bilal has two motivations for trying to swim across the Channel to Britain. First, he wants to be reunited with his teenage love Mina (Derya Ayverdi), who lives in London and who is being forced by her father into a marriage with his middle-aged, unattractive cousin. Second, Bilal is a keen amateur

222   *Republican Citizens, Precarious Subjects*

footballer and dreams of playing for Manchester United. Each of these motivations endows Bilal with considerable agency in a way that prevents his straightforward reduction to the status of passive suffering victim. Yet each of these motivations is potentially problematic and this in two principal ways.

First, by depicting Bilal as an admirable young man, struggling to get to Britain to be reunited with his young love and achieve his idealistic sporting ambitions, Lioret renders him immediately sympathetic to a Western audience. The problem here is that these audience responses of sympathy and empathy are secured at the cost of occluding what are surely the more representative drivers of undocumented migration, namely the range of geopolitical and economic issues that have destabilised locations such as Iraqi Kurdistan while producing the demand for undocumented migrant labour in developed economies such as Britain. These are factors from which Western viewers themselves benefit and in which they are implicated in ways that our immediate empathetic identification with the admirable Bilal risks occluding. Second, within the narrative of *Welcome* itself, Bilal's idealised motivations for migrating to Britain both infantilise him and reduce him to being merely the means by which Simon seeks to overcome his own personal and emotional crises.

In a conversation with his now ex-wife Marion immediately after they have signed their divorce papers, Simon expresses his admiration for the dangers Bilal has run in order to be with his love Mina, contrasting this to his lack of commitment to saving his own marriage. By helping Bilal to be reunited with Mina, Simon is clearly seeking to compensate symbolically for this lack of commitment to his own failed marriage. Meanwhile, in helping Bilal achieve his sporting ambitions, Simon is also seeking compensation for his own unrealised ambitions as a former member of the French national swimming squad. Bilal is thus infantilised, becoming the son Simon failed to have with Marion and the means through which Simon lives out his unrealised romantic, paternal, and sporting ambitions. In this way, Simon risks exploiting Bilal, instrumentalising his plight as a *sans papiers,* subordinating it to the role it plays in helping Simon to overcome his own sense of emotional and spiritual crisis. Moreover, if we read Simon's divorce as an allegory for the breakdown of French society as a whole – and the film certainly encourages such a reading – then *Welcome* seems to advocate supporting the *sans papiers'* cause less because of their legitimate claims to equal rights than on account of the role such humanitarianism might play in making French society whole again.

Lioret encourages us to see Simon and Marion's divorce as merely one small symptom of a broader societal breakdown by showing us a society characterised by surveillance, by whispered conversations in under-lit locations, by neighbour shopping neighbour to the police, by fear, suspicion, and mistrust. This atmosphere combines with a series of allusions to the persecution of Jews in France in the Vichy/Occupation era to imply that the French authorities' treatment of the *sans papiers* contradicts certain fundamental republican values and is hence eroding the social bond in its entirety. Early in the film, Simon bumps into Marion in a Calais supermarket. As they leave together, they come across a security guard trying to expel a small group of *sans papiers*. Marion intervenes, demanding to know what the *sans papiers* have done wrong. The supermarket manager's response, that the security guard 'has his orders', represents a clear allusion to the infamous 'Nuremberg defence': 'I was only obeying orders.' Sequences showing the *sans papiers* having numbers stamped on their hands as they are processed by the police or congregating in a railway marshalling yard to receive food and clothing spark visual memories of Jews being herded onto cattle trucks or being tattooed with serial numbers on their arrival at concentration camps. When Simon's neighbour informs on him to the police, this both recalls Henri Clouzot's classic film *Le Corbeau* (1943) and taps into broader folk memories of the Occupation years as a time of intra-communal rivalries sparked by vindictive neighbours informing the police of their fellow citizens' alleged role in sheltering Jews. These allusions to the Vichy/Occupation era also have a paratextual element, as in the course of publicising his film Lioret drew a parallel between the situation of migrants and volunteers in and around Calais today and that of Jews and the Righteous who helped them during the Occupation, provoking a public spat with the then Minister for Immigration, Éric Besson.

There is no doubt that these allusions to Vichy and the Occupation have a powerful rhetorical force, emphasising that Lioret considers the current treatment of the *sans papiers* as being wholly incompatible with French republican values and hence beyond the pale. They recall the position taken by a collective of filmmakers in 1997 when they pointed to the similarity between the Debré Law of that year, which compelled French citizens to inform the police of the arrival

224 Republican Citizens, Precarious Subjects

and departure of any non-EU citizen in their homes, and the legal obligation in the Vichy/Occupation era to inform the authorities of the presence of any Jews in the locality. This evocation of the memory of Vichy and the Occupation was to be echoed in the establishment of the *Réseau d'éducation sans frontières* (RESF – Network for Education without Frontiers) in June 2004, an organisation founded in response to Sarkozy's expulsion quotas that seeks to protect the children of *sans papiers* from being rounded up and expelled. In its founding text the RESF appealed to the image of Jewish children being dragged out of class by the authorities during the Occupation years, citing Paul Éluard's 1942 underground resistance poem, 'La Liberté', as emblematic of the French values current expulsions were flouting.[2]

This combination of appeals to both memories of Vichy and innocent child victims is evident in two other films about the *sans papiers*, Aki Kaurismäki's *Le Havre* (2011) and Romain Goupil's *Les Mains en l'air* (2010). In *Les Mains en l'air*, Vichy is evoked when the actions of the French mother, Cendrine (Valeria Bruni Tedeschi), in sheltering the *sans papiers* child, Milana (Linda Doudaeva), are compared to those of the Righteous who sheltered Jewish children under the Occupation. In *Le Havre*, Jean-Pierre Léaud plays a neighbour who informs the police that the central French character Marcel Marx (André Wilms) is sheltering the photogenic African child, Idrissa (Blondin Miguel). Once again, this evokes collective memories that associate vindictive police informers with the Occupation years. Over the course of the film, the young *sans papiers* Idrissa inspires and reinvigorates the working-class community inhabited by Marcel and his wife Arletty (Kati Outinen). As those two names (Marcel and Arletty), not to mention the appearance of Jean-Pierre Léaud, suggest, *Le Havre* is extraordinarily nostalgic for a certain idea of French working class and filmic culture, so that, once again, the role of the *sans papiers* Idrissa is to restore France to itself, or, at least, to restore the rather idealised conception of what France should be that the Finnish director Kaurismäki appears to possess. In both Goupil's and Kaurismäki's films, then, the ultimate purpose of the *sans papiers* seems to be to redeem the French nation through their suffering, a function they can more easily perform on account of, first, their depiction as helpless children and, second, multiple allusions to the Vichy era.

In their multiple allusions to the Vichy era, all of these films thus ally their humanitarianism to a particular take on questions of collective historical memory. They all imply that it is France's failure to come to terms with its role in the Holocaust that has enabled the authorities to persecute undocumented migrants today in just the way they persecuted Jews in the war years. As we have pointed out, these allusions to Vichy and the Occupation *do* have a strong rhetorical and moral force. Indeed, there is no doubt that Lioret's *Welcome* in particular contributed to the campaigns to repeal the so-called 'délit de solidarité', which made aiding undocumented migrants a criminal offence. With Hollande's election as president in 2012, this was partially repealed so that humanitarian aid to those already on French territory is no longer a cause for criminal prosecution. However, helping undocumented migrants to enter France remains illegal and members of refugee support groups have continued to find themselves subject to prosecution as a result (Mouzon 2018).

If *Welcome* thus contributed to a partial success in terms of concrete political change, any assessment of the contribution of the film's various allusions to the Vichy era to its political message must be similarly mitigated. For these allusions surely risk reinforcing some of the limitations inherent to what we have termed apolitical humanitarianism. They encourage us to see *sans papiers* as contemporary incarnations of a kind of universal victimhood, of which Jewish victims of the Holocaust are the archetype. Yet the juridical, political, and economic conditions that govern the *sans papiers'* presence in France are quite different to those under which European Jews suffered in the early 1940s. Finding durable solutions to the migrant crisis will require attending to precisely these political, economic, and juridical specificities. Allusions to the Vichy era, however well-intentioned, risk obscuring such specificities, as can be illustrated by returning to the plot of *Welcome*.

After his neighbour has informed on him, Simon is arrested and interrogated by a local police lieutenant. He pressures Simon to hand over the names of other volunteers who have been helping the *sans papiers*, so that he can charge them with the offence of 'assisting a person in an irregular situation'. The police lieutenant explains that he is under pressure from his superiors to increase the number of such charges: 'They've been asking me for months where the volunteers are, Monsieur Clamart. They keep on at me about it … and thanks to you, I'm finally going to be able to catch them.' As we have mentioned, the film implies this kind of effort forms one part of a more

226 Republican Citizens, Precarious Subjects

generalised climate of surveillance that it figures as corresponding to a reversion to the totalitarian policing tactics of the Vichy era. Yet, in fact, the kind of pressure to deliver to which the policeman is subject reflects something very specific to contemporary forms of neo-liberal governance, namely the imposition of a 'targets culture' on the French public services in accordance with the doctrine of 'new public management'. First introduced in the Public Finances Law of 2001, this kind of target culture was heavily promoted by Nicolas Sarkozy, as a means of driving up efficiency in public services. The introduction of targets and individualised performance audits is intended to act as a proxy for market discipline and an alternative to promotion based on professional status and time served (Laval, et al. 2012:30–32). One of its manifestations was the annual quotas for *sans papiers* expulsions (Cette France-là 2012a:61). Another is the pressure to which the police lieutenant is evidently subject in *Welcome* to deliver his target of arrests of volunteers from the *sans papier* movement.

If the targets chased by the police lieutenant exemplify the workings of neo-liberal governance in the developed world, Bilal's footballing ambitions could be interpreted as one symptom of that form of governance as it has been imposed on the developing world. As we have argued, within the film's narrative Bilal's sporting ambitions play an important role in rendering him sympathetic to Simon, allowing Bilal to adopt the role of the son Simon never had. However, there is an observable sociological phenomenon behind this plot detail in the form of the significant numbers of young men from the developing world who do migrate to countries like Britain or France in the hope of playing professional football. Sometimes these young men are trafficked, often they are exploited, abandoned by clubs or agents if they fail to perform, their visas expired and their situation hence highly precarious. As James Esson (2015) has argued, we should not, however, see these exploited young men as wholly passive victims. Their ambitions reflect their active agency faced with the situation in which they typically find themselves in their native countries. As Esson argues, under the aegis of successive structural adjustment programmes developing countries have dismantled significant elements of their public sectors, cut back on investments in education, and ceased subsidising indigenous industries, hence vastly reducing educational and employment opportunities, while promoting the notion that individuals, rather than the State, are responsible for their own life chances. In this context it is understandable that significant numbers of young men in the developing world should turn to the only resource they have, their embodied skills on the sports field, and seek to exploit that particular form of human capital by migrating to the West. In this way, Esson maintains, young male migrants can become versions of Foucault's 'entrepreneurs of the self', personifications of the 'sense of individuation, competition and treatment of the body as capital' inherent to that form of subjectivity (Esson 2015:53).[3] Suitably adapted to the specific situation of post-Saddam Kurdistan, Esson's interpretative schema can illuminate Bilal's sporting ambitions in *Welcome*.

It would thus be possible to link Bilal's ambition to become a professional footballer to the police lieutenant's subjection to target culture, insofar as both are symptoms of neo-liberal forms of governance, the first as it relates to the economics of debt and development in the developing world, the second as it relates to the management techniques now routinely applied to public sector institutions in the developed economies. Yet these kinds of link, which offer genuine insights into the political economy of both undocumented migration and its management in the West, are obscured by *Welcome*'s allusions to the Vichy era, its romantic plotline, and its associated ethics of humanitarianism. It is instructive in this context to turn to Gauz's 2014 novel *Debout-Payé*, a novel that incorporates a pointed satire of the limitations of humanitarianism while demonstrating that it is possible to highlight the more political and economic determinants of undocumented migration with perspicacity and concision in an engaging fictional text.

Debout-Payé

Debout-Payé focuses on the experiences of two young *sans papiers* from the Ivory Coast, Kassoum and Ossiri, who find work as security guards, sometimes in high-end Parisian stores, sometimes in disused factories. The novel is semi-autobiographical, drawing on the experiences of its author, Gauz, whose real name is Armand Gabaka-Brédé and who left his native Abidjan with a Masters in Biochemistry to work for a number of years in France in the informal economy. One of Gauz's two central protagonists, Ossiri, has a similar social and educational profile, having taught natural sciences in a private *lycée* in Abidjan before migrating to France, not to escape poverty or political repression

228 Republican Citizens, Precarious Subjects

but rather in search of adventure. As the narrator explains: 'Ossiri had made the decision to come to France all by himself. He was not in any way living in poverty in Abidjan' (Gauz 2014:129). The suggestion here that Gauz is consciously seeking to break with the depiction of the *sans papiers* as suffering victims is confirmed by his description of the support offered to Ossiri and his kind by French members of the *sans papiers* movement.

Ossiri and Kassoum live in a student hostel, the *Maison des étudiants de la Côte d'Ivoire* or 'MECI', in Paris. Towards the end of the novel, the French authorities decide to clear the hostel of its population of predominantly undocumented young migrants and close it down. A campaign is immediately launched by various French 'humanitarian organisations' to prevent the expulsions, prompting the narrator to reflect wryly:

> [A]ll these humanitarian organisations, the closer they got to you, the more you knew you were in the shit up to your neck. Their members often had the Christ-like feeling of being bearers of a hope rooted in their social commitment alone. But for the *sans papiers* and other social cases, they represented walking talking symbols of their despair and a realistic photograph of their desperate situation. (Gauz 2014:193)

The inhabitants of the MECI feel obliged to adopt the roles expected of them by these well-intentioned activists: 'Everyone had become an innocent expiatory victim of the *"xenophobic policies"* of a *"government of fascists"'* (194). The threatened expulsion of the MECI's inhabitants sparks memories in the narrator of the expulsions from the Saint Bernard Church in 1996 and an ironic reflection on the eagerness of the mass media to find a spokesperson from among the *sans papiers* who corresponds to their stereotype of an African migrant:

> Throughout the siege [of the Saint Bernard Church], the left and right-wing press alike found their darling in a man from Senegal who answered to the name of Mamadou. In reality his name was Diop but everyone knows that black men are called Mamadou; it's simpler, easier to pronounce. [...] From then on, whenever an expulsion was covered by the media, everyone dreamed of being The Mamadou: *the MSB syndrome, the Mamadou from Saint-Bernard syndrome.* (Gauz 2014:195–96)

Sans Papiers   229

Unfortunately for the inhabitants of the MECI, the media show little interest in their struggle:

> There must have been more spectacular things to report in the national and international news at the time. Also, not long before, the expulsion of some Africans from a squat in Arceuil had rather exhausted the topic. In that case, famous actors and actresses had even shown up to defend The Cause, stealing the limelight from all sorts of black spokespeople in the process. So the riot police were able to evacuate the MECI without any great difficulty or fuss. (Gauz 2014:196–97)

In *Debout-Payé*, Gauz thus offers an acerbic, incisive critique of the kind of limitations of apolitical humanitarianism we have already enumerated – its taste for photogenic images of suffering victimhood; its eagerness to reduce the *sans papiers* to the role of 'innocent expiatory victims' whose cause can redeem the sins of French society, as exemplified by the redemptive role played by Bilal in *Welcome*, Idrissa in *Le Havre*, or the eponymous hero of *Samba*. In seeking to escape this stereotype of the expiatory victim, Gauz offers a subtle and detailed depiction of the *sans papiers'* place within the contemporary political economy of France, a depiction that involves him not merely situating the *sans papiers* within the contemporary labour market, but also locating that situation within a longer history of exchanges of commodities, labour, and images between France and its colonial and post-colonial periphery. The extraordinary subtlety and economy with which Gauz is able to achieve this is exemplified by an apparently simple scene in which Ossiri, bored by his duties as a security guard protecting a huge abandoned Parisian flour mill, gazes across the street at an advertising hoarding for Western Union. The hoarding shows an African mother and child, dressed in apparently traditional African, brightly coloured, batik-printed dress. This image is framed as though it were contained in the wallet of an African migrant worker, whose 'large black thumb' appears at the bottom of the photograph. The image is accompanied by the strapline, 'Send some money back to the home country'.

This advertising image, or rather the scene in which Ossiri gazes at it, might be interpreted as a kind of 'dialectical image', in Walter Benjamin's sense of that term, a moment when 'what has been comes together in a flash with the now to form a constellation' (1999:463). This is a constellation composed of those historical, political, and

230   *Republican Citizens, Precarious Subjects*

economic determinants that account for the *sans papiers'* presence and role in contemporary France. Ossiri works in the massive abandoned flour mill, the *Grands Moulins de Paris*, during what the novel describes as 'the Golden Age, 1990–2000'. He is given the job by an older Ivoirian immigrant, an old friend of his mother's, Ferdinand, who arrived in France in 1973 and himself worked at the *Grands Moulins*, when it still processed hundreds of thousands of tons of flour a week. When Ossiri works there at the end of the twentieth century, however, it has been reduced to the status of 'a huge ghostly pile' (111) and, as he conducts his rounds, 'he had the impression of being in one of those Hollywood films in which a solitary hero walks across a post-apocalyptic land in search of some redemptive truth hidden far away somewhere beyond the chaos' (119).

The apocalypse in question is, of course, the deindustrialisation of France that followed the sudden end of the *trente glorieuses*, itself exacerbated by the Oil Crisis of 1973–74 just a few months after Ferdinand first arrived in France. As the narrator explains, it was the sudden downturn of the early 1970s that prompted the French government to 'suspend' all further mass labour migration into France in 1974 and to initiate a much more rigorous system of registration and papers for legal immigrants, hence creating the new category of the *sans papiers* for the first time (74). As Ossiri completes his rounds in the *Grands Moulins*, he is thus haunted by the historical memory of a lost age of industrial grandeur and of the very different legal and economic conditions it guaranteed to an earlier generation of African immigrants. Now, however, the flour mill is abandoned, the formerly industrialised Parisian *quartier* in which it is situated is becoming gentrified, transformed into smart flats and office blocks (122), while immigrants of Osiri's generation live the precarious existence of the *sans papiers*.

Ferdinand, who arrived in France just before the 'suspension' of immigration, has been able to remain, setting up a successful security business. Thus, he works in the new world of a subcontracted service economy, relying on employing *sans papiers*, on exploiting this pool of precarious, flexible, and hence cheap labour to keep his costs down. As Ossiri explains to Kassoum, major French employers know that Ferdinand employs *sans papiers* but by subcontracting their security services to him they can avoid both the costs of employing security guards legally in-house and any direct responsibility for breaking the law (183–84). If these forms of subcontracting reflect the functioning of the modern economy, they nonetheless rehearse much older hierarchies of ethnicity and class that can be traced back to the colonial era. The predominance of African men in low-paid security jobs reflects a 'jumble of clichés of the noble savage', according to which 'Blacks are tough, Blacks are big, Blacks are strong, Blacks are compliant, Blacks are scary' (14). These kinds of assumption also have an impact on hierarchies within the security industry, as jobs at sensitive sites such as nuclear plants or banks are reserved for whites, while shops, restaurants, abandoned factories, and nightclubs are typically guarded by blacks. This remains the case until the attacks of 9/11, in response to which stricter controls are placed on the recruitment of security guards, locking many *sans papiers* out of the security industry altogether, driving businesses like Ferdinand's into bankruptcy and hence signalling the end of 'the Golden Age' (184–85).

Older racial stereotypes and assumptions rooted in the colonial era are thus re-inflected through the contemporary economic and political conjuncture to produce the specific forms of labour exploitation to which the *sans papiers* are subjected. This process of historical layering and re-inflection is represented visually in the advertisement for Western Union, which Ossiri contemplates from his hut at the entrance to the now abandoned flour mill. Reflecting on its idealised image of a mother and child in traditional African dress, with its accompanying slogan 'Send some money back to the home country', Ossiri remarks: 'The advertising creatives really knew their dictionary of clichés. What's more, with the place phrase, "the home country", you could also say they'd mastered their pidgin French [*petit-nègre de poche*]' (110). However, if the poster offers a cliché of traditional African-ness, its appeal to tradition is bogus. For, as Ossiri knows, and as the reader is informed via a footnote, the batik dress worn by the mother and child is not traditionally African but was first 'imported into Africa by Ghanaian soldiers who were fighting for the Dutch in Java and Sumatra' (107n.1). It is for this reason that Ossiri's mother, an adherent of Amilcar Cabral's brand of anti-imperialism, always refused to wear such garments, just as when the *Grands Moulins de Paris* set up a plant in Abidjan she refused to buy their products, hence refusing to be implicated in the networks of unequal colonial and neo-colonial exchange.

Gazing at the Western Union advertisement, Ossiri is thus prompted into a lengthy reflection on the history of colonial and neo-colonial exchanges of people, commodities, images, and stereotypes between

232   Republican Citizens, Precarious Subjects

France and Africa, as well as the unrealised dreams for socialist transformation in post-independence Ivory Coast personified by his own mother (112–21). His mother's old friend, Ferdinand, belongs to that same generation and the account of his time living in the MECI in the early 1970s is replete with details of the anti-imperialist and socialist ideals of his fellow young Ivoirians. Yet, the reader learns, these dreams were soon extinguished by a shift to authoritarianism and corruption in post-independence African regimes, epitomised by Jean-Bedel Bokassa, notorious ruler of Central Africa, whose hypocritical tears of sadness at Georges Pompidou's Paris funeral in 1974 disgust the radical students of the MECI (65–66).

As Ossiri gazes at the Western Union advertisement, reflecting on its multiple connotations, he thus situates himself in a long history of uneven economic and cultural exchange between France and Africa. The bright-coloured, batik-patterned dress worn by the mother and child take him back to nineteenth-century colonialism, suggesting his own presence in France is merely a recent episode in a much longer history of exploiting the natural and human resources of his native West Africa. These garments also remind him of his mother, the unrealised dreams she personifies, and the corruption and authoritarianism of post-independence regimes that provide one driver of migration. The remittances immigrants such as Ossiri are able to send back to their countries of origin represent another such driver and this is precisely the service Western Union is advertising here. Furthermore, the advertisement embodies the ethnic stereotypes and assumptions that govern the terms of Ossiri's precarious job in the informal labour market. It is this job that has brought him to the sentry box at the entrance to the *Grands Moulins*, the perfect location from which to both gaze at the Western Union advertisement and ponder the shift from Fordism to post-Fordism, from the industrial jobs performed by an earlier generation of immigrants to the precarious service-sector position he now occupies. It is in this sense that the advertisement represents a 'constellation' in which, to quote Benjamin again, 'what has been comes together in a flash with the now'. Through his description of Ossiri gazing at the advertising hoarding, Gauz offers a nuanced and insightful account of the situation of the *sans papiers*, precisely by showing how the legacies of colonialism are mediated through and re-inflected by the dynamics of the contemporary French labour market. If the effects of Gauz's novel remain inevitably limited to the realm of cultural representation, from late 2006 onwards significant numbers of *sans papiers* themselves began to mobilise politically, highlighting their role as workers as a means of asserting their agency and political subjectivity.

'We Work Here! We Live Here! We're Staying Here!'

In their 2011 book, *On Bosse ici, on reste ici!*, Pierre Barron and his co-authors examine what they term an 'innovative' or previously 'unheard of' form of struggle adopted by the *sans papiers* from late 2006 on. In concrete terms, they focus on a series of strikes by *sans papiers* at a variety of their workplaces – well-known restaurant and hotel chains, building sites, maintenance crews on the Paris metro, and so on – demanding that they have their situations 'regularized', on the basis that, as their slogan had it: 'We work here! We live here! We're staying here!' As Barron and his co-authors argue, these strike movements 'allowed the strikers to speak in their own name rather than leaving external activists to speak for them' as had been the case in earlier occupations, such as that of the Saint Bernard Church. Further, these strike movements moved beyond the purely humanitarian emphasis placed in earlier campaigns by an organisation such as the RESF on protecting children and families: 'The fact that the strikers highlighted their status as employees led to an extension of their demands to include the unmarried, who had been excluded from the minor wave of regularisations in 2006 that had been centred on those families supported by the RESF' (Barron, et al. 2011:33).

The importance of the *sans papiers* having their status as salaried workers recognised was also emphasised by the *Cette-France-là* collective, a group of sociologists, activists, and politicians from across the political spectrum set up to monitor the results of the immigration policies enacted under Sarkozy's presidency. As the collective notes in the Introduction to their study of the effects of Sarkozy's expulsion quotas, the *sans papiers* 'are asserting themselves in social movements, that is to say they are redefining themselves to constitute themselves, in particular, as *workers* without papers' (Cette France-là 2012:8). This insistence on the role of *worker* is also evident in the intervention of one of the *sans papiers* interviewed in the 2010 short film, *On bosse ici! On vit ici! On reste ici!*, a documentary produced by the *Collectif des cinéastes pour les sans*

234   *Republican Citizens, Precarious Subjects*

papiers. As one of the strikers puts it: 'We are workers, we aren't just *sans papiers*. We've moved from being without papers [*sans papiers*] to being workers without papers [*travailleurs sans papiers*].'

Clearly, it would be naïve to imagine that the fact of asserting their status as workers resolved all of the problems faced by undocumented migrants at one stroke. Focusing on the position occupied by the *sans papiers* in the contemporary labour market reveals little, for example, about the role of Western foreign policy and military interventions in the developing world as motors of mass migration. Further, as we have noted, there is no absolute opposition between supporting the *sans papiers* in their struggles to be recognised as workers, on the one hand, and, on the other, adopting a more limited, strictly humanitarian approach to such issues. The RESF, whose focus on suffering children and families we questioned above, nonetheless gave their active support to the wave of strikes by *sans papiers*, married and unmarried, with or without children, from 2007 on. Similarly, filmmakers such as Romain Goupil and Philippe Lioret, the humanitarianism of whose films *Les Mains en l'air* and *Welcome* we criticised above, contributed to supporting and documenting those strikes through their involvement with the *Collectif des cinéastes pour les sans papiers*. At the same time, it is clear that for a number of commentators, as for many *sans papiers* themselves, having their status as workers recognised represented an important political step. Hence, in what follows, we will seek to clarify quite how and why this political step had become possible from 2007 on, before examining the benefits of situating the *sans papiers* within those broader shifts in political economy and the governance of the labour market that we have analysed throughout this study.

There is little doubt that the *sans papiers* movement of the late 1990s and events such as the violent evacuation of the Saint Bernard Church played a significant role in discrediting the mainstream right-wing parties and enabling Lionel Jospin to be elected Prime Minister at the head of a Socialist-led coalition in 1997. One element of the new government's less repressive approach to immigration policy was the inclusion in the 1998 immigration law of a series of clauses according to which undocumented migrants who could prove they were ill or had been victims of violence against women or of human trafficking were protected against expulsion from France. Both Didier Fassin (2011) and Miriam Ticktin (2011) have examined the perverse effects of these humanitarian clauses in their respective critiques of the limitations of

Sans Papiers   235

what the former terms 'humanitarian reason'. As Ticktin (2011:4–5) argues, the problem with these measures is that they give immigrants 'rights, not as equal citizens, but only insofar as they are – and remain – disabled' in some way. She continues: '[n]oticeably absent are the labouring bodies, the exploited bodies: these are not the exception, but the rule, and hence are disqualified as morally legitimate'. In short, in a striking confirmation of the limitations of a purely humanitarian approach, undocumented migrants were permitted to remain in France provided they could prove that they were indeed suffering victims.

In an unexpected and certainly unintended way, the election of a right-wing government in 2002, followed by Sarkozy's election as president in 2007, would provide the conditions under which Ticktin's 'labouring' and 'exploited bodies' would be given a moral legitimacy and hence an opportunity to subjectivise their situation not purely as suffering victims but also as active agents performing an important role within the French economy.

With the election of Jacques Chirac in 2002, Sarkozy was appointed Minister of Interior, a role he would perform from 2002 to 2004 and from 2005 to 2007 and that gave him primary responsibility for immigration policy. As president from 2007 to 2012, he would continue to set the agenda in this area. Initially, Sarkozy appeared to pursue the policies set by previous right-wing governments of the 1980s and 1990s, policies with the stated goal of achieving 'zero immigration'. This much was evident in his introduction of annual expulsion quotas and the further limitations on family reunification included in his 2003 immigration law. From 2006 on, however, he began to give a series of speeches in which he declared the goal of zero immigration to be unrealistic, unachievable, and undesirable since it ignored the real economic benefits for France of continuing labour migration. As Minister of Interior in 2006 and then in 2007 as president he piloted two new immigration laws intended to achieve his new goal of 'selective' labour immigration. For the first time since 1974, the French State would actively encourage new labour migration into France: on a region-by-region basis, unions, employers, and the State would identify job functions with unfilled vacancies and would then encourage immigrants from both outside the EU and from the new EU accession states, who had yet to achieve free access to the French labour market, to fill those jobs. Immigrants from the EU accession states would be given preference, as evidenced in the much

236 *Republican Citizens, Precarious Subjects*

greater number of jobs open to them and the lower level of qualifications required to fill those jobs. A much smaller number of more highly qualified jobs would be offered to immigrants from outside the EU (Carvalho and Geddes 2012).

Sarkozy's adoption of this new, 'selective' immigration policy was clearly inspired by theories of human capital, that is to say by the notion that immigrants are to be valued and encouraged insofar as they can be shown to contribute to any nation state's stock of human capital, itself seen as a fundamental determinant of economic growth.[4] This was a version of human capital theory that was inflected through some rather questionable assumptions about the relative assimilability of different ethno-national groups, assumptions rooted in French colonial history. Thus, Eastern European immigrants were to be favoured over Africans, with the higher qualifications demanded of the latter group intended to act as guarantees of their proximity to an implicitly European norm of culture and education.

The effects of these new policies, meanwhile, were highly ambiguous. On the negative side, they set up an opposition between 'good' economically productive immigrants and 'bad' economically unproductive ones; the latter were to be expelled in accordance with the new annual quotas, while supposedly unproductive family members and dependants would find it harder to gain legal entry as the regulations governing family reunification were made ever stricter. On the positive side, inherent to the logic of 'selective' immigration was the notion that undocumented immigrants who were already employed in France could now make a strong case for being allowed to remain on the basis of their positive contribution to the French economy. Indeed, this was the logic behind an amendment to the 2007 immigration law moved by Frédéric Lefebvre, a member of Sarkozy's ruling Union for a Popular Movement (UMP) party. The amendment allowed *sans papiers* to make a case for their status to be 'regularized' if they could show they had a work contract in an area of the jobs market in which French employers were struggling to recruit (Barron, et al. 2011:40–41).

Thus, one of the unintended outcomes of Sarkozy's immigration policies was to realise a fundamental shift in relation to the humanitarian exceptions written into immigration legislation under the previous socialist coalition government. Where those humanitarian exceptions had compelled *sans papiers* to adopt the subjective position of victims – whether of illness, domestic abuse, or human trafficking

– Sarkozy's selective immigration policies enabled them to adopt the position of workers, of active agents. The political implications of that shift are clearly reflected in the short documentary *On bosse ici! On vit ici! On reste ici!*, which features a series of interviews with striking *sans papiers* at or in front of their workplaces – the Paris metro, the major buildings they have helped construct, refuse centres, even the French National Assembly. Typically, in addition to describing the role they play in the French economy, these striking *sans papiers* brandish wage slips that detail their contributions to taxes and social insurance funds. The fact that such contributions are not rewarded with recognition of these workers' civic and social rights is, of course, in contradiction with that long-established French republican tradition of corporatism, according to which social rights and salaried labour are seen as consubstantial. As one of the striking *sans papiers* puts it:

> We work. We're building France just like all French people are. We've found fraternity with French people. On the other hand, we haven't found equality in the State and we haven't found liberty.

By emphasising his status as a worker, this man hence stakes a claim to inclusion within the French Republic on equal terms with other citizens. As we have argued throughout this study, the French post-war model was based on a particular articulation between salaried labour, social rights, and inclusion within the Republic. Those *sans papiers* protests that involve undocumented migrants emphasising their roles as workers, rather than merely victims, seek to exploit that historical articulation between employment, rights, and social inclusion. Yet they simultaneously stretch its traditionally national parameters to suggest that inclusion should not be predetermined by questions of national or ethnic origin.

It would be wrong to idealise or exaggerate the political implications of this phenomenon. For, there is arguably a fundamental contradiction inherent to appealing to the logic of Sarkozy's selective immigration policies as the key to securing immigrants' rights. As the *Cette France-là* collective points out (2012a:67), those selective immigration policies rested on the same philosophy as do 'back-to-work programmes and programmes aiming to make civil servants more accountable' by subjecting them to target culture. In all three cases, it is a matter of making these recipients of the State's alleged largesse show they are

238   *Republican Citizens, Precarious Subjects*

worthy of such generosity by proving their economic worth. Claiming rights on the basis of economic worth may thus risk conceding too much to contemporary modes of economic governance that reduce human beings to nothing more than units of monetary value or stocks of exploitable human capital.

As Barron and his co-authors (2011:297) point out, in the wake of the strikes of 2008, the number of 'regularisations' accorded to undocumented immigrants in France did increase significantly. Yet, as they also acknowledge and as we have argued, these strikes certainly did not definitively resolve all the issues faced by the *sans papiers*. Nonetheless, it is possible to concur with Barron at al. that those strikes did represent 'a political victory' of sorts and this for a number of reasons. First, the *sans papiers'* self-representation as workers and not simply victims was a significant step: 'for the path of collective action henceforth seems more profitable than that of solitary suffering. Gaining one's papers, rather than receiving them as a favour is also to train oneself for future struggles' (Barron, et al. 2011:297). Further, by highlighting their place in the contemporary French labour market, the striking *sans papiers* moved their struggle beyond the limited terrain of humanitarianism to raise a series of important questions about contemporary global and national economic governance: the political implications of French employers' need for a pool of flexible, precarious labour; the relationship between the structural adjustment programmes applied in the developing world, neo-liberal governance in the developed world, and the phenomenon of labour migration; the possible links to be drawn between the increasing incidence of burn-out and workplace suffering among French citizens and the precarious conditions in which the *sans papiers* live and work.

Indeed, as we have argued throughout this chapter, the emergence of the *sans papiers* as a recognisable socio-political category in France is inseparable from those shifts in political economy that explain the increasingly high profile acquired by the social categories that have formed the subjects of preceding chapters, from middle-aged male workers, through working women of different social classes, to doomed youth. The *sans papiers* are among those who find themselves occupying the most precarious and flexible positions within the contemporary French labour market. Their very presence in France poses questions of republican citizenship, of who belongs in France and who should have access to social and political rights, in a peculiarly acute form. It is not necessary to idealise their struggles in order to acknowledge the role these have played in stretching and reformulating established notions of the relationship between salaried labour, republican citizenship, and social rights. In this sense, the *sans papiers* can be seen as paradigmatic of those more general phenomena examined throughout this study whereby post-Fordist forms of salaried labour have posed fundamental challenges to older notions of French republican citizenship. However, in the case of the *sans papiers*, these are challenges that work in a progressive direction, expanding established notions of citizenship, inclusion, and social solidarity.

Notes

1 Béart's interview can be seen in full at: http://www.ina.fr/video/CAB96044493/plateau-emmanuelle-beart-video.html (accessed 12 September 2018).

2 In their *La Chasse aux enfants* (2008), published under the aegis of the RESF, Miguel Benasayag and Angélique del Rey do warn against too hasty analogies between the Vichy years and the situation of the *sans papiers* today, before concluding that such 'appeals to history' are 'legitimate' if not strictly necessary in securing commitment to the *sans papiers*' cause (Benasayag, et al. 2008:79–84). Yet elsewhere in the book they evoke images of children being dragged out of class and of French citizens subject to an ambiance of 'organised informing' in a way that cannot help but tap into collective memories of Vichy and the Occupation (19–20).

3 This role of the aspirant footballer as 'entrepreneur of the self' has been depicted fictionally in Fatou Diome's novel, *Le Ventre de l'Atlantique* (2003). Moussa, a young man from a Senegalese fishing village whose dream of a job in an 'air-conditioned office as a civil servant' has been frustrated, migrates to France having been recruited by a French football scout. Having failed to impress, Moussa is dropped by his club and forced to engage in hard physical labour in the informal economy to reimburse the price of his ticket and visa. He is picked up by the police, expelled as an undocumented migrant, and returns in shame to his native village (Diome 2003:95–117).

4 For a more detailed analysis of the economic benefits of immigration from the point of view of the founder of human capital theory, see Becker (2011).

Conclusion

In November 2018 a new nationwide protest movement emerged in France, a movement that has continued to stage periodic and sometimes violent protests to this day (early summer 2019). The proximate cause of the *gilets jaunes* movement was Macron's new environmental fuel tax. However, this measure only proved so inflammatory on account of the broader context of stagnating real wages, labour market flexibility, and resulting socio-economic precarity. Such are the conclusions of the authors of the *Observatoire des inégalités*'s 2019 report into socio-economic inequalities in France. As Anne Brunner and Louis Maurin point out, one in seven French workers, or some 8.1 million individuals, now find themselves in what they term 'une situation de mal-emploi', where 'mal-emploi' or 'poor employment' is defined as being either unemployed or employed on precarious terms. It is 'this France of social insecurity', they suggest, that 'has driven the demonstrations of the *gilets jaunes*' (Brunner and Maurin 2019:12–13).

Indeed, one of the most striking characteristics of the numerous analyses of the *gilets jaunes* movement is the frequency with which they rehearse themes and ideas that have been at the centre of this study. For example, in an opinion piece in the daily newspaper *Libération*, the economist Alain Lipietz coins the term 'social uberisation' to explain the genesis of the *gilets jaunes* protests. 'Uberised' forms of employment erode the kinds of social solidarity secured by Fordism's combination of stable employment and associated welfare rights, leaving workers as atomised individuals, solely responsible for their fate. 'Social uberisation', according to Lipietz, represents the extension of these atomising tendencies across the entirety of the social field, as cutbacks in welfare payments and social programmes leave the individual 'responsible for

242   *Republican Citizens, Precarious Subjects*

an increasing share of the reproduction of the labour force', while 'the share socialised by two centuries of struggles (the Welfare State, public services) diminishes'. Since welfare and care-giving responsibilities have traditionally fallen disproportionately on women, the negative effects of these phenomena have affected them in particular. Hence, Lipietz concludes, if the *gilets jaunes* movement represents 'the first revolt against the uberisation of society', female workers – 'care workers, home helps, female tertiary sector employees' – have played a conspicuous role in the protests, since they find themselves 'in the front line of social uberisation' (Lipietz 2018).

A second recurrent theme in much commentary on the *gilets jaunes* movement relates to the central role accorded to the so-called 'intermediary bodies' under the terms of the French republican-corporatist model. As we have noted, the essential role of the 'intermediary bodies' in mediating between citizen and State, while securing social solidarity, had first been theorised by Émile Durkheim in the late nineteenth century, before being given institutional form at the end of the Second World War. The role of these 'intermediary bodies' was secured, first, by the linking of welfare rights to membership of a particular occupational group or corporation and, second, by the role accorded to the so-called 'social partners' – trades unions, employers, and the State – in the joint governance of industry, employment, and social insurance funds.

As we have shown over preceding chapters, the bases of this peculiarly corporatist social model have been significantly eroded over recent decades by a combination of shifting patterns of salaried employment and reforms to the French labour code. The profusion of atypical forms of employment, epitomised by 'uberised' work in the platform economy, has eroded the link between work, membership of a professional corporation, and rights to social protection. Labour market reforms brought in under the successive presidencies of Sarkozy, Hollande, and Macron have actively sought to bypass the 'social partners' in the name of fostering 'social dialogue' at the level of the individual workplace. The measures of 'flexicurity' introduced under those three presidencies, meanwhile, have eroded the linkage between employment and rights to social protection, hence bypassing the role of the 'intermediary bodies' in this domain also.

Macron's recourse to 'ordonnances', or rule by decree, to introduce his labour market reforms represents a more specific instance of

Conclusion 243

his bypassing the all-important 'intermediary bodies' and hence of undermining one of the fundamental tenets of the French post-war compromise. 'Can we all at least agree on the fact', asks the economist Philippe Frémeaux, that 'the bypassing of the intermediary bodies practised by Emmanuel Macron, in a style of government that conjoins plebiscitary populism with technocratic hauteur, has left him today directly exposed to popular anger?' (Frémeaux 2018). The political commentator Alain Duhamel echoes this, arguing that the *gilets jaunes* protests have been sparked by Macron spending 'eighteen months forcing through reforms while ignoring the intermediary bodies'. He concludes that Macron will have to negotiate and this will necessitate 'a return to origins with the intermediary bodies' (Duhamel 2018). It is not simply Macron, of course, who has bypassed the 'intermediary bodies'; this is also true of the *gilets jaunes* protestors themselves. For this is a mass protest movement that has conspicuously eschewed any mediation through the traditional, institutional forms of social or political protest – the trades unions or established left-wing parties – opting instead for more diffuse, non-hierarchical modes of organisation and expression that rely heavily on social media.

A third theme that recurs in much commentary on the *gilets jaunes* relates to the geographical origins of the movement, its roots in provincial, rural, and suburban or 'peri-urban' France. These are the small towns and communities to which large numbers of French lower-middle- and working-class people have migrated, as rents and property prices in the urban centres have risen beyond their reach. In this sense, the *gilets jaunes* movement reflects the uneven economic geography, the increasing disparity between metropolitan centres and periphery that is so frequently depicted in the various fictional and documentary texts we have studied in preceding chapters. The effects of this uneven geography have also been evident in the form taken by the *gilets jaunes* protests. It is notable that the *gilets jaunes* have repeatedly opted to demonstrate in Paris's wealthy western *quartiers*, along the Champs Elysées, for example, rather than in the more traditional locations of street protest, whether in the city's eastern, historically working-class districts or in the Quartier Latin, the typical site of student radicalism. If this seems to represent a conscious targeting of ostentatious symbols of metropolitan wealth, the typical location of *gilets jaunes* protest in the provinces themselves is equally revealing. The mounting of barricades at major road junctions and roundabouts contrasts with an established

244 *Republican Citizens, Precarious Subjects*

tradition in which the factory serves as the primary site of worker protest, as epitomised by the strikes of May 1968 or of May–June 1936, as well as the more recent occupations of factories threatened with closure. In the context of the more mobile circuits of post-Fordist capital accumulation, of just-in-time production, and tertiary-sector employment, road junctions and roundabouts have apparently emerged as an alternative strategic location for labour struggle. Further, as the sociologist Camille Peugny has argued, one of the effects of the tertiarisation of the French workforce in recent decades has been the increasingly isolated nature of many people's working lives, as workers no longer congregate in the old 'collectifs de travail' in a factory but have a more lonely existence as delivery drivers, peripatetic care workers, and the like. The *gilets jaunes*'s occupation of road junctions and roundabouts hence may also reflect a desire to reconfigure these places of fleeting, anonymous passage into sites of social interaction, political debate, and potential community (Peugny 2019).

In this sense, the *gilets jaunes* manifest certain similarities with the protest movement we first mentioned at the very beginning of this book, those *Nuit debout* protestors who, in 2016, occupied town and city squares throughout France, transforming these spaces of commerce, tourism, and official commemoration into locations for some new political community. There are significant differences between the ideological affiliations and sociological profile of the *gilets jaunes* and the *Nuit debout* protestors, the latter being more urban, often more highly educated and more clearly affiliated to non-mainstream left-wing movements and parties. Nonetheless, both groups of protestors are clearly responding to equivalent phenomena of labour market deregulation and consequent socio-economic precarity. Both groups have also sought modes of organisation and expression outside of the institutionalised forms and locations – the trades union, the established left-wing party, the factory floor – characteristic of Fordism.

The *gilets jaunes*, then, like the *Nuit debout* protestors before them, might reasonably be characterised as one further group of precarious subjects rebelling against the erosion of the rights that their status as French republican citizens had previously promised to guarantee them. They demand to be included alongside those other social categories and character types whose difficulties in adapting to the demands of a post-Fordist workplace we have examined in the main body of this study – middle-aged male workers struggling to modulate their professional and personal identities, *femmes fortes*, doomed youth, *sans papiers*. Indeed, the *gilets jaunes* movement seems to represent, in peculiarly condensed form, nearly all of the phenomena we have identified in earlier chapters as characteristic of the long-drawn-out crisis of the French republican-corporatist post-war model – the proliferation of precarious forms of employment, the increasing polarisation between prosperous metropolitan centres and a marginalised periphery, the tertiarisation and feminisation of the labour market, the declining importance of the 'intermediary bodies', the growing rift between the promises inherent to French republican citizenship and the lived realities of precarious subjecthood. As we have shown, it is these very phenomena that are at the heart of the educational and career trajectories followed, as well as the uneven geographies inhabited by the range of recurrent character types depicted in our corpus of fictional and documentary texts.

By focusing on documentary and fictional depictions of a representative sample of such character types, the trajectories they follow, and the spaces they inhabit, we have sought to cast some light on the different ways in which these phenomena have been experienced and narrativised. As we have argued, the profusion of often flexible and immaterial forms of labour in France today has not merely challenged the material well-being of many French citizens, it has also forced them to modulate their professional and social identities in a number of ways, imposing more precarious forms of subjectivity that challenge established notions of republican citizenship. Reactions to those different challenges range from nostalgia for the most conservative aspects of French republican citizenship to laments at the erosion of its more progressive characteristics. Hence the different ways in which particular authors or filmmakers select and combine the character types, spaces, and trajectories that recur throughout our corpus are by no means politically neutral in their implications. Rather those elements are combined and inflected in various ways to produce distinct meanings that range from the nostalgic or conservative to the more critical and incisive. The work of Michel Houellebecq can be situated at the conservative pole of that spectrum. His novels repeatedly focus on the dilemmas of middle-aged men forced to modulate their personal and professional identities in accordance with more liberalised socio-sexual mores and economic practices. These dilemmas are depicted in a manner that betrays a questionable nostalgia for the supposed certainties of *terroir*,

246   Republican Citizens, Precarious Subjects

nation, family, masculinity, and industrial labour. In Beinstingel's novel, *Retour aux mots sauvages*, Cantet's film *L'Emploi du temps*, and Kechiche's *La Graine et le mulet*, these interrelationships between post-Fordist labour, masculinity, and the family are explored in a subtler and more reflective fashion. These narratives offer valuable insights into the links between family breakdown, social class, ethnicity, and global capitalism without engaging in uncritical nostalgia for the certainties of Fordism.

It would, however, be too convenient to imagine that Houellebecq's appeals to conservative notions of nation, family, and gender are unique to him and hence aberrations in a field of otherwise generally progressive French reactions to the interrelated crises of both Fordism and the French republican-corporatist model. In articulating their criticisms of the current economic conjuncture, apparently more progressive authors and filmmakers often appeal to less extreme but nonetheless questionable notions of nation, gender, and *terroir*. This much is evident in the remarkable frequency with which the prime movers behind labour market de-regulation or exploitative management practices are characterised as being foreign, typically of 'Anglo–Saxon' origin. These may be individuals who are literally British or American, like Christine in Corneau's *Crime d'amour*, or French citizens who have in some way been contaminated by 'Anglo–Saxon' business mores, like Paul Cathéter in Kuperman's *Nous étions des êtres vivants*. Alternatively, they may be institutions, like the two fictional US consultancies for which Philippe in *Violence des échanges en milieu tempéré* and Isabelle in *Crime d'amour* respectively work.

The antagonism between a putatively good French mode of life and the 'Anglo–Saxon' forces that threaten its continued existence is typically also spatialised in particular ways. This is evident in the recurrent depiction of La Défense, in *Violence des échanges en milieu tempéré*, *Crime d'amour*, *Le Système Victoria*, and Viallet's documentary *La Dépossession*, as the locus in which these destructive 'Anglo–Saxon' values are concentrated and from which they threaten to seep out into broader French society. As we have argued, there is a strong sense in which La Défense is depicted in these films and novels as being in France but not of France, a kind of portal through which a set of fundamentally destructive, foreign values has entered the French nation, threatening to overwhelm its defining characteristics and customs.

Conclusion   247

Through its position on the margins of the French capital city, as in the faceless anonymity of its modernist towers, La Défense shares a surprising spatial and visual affinity with its apparent antipodes, the economically deprived, semi-dilapidated residential towers of the *banlieue*. Like La Défense, the *banlieue* is widely perceived to be in France but not of it, the locus not of the foreign forces of global capital but of the equally alien forces of Islamic radicalism or of an American-inspired ghetto culture that may yet invade and destroy the culture and identity of the society on whose margins the *banlieue* stands as a looming, threatening presence. Through its geographical location, its starkly modernist architecture, and its symbolic resonances, the *banlieue* represents a kind of inverted mirror image of its apparent antithesis, the new centre of financial power that is La Défense.

Indeed, we might say that La Défense and the *banlieue* are post-Fordist spaces par excellence, the first in its role as the location of and conduit for globalised financial forces, the second as the place in which the destructive effects of Fordism's crisis have been felt most acutely. Situated on the margins of the French city and characterised by a rebarbatively modernist architectural style, these two spaces lend themselves to depiction as alien forces threatening to engulf that city. The term 'city' here should be understood in both its literal sense and the more figurative sense it has inherited from Greek philosophy as designating the locus of a civilised society and polity, the core of the Republic itself. When the staff at the publishing firm in Kuperman's novel *Nous étions des êtres vivants* chant the name of Paris's Place de la République to celebrate the fact that their new boss, Paul Cathéter, has decided not to relocate them to an anonymous Parisian *banlieue*, it is this more figurative conception of the 'city' that they implicitly evoke.

The marginal, alien, and hence threatening spaces of La Défense and the *banlieue* are not merely opposed to the civilised space of the city, however. That space of more civilised, specifically French values is also typically represented by the provincial factory or industrial plant. This is the case in films like *Violence des échanges en milieu tempéré* and *Ressources humaines*, where provincial factories are figured as embodying a sense of certainty, solidity, and working-class solidarity in opposition to the destructive forces that the two young products of elite French business schools, Philippe and Frank, unwittingly embody. The Lorraine steel plant, whose sale to a Brazilian asset-stripper Victoria is negotiating, plays an analogous role in *Le Système Victoria*. In some

248   *Republican Citizens, Precarious Subjects*

cases, the location of such manufacturing plants in the French provinces serves as a pretext to resuscitate powerful myths of *terroir*, itself posited as the antidote to the corrosive forces of global capital. These myths of *terroir* achieve their most explicit form in the work of Houellebecq, epitomised by both Jed Martin's sense of the 'sublime' when confronted with a Michelin map and his ultimate retreat to the French countryside to escape the post-Fordist dystopia that deindustrialised France has become. A less explicit appeal to *terroir* lies behind Bon's claim to have located 'the elementary idea of work' in a limestone quarry in the Lorraine, whose physically demanding, predominantly masculine labour he contrasts to the inauthenticity of both feminised work in Daewoo's screwdriver factories and the low-paid service-sector labour that has now replaced even that degraded form of employment. When, at the end of *Le Système Victoria*, David retreats to a hotel close to the rural village in which his mother and grandmother were both born, Reinhardt is staging one further appeal to the supposed certainties of *terroir* as antidote to contemporary capitalism.

In all these narratives, then, old myths of *terroir* are resuscitated and articulated to peculiarly gendered notions of supposedly authentic, wholesome male industrial labour. Indeed, as the chapter we dedicated to the figure of the *femme forte* demonstrated, depictions of the contemporary French workplace have struggled to represent the reality of its increased feminisation as anything other than an aberrant departure from traditional and allegedly natural gender roles. The figure of the female executive as a *femme forte* who has betrayed her 'natural' destiny, renouncing marriage and motherhood to pursue her career, appears very well established in French novel and film. Depictions of her working-class counterpart, the *femme forte* struggling to keep family and community together in a context of mass male unemployment, seem less conservative in their implications. Yet it is difficult not to suspect that this second group of working women is the subject of less censorious depiction precisely because they remain relatively powerless while still being defined by their maternal, care-giving function. It seems that the assumptions regarding a woman's proper social role that were institutionalised in the gendered forms of the republican-corporatist post-war compromise continue to cast a long shadow.

A less conservative, if perhaps equally idealised appeal to French republicanism is evident in the various narratives that focus on the figure of the doomed youth. In the modern era the French Republican

Conclusion 249

School was supposed to work closely alongside the labour market to ensure the integration of all the nation's citizens into a cohesive society and polity. At the lower end of the republican education system, formal qualifications delivered in accordance with objective measures of academic achievement were intended to secure jobs with associated rights to social welfare for their holders. At the summit of that system, a republican elite, selected on purely objective academic criteria, would exercise its knowledge in the general interest of all citizens. The possibility that the relationship between republican education, employment, and social integration might be breaking down was perhaps first raised in relation to the *banlieue*. The emergence, from the 1980s onwards, of the figure of the ethnic minority youth, supposedly doomed to educational failure, unemployment, and delinquency, expresses widespread anxieties at the combined effects of deindustrialisation and increased ethnic diversity on France's deprived suburban housing projects. More recently, the figure of the young graduate of a business-oriented *grande école*, doomed by the nature of their education and employment to betray the traditional ideals of the republican elite, expresses equally widespread anxieties at the dominance of narrowly financial imperatives over elite education in France. Doubtless, there is something both idealised and nostalgic in these appeals to a now threatened tradition of egalitarian republican education, a blindness to the role the Republican School actually played in reproducing class distinctions or training a republican elite that was often more self-interested than genuinely committed to promoting the general interest. Such nostalgia does nonetheless betray a fundamentally progressive impulse, in the form of a desire to see the Republican School realise its egalitarian ideals. Moreover, such egalitarian ideals, however compromised in practice, did form part of official public discourse and could hence be appealed to in order to curb more nakedly commercial imperatives. Appeals to those founding republican ideals, however idealised or nostalgic, can thus express a justified lament at their disappearance from the sphere of public debate.

If the emergence of the figure of the doomed youth suggests there are elements in the French republican tradition that merit safeguarding, the *sans papiers* movement, by contrast, represents a powerful call for that tradition to be reformed to become more inclusive. As we have argued, the phenomenon of mass undocumented migration has a number of different determinants, 'push' factors that

250   *Republican Citizens, Precarious Subjects*

reflect political and economic instability in the developing world, alongside 'pull' factors that explain the continuing demand for a pool of cheap, flexible labour in the developed economies. Many of these factors are intimately related to the shifts in both global economic governance and the domestic labour market that have propelled the question of labour market precarity to the top of the French political, intellectual, and cultural agenda. As we noted, the strike movements of the late 2000s and early 2010s saw the *sans papiers* arguing for residency, labour, and welfare rights based on the significant role they play in the contemporary French labour market. This involved not merely looking backwards, as it were, appealing to established French republican traditions in which rights and employment are closely interrelated. It also involved reformulating that republican tradition, rendering it more inclusive of workers of different nationalities and ethnicities, hence reimagining the relationships between rights, employment, and citizenship inherent to the republican-corporatist model in its traditional form.

Each of these recurrent character types – the male worker in crisis, the *femme forte*, the doomed youth, the *sans papiers* – hence embodies a challenge to the republican-corporatist terms of the French post-war compromise. Typically, those challenges have been portrayed as something to be regretted, generating recurrent narratives of *loss*, the loss of older certainties of nation and gender, the loss of stable jobs, the loss of hard-won social rights, the loss of hopes for future socio-economic progress. One contributory factor here is surely the absence of a consensus on the French left regarding how best to respond to the proliferation of flexible, precarious forms of labour, the absence, that is to say, of a shared vision around which trade unions, political parties, and workers might unite. Indeed, as we argued in Chapter 2, the French left appears to be characterised by a fundamental division in this respect. On the one hand, there are those commentators who believe labour market precarity to be the product of an ideologically driven assault on the gains embodied in the French post-war model, an assault that can best be reversed by deepening and extending the system of social protection established at the Liberation. On the other hand, a range of commentators argue that there has been a profound shift in the regime of capital accumulation that has rendered the corporatist system of work and welfare established in the immediate post-war decades obsolete. For these thinkers it is therefore essential

Conclusion 251

to conceive of a new form of social protection adapted to the changed realities of a post-Fordist conjuncture characterised by the proliferation of atypical and precarious forms of employment. This second group of commentators is further divided between those who thus argue in favour of a social-democratic form of flexicurity and those who insist that some form of guaranteed income represents the best response to this changed conjuncture. Advocates of a guaranteed income are further divided among themselves in terms of the level and potential universality of any such income (Le Naire and Lebon 2017).

There has, thus, been a proliferation of proposals emanating from left-wing thinkers and activists in France regarding how best to combat mass unemployment, labour market deregulation, flexibility, and precarity. However, no clear consensus has emerged as to which proposal should be pursued. Hence, although France has seen waves of protest over recent decades, from factory occupations to the nationwide *Nuit debout* and *gilets jaunes* movements, none of these has prevented the passing of labour market reforms, under the successive presidencies of Sarkozy, Hollande, and Macron, that have further deregulated the labour market and eroded social protections. As we have noted, these reforms have been legitimated by reference to real problems of welfare and labour dualisation inherent to the French republican-corporatist model. Yet, the forms of flexicurity they have thus put in place have clearly emphasised the *flexibility* side of that equation to the detriment of any genuine form of social *security*. Moreover, Macron's proposed future reforms in this area all seem destined to strengthen these tendencies, further eroding the bases of France's corporatist model of social welfare and replacing them with exacerbated forms of flexibility and precarity.

Macron's pension reforms, announced for 2019 but temporarily delayed by the need to respond to the *gilets jaunes* crisis, are a case in point here. For the proposed reduction in the number of separate occupational funds and the imposition of greater uniformity in calculating pension rates will give central government greater powers to reduce the overall level of expenditure. In 2020, Macron has promised to introduce a new benefit, the 'revenu universel d'activité'. Modelled on the UK's highly controversial 'universal credit', this will be an amalgamation of a range of existing 'social minima', including the RSA or Active Solidarity Income, into a single payment. Recipients will have to sign up to 'un parcours d'intégration' or 'integration

252 *Republican Citizens, Precarious Subjects*

pathway', while risking sanctions if they fail to be sufficiently 'active' in their search for work (Foulon 2019:11).

Macron's most recent and proposed future reforms hence all move in the direction of a further erosion of the terms of the republican-corporatist post-war model. They promise to reinforce the tendencies we have identified in the main body of this study, institutionalising the shift away from viewing citizens as members of an occupational group with its associated status and welfare rights to seeing them as 'entrepreneurs of the self', compelled constantly to modulate their personal and professional identities in response to changing market conditions and meriting welfare payments only insofar as they can prove they are sufficiently 'active' in that respect. As we have argued, this model of personal and professional subjectivity is epitomised by the 'uberised' platform worker and some commentators, government officials among them, have actively promoted 'uberised' labour as one solution to the alleged rigidities of France's corporatist model. There is a striking irony in this faith in the ability of 'uberised' employment to offer solutions to France's problems of high working-class unemployment and discriminatory recruitment practices. For it seems clear that Uber itself is committed, as soon as proves possible, to replacing all its drivers with driverless vehicles and hence offering no jobs at all to unemployed French youth. Uber's potential recourse to driverless technology represents just one example of the possible future effects of Artificial Intelligence (AI) and robotisation on labour markets. Predictions as to those future effects vary from almost apocalyptic visions of the destruction of hundreds of thousands of jobs to more sanguine assessments of the new forms of labour that emerge in the wake of any technological revolution (Arntz, et al. 2016). It seems nonetheless clear that the radical transformation of salaried employment that such developments promise will further challenge the republican–corporatist forms of the French social model.

The technological impetus behind AI demonstrates that such challenges are not wholly attributable to the hegemony of neo–liberalism as an ideology. Throughout this study we have insisted that, alongside technological change, worker resistance to the disciplinary rigidities of Fordism, the fall in the rate of profit secured through Fordist production, cultural and social shifts all had a role to play in both the crisis of Fordism and the subsequent proliferation of more precarious forms of employment. These shifts have certainly been exploited by

Conclusion 253

the adherents of neo-liberal solutions and their destructive effects exacerbated by the hegemony of neo-liberal ideas at both national and global levels. Finding progressive solutions to the problems of labour market precarity will certainly require challenging that ideological hegemony, not least in an effort to impose new forms of regulation over the global financial system and to defend the legitimacy of new forms of social protection at the national level. Inventing forms of regulation and social protection that draw on earlier ideals of justice and social solidarity but are adapted to the technological, social, and political realities of the current conjuncture will be a demanding task. It will nonetheless surely be a vital first step in the formation of a consensus around which trades unions, left-wing parties, and workers can unite in their struggles against precarity and in defence of the more progressive forms of republican citizenship.

Bibliography

Abdelnour, Sarah. (2017) *Moi, petite entreprise. Les auto-entrepreneurs, de l'utopie à la réalité*. Paris: Presses universitaires de France.

Aglietta, Michel and Antoine Rebérioux. (2004) *Dérives du capitalisme financier*. Paris: Albin Michel.

Algan, Y., P. Cahuc, and A. Zylberberg. (2012) *La Fabrique de la défiance … et comment s'en sortir*. Paris: Albin Michel.

Altes, Liesbeth Kortals. (2008) 'Traces: Writing the Visual in François Bon's *Daewoo*', *Yale French Studies*, vol.114, pp.80–94.

Amable, Bruno. (2017) *Structural Crisis and Institutional Change in Modern Capitalism: French capitalism in transition*. Oxford: Oxford University Press.

Amar, Nicolas and Louis-Charles Viossat. (2016) *Les Plateformes collaboratives, l'emploi et la protection sociale*, IGAS Rapport no.2015–121R.

Arnold, Martin. (2005) 'French Minister Says Polygamy to Blame for Riots', *Financial Times*, 15 November, p.12.

Arntz, Mikael, Timothy Gregory, and Ute Zierahn. (2016) 'The Risk for Automation for Jobs in OECD Countries', *OECD Social and Migration Working Papers*, no.189, Paris: OECD.

Attali, Jacques, ed. (2008) *Rapport de la Commission pour la libération de la croissance française*. Paris: XO Éditions/La Documentation française.

Aubenas, Florence. (2010) *Le Quai de Ouistreham*. Paris: Éditions de l'Olivier.

Balibar, Étienne. (1998) *Droit de cité*. Paris: Quadrige/Presses universitaires de France.

Balibar, Étienne, Monique Chemillier-Gendreau, Jacqueline Costa-Lascoux, and Emmanuel Terray. (1999) *Sans papiers: l'archaïsme fatal*. Paris: La Découverte.

Balzac, Honoré de. (1837–43 [1966]) *Illusions perdues*. Paris: Garnier-Flammarion.

Barron, Pierre, Anne Bory, Lucie Tourette, Sébastien Chauvin, and Nicolas Jounin. (2011) *On Bosse ici, on reste ici! La Grève des sans papiers: une aventure inédite*. Paris: La Découverte.

Baumard, Maryline. (2016) 'En Banlieue, l'"ubérisation" au secours de l'intégration', *Le Monde Économie et Entreprise*, 19 mai, p.6.

256 Republican Citizens, Precarious Subjects

Beaud, Stéphane and Gérard Mauger, eds. (2017) *Une Génération sacrifiée? Jeunes des classes populaires dans la France désindustrialisée.* Paris: Éditions Rue d'Ulm.

Beaud, Stéphane and Michel Pialoux. (1999) *Retour sur la condition ouvrière.* Paris: Fayard/10/18.

———. (2003) *Violences urbaines, violence sociale. Genèse des nouvelles classes dangereuses.* Paris: Fayard/Hachette Pluriel.

Becker, Gary S. (2011) *The Challenge of Immigration: a radical solution.* London: Institute of Economic Affairs.

Begag, Azouz and Christian Delorme. (1994) *Quartiers sensibles.* Paris: Seuil-Points.

Beinstingel, Thierry. (2010) *Retour aux mots sauvages.* Paris: Fayard.

———. (2012) *Ils désertent.* Paris: Fayard.

Benasayag, Miguel and Angélique del Rey. (2008) *La Chasse aux enfants. L'effet miroir de l'expulsion des sans papiers.* Paris: La Découverte.

Benguigui, Yamina. (1997) *Mémoires d'immigrés.* Paris: Canal + Éditions.

Benjamin, Walter. (1999) *The Arcades Project,* trans. H. Eiland and K. McLaughlin. Cambridge (MA): Belknap Press.

Bergeron, Marion. (2010) *En CDD à Pôle Emploi. 183 jours dans les coulisses du système.* Paris: Plon/Presses Pocket.

Bernard, Philippe. (2002) *Immigration: le défi mondial.* Paris: Gallimard-Folio.

Berthaut, Jérôme. (2013) *La Banlieue du '20 Heures'.* Marseille: Agone.

Bhabha, Jacqueline. (2018) *Can We Solve the Migration Crisis?* Cambridge: Polity Press.

Blin, Thierry. (2010) *L'Invention des sans papiers.* Paris: Presses universitaires de France.

Boltanski, Luc and Eve Chiapello. (1999) *Le Nouvel Esprit du capitalisme.* Paris: Gallimard.

Bon, François. (2004) *Daewoo.* Paris: Fayard/Livre de poche.

Bourdieu, Pierre. (1979) *La Distinction. Critique sociale du jugement.* Paris: Minuit.

———. (1989) *La Noblesse d'état. Grandes écoles et esprit de corps.* Paris: Minuit.

Boyer, Robert. (2015) *Économie politique des capitalismes. Théorie de la régulation et des crises.* Paris: La Découverte.

Boyer, Robert and Jean-Pierre Durand. (1993) *L'Après-fordisme.* Paris: Syros.

Brown, Philip, David Ashton, and Hugh Lauder (2010) 'Skills Are Not Enough: The Globalization of Knowledge and the Future UK Economy', *Praxis,* no.4, pp.1–33.

Brunel, Valérie. (2008) *Les Managers de l'âme. Le développement personnel en entreprise, nouvelle pratique de pouvoir?* Paris: La Découverte.

Brunner, Anne and Louis Maurin. (2019) *Rapport sur les inégalités en France,* édition 2019. Paris: Éditions de l'observatoire des inégalités.

Burke, Edmund. (1990 [1757]) *A Philosophical Enquiry into our Ideas of the Sublime and the Beautiful.* Oxford: Oxford University Press.

Cahuc, Pierre and André Zylberberg. (2009) *Les Réformes ratées du président Sarkozy.* Paris: Flammarion/Champs Actuel.

Bibliography   257

Camfield, David. (2007) 'The Multitude and the Kangaroo: A Critique of Hardt and Negri's Theory of Immaterial Labour', *Historical Materialism*, vol.15, no.2, pp.21–52.

Caroli, Eve and Jérôme Gautié, eds. (2009) *Bas salaires et qualité de l'emploi: l'exception française.* Paris: Éditions Rue d'Ulm.

Carvalho, Joao and Andrew Geddes. (2012) 'La Politique d'immigration sous Sarkozy', in Jacques de Maillard and Yves Surel, eds. *Les Politiques publiques sous Sarkozy.* Paris: Presses de Sciences Po, pp.279–98.

Castel, Robert. (2009) *La Montée des incertitudes. Travail, protections, statut de l'individu.* Paris: Seuil.

Castel, Robert and Nicolas Duvoux, eds. (2013) *L'Avenir de la solidarité.* Paris: Presses universitaires de France.

Castells, Manuel. (2007) *The Power of Identity*, second edition. Oxford: Blackwell.

Céreq. (2017) 'Quand l'école est finie. Premiers pas dans la vie active de la generation 2013', *Céreq Enquêtes*, no.1, pp.1–92.

Cette France-là. (2012) *Sans-Papiers et Préfets. La culture du résultat en portraits.* Paris: La Découverte.

———. (2012a) *Xénophobie d'en haut. Le choix d'une droite éhontée.* Paris: La Découverte.

Clarke, Jackie. (2011) 'Closing Moulinex. Thoughts on the Visibility and Invisibility of Industrial Labour in France', *Modern & Contemporary France*, vol.19, no.4, pp.443–58.

———. (2013) *France in the Age of Organisation. Factory, home and nation from the 1920s to Vichy.* New York: Berghahn Books.

Clot, Yves. (2010) *Le Travail à Coeur. Pour en finir avec les risques psychosociaux.* Paris: La Découverte.

Collovald, Annie. (2004) *Le Populisme du FN, un dangereux contresens.* Paris: Éditions du croquant.

Combrexelle, Jean-Denis. (2015) *La Négociation collective, le travail et l'emploi.* Paris: France Stratégie.

Conseil d'État. (2017) *Puissance publique et plateformes numériques. Accompagner l' 'ubérisation'.* Paris: La Documentation française.

Cour des comptes. (2013) *Le Marché du travail: face à un chômage élevé, mieux cibler les politiques.* Paris: La Documentation française.

Crawley, Heaven, Franck Düvell, Katherine Jones, Simon McMahon, and Nando Sigona. (2018) *Unravelling Europe's 'Migration Crisis'.* Bristol: Policy Press.

Crozier, Michel. (1964) *Le Phénomène bureaucratique.* Paris: Seuil.

———. (1970) *La Société bloquée.* Paris: Seuil.

Curiel, Jonathan. (2012) *Génération CV.* Paris: Fayard/Points Seuil.

Dardot, Pierre and Christian Laval. (2013) *The New Way of the World: on neo-liberal society*, trans. Gregory Elliott. New York and London: Verso.

DARES. (2015) 'Femmes et hommes sur le marché du travail', *DARES Analyses*, no.017 (mars), pp.1–12.

258   *Republican Citizens, Precarious Subjects*

——. (2018) 'CDD, CDI: comment évoluent les embauches et les ruptures depuis 25 ans?', *DARES Analyses*, no.026 (juin), pp.1–11.

Darmon, Muriel. (2013) *Classes préparatoires. La fabrique d'une jeunesse dominante.* Paris: La Découverte.

Dayan, Jean-Louis. (2002) *35 Heures. Des ambitions aux réalités.* Paris: La Découverte.

Défenseur des droits. (2014) *Le Refus de soins opposé aux bénéficiaries de la CMU-C, de l'ACS, et de l'AME*, https://www.defenseurdesdroits.fr/sites/default/files/atoms/files/ddd_r_20140301_refus_soins.pdf, accessed 17 July 2017.

De Gaulejac, Vincent. (2005) *La Société malade de la gestion. Idéologie gestionnaire, pouvoir managerial et harcèlement social.* Paris: Seuil/Collection Points.

Dejours, Christophe. (1998) *Souffrance en France: la banalisation de l'injustice sociale.* Paris: Seuil/Collection Points.

——. (2003) *L'Évaluation du travail à l'épreuve du reel. Critique des fondements de l'évaluation.* Paris: INRA Éditions.

Dejours, Christophe and Florence Bègue. (2009) *Suicide et travail. Que faire?* Paris: Presses universitaires de France.

Deleuze, Gilles. (2003) *Pourparlers, 1972–1990.* Paris: Éditions de minuit.

Dembele, Dembe Moussa. (2003) *Debt and Destruction in Senegal: a study of twenty years of IMF and World Bank policies.* World Development Movement (November).

De Rauglaudre, Timothée. (2015) 'Seuls 14% des postes de direction sont occupés par des femmes', *Les Échos*, 18 juin, p.16.

Dermine, Elise and Daniel Dumont, eds. (2014) *Activation Policies for the Unemployed, the Right to Work and the Duty to Work.* Brussels: Peter Lang.

Des Isnards, Alexandre and Thomas Zuber. (2008) *L'Open Space m'a tuer.* Paris: Hachette/Livre de poche.

Diamond, Hannah. (2011) 'Miners, Masculinity and the *Bataille du Charbon* in France, 1944–1948', *Modern & Contemporary France*, vol.19. no.1, pp.69–84.

Diome, Fatou. (2003) *Le Ventre de l'Atlantique.* Paris: Livre de poche.

D'Iribarne, Philippe. (1993) *La Logique de l'honneur. Gestion des entreprises et traditions nationales.* Paris: Seuil-Points.

DRESS. (2015) *La Protection sociale en France et en Europe en 2013.* Paris: Direction de la recherche, des études, de l'évaluation et des statistiques.

Duchaussoy, Vincent. (2014) 'L'État livré aux financiers? La Loi du 3 janvier sur la Banque de France', *La Vie des idées*, 1 juillet, www.laviedesidées.fr/L-Etat-livre-aux-financiers.html, accessed 1 February 2018.

Duhamel, Alain. (2018) 'La Fin de l'innocence', *Libération*, 28 novembre, p.5.

Duménil, Gérard and Dominique Lévy. (2000) *Crise et sortie de crise: ordres et désordres néolibéraux.* Paris: PUF.

Durkheim, Émile. (2007 [1893]) *De la division du travail social.* Paris: PUF/Quadrige.

Du Roy, Ivan. (2009) *Orange stressé: le management par le stress à France Télécom.* Paris: La Découverte.

Duval, Guillaume. (2018) 'Les Aides sociales sur la sellette', *Alternatives économiques*, no.381 (juillet–août), pp.12–14.

Duvoux, Nicolas. (2012) *Le Nouvel Âge de la solidarité. Pauvreté, précarité et politiques publiques*. Paris: Seuil/République des idées.

Ellwood, Wayne. (2002) *The No-Nonsense Guide to Globalization*. London: Verso.

Emmenegger, Patrick, Silja Häusermann, Bruno Palier, and Martin Seeleib-Kaiser, eds. (2012) *The Age of Dualisation. The changing face of inequality in deindustrialising societies*. Oxford: Oxford University Press.

Esping-Andersen, Gosta. (1989) *The Three Worlds of Welfare Capitalism*. Cambridge: Polity Press.

Esson, James. (2015) 'Escape to Victory: Development, Youth Entrepreneurship and the Migration of Ghanaian Footballers', *Geoforum*, vol.64, pp.47–55.

Etcherelli, Claire. (1967) *Élise ou la vraie vie*. Paris: Denoël.

Evrard, Audrey. (2018) '*Rêve d'usine* (Luc Decaster, 2003): Presenting the Vanishing Workplace', *Modern and Contemporary France*, vol.26, no.3, pp.307–21.

Fanon, Frantz. (1986) *Black Skin, White Masks*, trans. C.L. Markmann. London: Pluto Press.

Farbiaz, Patrick. (2016) *Nuit debout: les textes*. Paris: Les Petits Matins.

Fassin, Didier. (2011) *Humanitarian Reason: a moral history of the present*. Berkeley and Los Angeles: University of California Press.

Feher, Michel. (2017) *Le Temps des investis. Essai sur la nouvelle question sociale*. Paris: La Découverte.

Filhol, Élisabeth. (2010) *La Centrale*. Paris: P.O.L./Gallimard-Folio.

——. (2014) *Bois II*. Paris: P.O.L.

Flaubert, Gustave. (1869 [2013]) *L'Éducation sentimentale*. Paris: Flammarion.

Fleming, Peter. (2015) *The Mythology of Work. How capitalism persists despite itself*. London: Pluto Press.

——. (2017) *The Death of Homo Economicus. Work, debt and the myth of endless accumulation*. London: Pluto Press.

Flocco, Gaëtan. (2015) *Des Dominants très dominés. Pourquoi les cadres acceptent leur servitude*. Paris: Liber-Raisons d'agir.

Flottes, Anne. (2013) *Travailler, quel boulot!* Paris: Syllepse.

Foucault, Michel. (1975) *Surveiller et punir. Naissance de la prison*. Paris: Gallimard.

——. (2004) *Naissance de la biopolitique. Cours au Collège de France, 1978–79*. Paris: Gallimard/Seuil.

Foulon, Sandrine. (2017) 'Le Code du Travail après les ordonnances', *Alternatives économiques*, no.372 (octobre), pp.24–25.

——. (2019) 'Les Chômeurs vont payer la facture', *Alternatives économiques*, no.392 (juillet–août), pp.8–11.

Frémeaux, Philippe. (2018) 'Le Bloc-notes', *Alternatives économiques*, no.385, décembre, p.98.

Friedmann, Georges. (1964) *Le Travail en miettes. Spécialisation et loisirs*, nouvelle édition revue et augmentée. Paris: Gallimard/Idées.

Friot, Bernard. (2017) *Vaincre Macron*. Paris: La Dispute.

260 Republican Citizens, Precarious Subjects

Gauz. (2014) *Debout-payé*. Paris: Le Nouvel Attila/Livre de poche.

Gilbert, Geoff. (2011) 'Amortissement: François Bon's *Daewoo*', *Textual Practice*, vol.25, no.2, pp.315–28.

Grandguillot, Dominique. (2009) *Revenu de solidarité active. Compléter les revenus du travail. Lutter contre l'exclusion. Accompagner vers l'emploi*. Paris: L'Extenso Éditions.

Granvaud, Raphaël. (2012) *Areva en Afrique: Une face cachée du nucléaire français*. Marseille: Agone.

Grimault, Solveig. (2008) 'Sécurisation des parcours professionnels et flexicurité: analyse comparative des positions syndicales', *Travail et Emploi*, no.113, pp.75–89.

Guattari, Félix. (1980) 'Présentation du séminaire', *Séminaires de Félix Guattari*, https://www.revue-chimeres/IMG/odf/801209.pdf, accessed 9 July 2019.

Guilluy, Christophe. (2010) *Fractures françaises*. Paris: François Bourin.

Hajjat, Abdellali. (2013) *La Marche pour l'égalité et contre le racisme*. Paris: Éditions Amsterdam.

Hall, Peter A. and David Soskice, eds. (2001) *Varieties of Capitalism. The institutional foundations of comparative advantage*. Oxford: Oxford University Press.

Harvey, David. (2006) *Spaces of Global Capitalism*. London: Verso.

Hayes, Graeme. (2012) 'Bossnapping: Situating Repertories of Industrial Action in National and Global Contexts', *Modern and Contemporary France*, vol.20, no.2 (May), pp.185–201.

Higbee, Will. (2004) '"Elle est où ta place?" The Social Realist Melodramas of Laurent Cantet: *Ressources humaines* and *L'Emploi du temps*', *French Cultural Studies*, vol.15, no.3, pp.235–50.

Houellebecq, Michel. (1994) *Extension du domaine de la lutte*. Paris: Nadeau/ Éditions 'J'ai lu'.

——. (1998) *Les Particules élémentaires*. Paris: Flammarion/Éditions 'J'ai lu'.

——. (2010) *La Carte et le territoire*. Paris: Flammarion/Éditions 'J'ai lu'.

——. (2015) *Soumission*. Paris: Flammarion/Éditions 'J'ai lu'.

Hudson, Michael. (2015) *Killing the Host. How financial parasites and debt destroy the global economy*. Frankfurt: Islet Verlag.

Husson, Michel. (2003) 'Sommes-nous entrés dans le "capitalisme cognitif"?', *Critique communiste*, no.169–70 (été–automne), pp.1–8.

IRES. (2009) *La France du travail. Données, analyses, débats*. Paris: Éditions de l'atelier/Éditions ouvrières.

ISO. (2017) *The ISO Survey*, https://www.iso.org/fr/the-iso-survey,html, accessed 2 February 2018.

Kokoreff, Michel and Jacques Rodriguez. (2012) *Une France en mutation. Globalisation, état, individus*. Paris: Petite Bibliothèque Payot.

Kuperman, Nathalie. (2010) *Nous étions des êtres vivants*. Paris: Gallimard.

Labadie, Aurore. (2016) *Le Roman d'entreprise français au tournant du XXIe siècle*. Paris: Presses Sorbonne nouvelle.

Laclos, Choderlos de. (1782 [1961]) *Les Liaisons dangereuses*. Paris: Flammarion.

Lallement, Michel. (2007) *Le Travail: une sociologie contemporaine*. Paris: Gallimard/ Folio.

Lallement, Michel and Olivier Mériaux. (2003) 'Status and Contracts in Industrial Relations. "La refondation sociale", a New Bottle for Old (French) Wine?', *Industrielle Beziehungen*, vol.10, no.3, pp.418–37.

Landier, Augustin, Daniel Szomoru, and David Thesmar (2016) *Travailler sur une plateforme internet: une analyse des chauffeurs utilisant Uber en France*, https://drive.google.com/file/d/0B1s08BdVqCgrTEZieTloQnRlazQ/view, accessed 12 March 2018.

Lapavitsas, Costa. (2013) *Profiting without Producing. How finance affects us all*. London and New York: Verso.

Laroque, Pierre. (2008 [1945]) 'Discours prononcé le 23 mars 1945 à l'école nationale d'organisation économique et sociale à l'occasion de l'inauguration de la section assurances sociales', reprinted in *Revue française des affaires sociales*, no.1 (janvier–mars), pp.153–63.

Laval, Christian, Francis Vergue, Pierre Clément, and Guy Dreux. (2012) *La Nouvelle École capitaliste*. Paris: La Découverte/Poche.

Lavoine, Lucie and Dominique Méda. (2008) 'Place et sens du travail en Europe: une singularité française?', *Centre d'études de l'emploi, Document de travail no.96–1* (février), pp.1–117.

Le Bras, Hervé. (1991) *Marianne et les lapins. L'obsession démographique*. Paris: Hachette Pluriel.

Lebtahi, Yannick and Isabelle Roussel-Gillet. (2005) *Pour une méthode d'investigation du cinéma de Laurent Cantet*. Paris: L'Harmattan.

Le Naire, Olivier and Claire Lebon. (2017) *Le Revenu de base: une idée qui pourrait changer nos vies*. Arles: Librairie Actes Sud.

Linhart, Danièle. (2015) *La Comédie humaine du travail. De la déshumanisation taylorienne à la sur-humanisation managériale*. Toulouse: Éditions érès.

Linhart, Robert. (1978) *L'Établi*. Paris: Minuit.

Lipietz, Alain. (2018) 'Gilets jaunes: l'insurrection contre l'ubérisaton sociale', *Libération*, 7 décembre, p.6.

Lordon, Frédéric. (2000) *Fonds de pension, piège à cons? Mirages de la démocratie actionnariale*. Paris: Liber-Raisons d'agir.

———. (2002) *La Politique du capital*. Paris: Odile Jacob.

———. (2008) *Jusqu'à quand? Pour en finir avec les crises financières*. Paris: Liber-Raisons d'agir.

———. (2010) *Capitalisme, désir et servitude. Marx et Spinoza*. Paris: La Fabrique.

———. (2010a) 'Finance: la société prise en otage. Entretien avec Yann Moulier Boutang et Jérôme Vidal', *La Revue internationale des livres et des idées*, no.8, pp.3–5.

———. (2013) 'Pour une monnaie commune sans l'Allemagne (ou avec, mais pas à la francfortoise)', *Le Monde diplomatique*, 25 mai, https://blog.mondediplo. net/2013-05-25-Pour-une-monnaie-commune-sans-l-Allemagne-ou-avec, accessed 13 February 2018.

———. (2016) 'Pour la République sociale', *Le Monde diplomatique*, mars, pp.17–19.

262　*Republican Citizens, Precarious Subjects*

Maier, Corinne. (2004) *Bonjour paresse. De l'art et de la nécessité d'en faire le moins possible en entreprise.* Paris: Éditions Michalon/Gallimard Folio.

Maris, Bernard. (2014) *Houellebecq économiste*. Paris: Flammarion.

Marks, John. (2011) '"Ça tient qu'à toi": Cartographies of Post-Fordist Labour in Laurent Cantet's L'Emploi du temps', *Modern and Contemporary France*, vol.19, no.4, pp.477–94.

Maurani, Margaret and Monique Meron. (2012) *Un Siècle de travail des femmes en France, 1901–2011.* Paris: La Découverte.

Maurin, Louis. (2018) 'La France dépense-t-elle trop?', *Alternatives économiques*, no.381 (juillet–août), pp.15–16.

Mazzucato, Mariana. (2013) *The Entrepreneurial State. Debunking public vs. private sector myths.* London: Penguin Books.

Méda, Dominique and Pierre Larrouturou. (2016) *Einstein avait raison: il faut réduire le temps du travail.* Paris: Éditions de l'atelier.

Ministère du Travail. (2015) *Bilan de la loi de la sécurisation de l'emploi du 14 juin 2013*, http://travail-emploi.gouv.fr/IMG/pdf/CONFERENCE_THEMATIQUE_DU_3_AVRIL_2015_-_Bilan_de_la_loi_de_securisation_de_l_emploi.pdf, accessed 25 April 2017.

———. (2016) 'Grands Dossiers: Loi Travail', http://travail-emploi.gouv.fr/grands-dossiers/LoiTravail/, accessed 7 May 2016.

Montel, Olivia. (2017) 'L'Économie des plateformes. Enjeux pour la croissance, le travail, l'emploi et les politiques publiques', *Documents d'études DARES*, no.213 (août), pp.1–39.

Mordillat, Gérard. (2014) *Xénia*. Paris: Calmann-Levy.

———. (2017) *La Tour abolie*. Paris: Albin Michel.

Moretti, Franco. (1998) *Atlas of the European Novel, 1800–1900*. London: Verso.

Morin, François. (2000) 'A Transformation in the French Model of Shareholding and Management', *Economy and Society*, vol. 29, no. 1 (February), pp.36–53.

———. (2006) 'Le Capitalisme de marché financier et l'asservissement du cognitif', *Cahiers du GRES*, no.2006–05 (janvier), pp.1–22.

Morini, Cristina (2007) 'The Feminization of Labour in Cognitive Capitalism', *Feminist Review*, no.87, pp.40–59.

Mouhoud, El Mouhoub. (2013) *Mondialisation et délocalisation des entreprises*, 4e édition. Paris: La Découverte.

Mouhoud, El Mouhoub and Dominique Plihon. (2009) *Le Savoir et la finance: liaisons dangereuses au coeur du capitalisme contemporain.* Paris: La Découverte.

Moulier Boutang, Yann. (2007) *Le Capitalisme cognitif. La nouvelle grande transformation.* Paris: Amsterdam.

———. (2008) 'Finance, instabilité et gouvernabilité des externalités', *Multitudes*, vol.32, no.1, pp.91–102.

———. (2010) *L'Abeille et l'économiste.* Paris: Carnets nord.

Moulier Boutang, Yann and Antoine Rebiscoul. (2009) 'Peut-on faire l'économie de Google?', *Multitudes*, vol.1, no.36, pp.83–93.

Mouzon, Céline. (2018) 'Aider un migrant, est-ce un crime?', *Alternatives économiques*, no.382, pp.56–58.

Bibliography 263

OFCE. (2010) *L'Industrie manufacturière française*. Paris: La Découverte.
——. (2012) *L'Économie française 2013*. Paris: La Découverte.
——. (2013) *L'Économie française 2014*. Paris: La Découverte.
——. (2017) *L'Économie française 2018*. Paris: La Découverte.
——. (2018) *L'Économie française 2019*. Paris: La Découverte.
O'Shaughnessy, Martin. (2007) *The New Face of Political Cinema. Commitment in French film since 1995*. London and New York: Berghahn Books.
——. (2015) *Laurent Cantet*. Manchester: Manchester University Press.
Palier, Bruno. (2005) *Gouverner la Sécurité sociale. Les réformes du système français de protection sociale depuis 1945*. Paris: PUF/Quadrige.
Paradeise, Catherine and Yves Lichtenberger. (2001) 'Compétences, compétences', *Sociologie du travail*, vol. 43, no.1 (janvier–mars), pp.33–48.
Parienty, Arnaud. (2015) *School Business. Comment l'argent dynamite le système éducatif*. Paris: La Découverte.
Paugam, Serge. (2007) 'Introduction: Durkheim et le lien social', in Émile Durkheim, *De la division du travail social*. Paris: PUF/Quadrige, pp.1–40.
Paugam, Serge and Nicolas Duvoux. (2008) *La Régulation des pauvres*. Paris: Presses universitaires de France.
Peugny, Camille. (2019) 'La Politique, des usines aux ronds-points', *Alternatives économiques*, no.389 (avril), pp.73–74.
Piketty, Thomas. (2013) *Le Capital au XXIe siécle*. Paris: Seuil.
——. (2019) *Capital et idéologie*. Paris: Seuil.
Quintreau, Laurent. (2006) *Marge brute*. Paris: Denoël/10/18.
Ramaux, Christophe. (2006) *Emploi: éloge de la stabilité. L'État social contre la flexicurité*. Paris: Mille et une nuits.
Ray, Jean-Emmanuel. (2017) 'Accords "offensifs", mode d'emploi', *Le Monde*, 17 janvier, p.13.
Reinhardt, Éric. (2011) *Le Système Victoria*. Paris: Stock/Gallimard-Folio.
Reynaud, Jean-Daniel. (2001) 'Le Management par compétences: un essai d'analyse', *Sociologie du travail*, vol.43, no.1 (janvier–mars), pp.7–31.
Ross, Andrew. (2009) *Nice Work if You Can Get it. Life and labour in precarious times*. New York: New York University Press.
Ross, Kristin. (1995) *Fast Cars, Clean Bodies. Decolonization and the reordering of French culture*. Cambridge (MA): The MIT Press.
Saada, Emanuelle. (2006) 'Un Racisme de l'expansion. Les discriminations raciales au regard des situations coloniales', in D. Fassin and E. Fassin, eds. *De la question sociale à la question raciale?* Paris: La Découverte, pp.63–79.
Saglio, Jean. (2007) 'Les Arrêtés Parodi sur les salaires: un moment de la construction de la place de l'État dans le système français de relations professionnelles', *Travail et emploi*, no.111 (juillet–septembre), pp.53–73.
Sam, Anna. (2008) *Les Tribulations d'une caissière*. Paris: Stock/Livre de poche.
Sartre, Jean-Paul. (1943) *Being and Nothingness: an essay on phenomenological ontology*, trans. H.E. Barnes, 2nd edition. London: Routledge, 2003.
Sayad, Abdelmalek. (1999) *La Double absence. Des illusions de l'émigré aux souffrances de l'immigré*. Paris: Seuil.

264 Republican Citizens, Precarious Subjects

Shin, Jang-Sup and Ha-Joon Chang. (2003) *Restructuring Korea Inc.* London: Routledge.

Silver, Beverly J. (2003) *Forces of Labour. Workers' movements and globalisation since 1870.* Cambridge: Cambridge University Press.

Southwood, Ivor. (2011) *Non-Stop Inertia.* Winchester: Zero Books.

Standing, Guy. (2011) *The Precariat. The new dangerous class.* London: Bloomsbury.

——. (2017) *Basic Income and How We Can Make it Happen.* London: Pelican Books.

Stiglitz, Joseph. (2002) *Globalization and its Discontents.* London: Penguin Books.

Streeck, Wolfgang. (2017) *Buying Time. The delayed crisis of democratic capitalism,*second edition. London and New York: Verso.

Taddei, Dominique and Benjamin Coriat. (1993) *Made in France. L'Industrie française dans la compétition mondiale.* Paris: Livre de poche-Essais.

Talneau, Sophie. (2004) *On vous rappellera. Une Bac +5 dans la jungle du recrutement.* Paris: Hachette/Livre de poche.

Tarr, Carrie. (2005) *Reframing Difference.* Beur *and* banlieue *filmmaking in France.* Manchester: Manchester University Press.

Taylor, Frederick W. (1911) *The Principles of Scientific Management.* New York and London: Harper Brothers Publishing.

Tesi, Francesca. (2008) 'Michelin et le Taylorisme', *Histoire, économie et société,* no.3, pp.111–26.

Tévanian, Pierre. (2013) *Chronique du racisme républicain.* Paris: Syllepse.

Thesmar, David. (2008) 'Retour sur la déréglementation financière', *Regards croisés sur l'économie,* vol.1, no.3, pp.67–74.

Thomas, Dominic. (2013) *Africa and France. Postcolonial cultures, migration, and racism.* Bloomington: Indiana University Press.

Ticktin, Miriam. (2011) *Casualties of Care: immigration and the politics of humanitarianism in France.* Berkeley and Los Angeles: University of California Press.

Triolet, Elsa. (1957) *Roses à crédit.* Paris: Gallimard.

Turner, Graham. (2008) *The Credit Crunch. Housing bubbles, globalisation and the worldwide economic crisis.* London: Pluto Press.

Vasset, Philippe. (2010) *Journal intime d'une prédatrice.* Paris: Fayard.

Vercellone, Carlo, ed. (2003) *Sommes-nous sortis du capitalisme industriel?* Paris: La Découverte.

Verschave, François-Xavier. (2003) *La Françafrique. Le plus long scandale de la République.* Paris: Stock.

Vlandas, Tim. (2013) 'The Politics of In-Work Benefits: The Case of the "Active Income of Solidarity" in France', *French Politics,* vol.11, no.2, pp.117–42.

Vouteau, Sophie. (2018) *Ma Vie d'auto-entrepreneur. Pas vraiment patron, complètement tâcheron.* Monaco: Éditions du Rocher.

Waters, Sarah. (2012) *Between Republic and Market: globalization and identity in contemporary France.* London: Continuum.

Weil, Simone. (1951) *La Condition ouvrière.* Paris: Gallimard.

Windebank, Jan. (1997) 'Men. Women, Work and Family Size in France: A Feminist Perspective', in Maire Cross and Sheila Perry, eds. *Population and Social Policy in France.* London: Pinter, pp.61–77.

Zamora, Daniel and Michael Behrent, eds. (2016) *Foucault and Neo-liberalism*. Cambridge: Polity Press.

Zarifian, Philippe. (2009) *Le Travail et la compétence: entre puissance et contrôle*. Paris: Presses universitaires de France.

Zimmer, Hélène. (2017) *Fairy Tale*. Paris: P.O.L.

Filmography

Abelanksi, Lionel, et al., dirs. (1997) *Nous, sans papiers de France*. Collectif des cinéastes pour les sans papiers.

——. (2007) *Laissez-les grandir ici!* Collectif des cinéastes pour les sans papiers.

——. (2010) *On bosse ici! On vit ici! On reste ici!* Collectif des cinéastes pour les sans papiers.

Balbastre, Gilles, dir. (2008) *Fortunes et infortunes des familles du Nord*. Point du jour Productions.

Benyamina, Houda, dir. (2016) *Divines*. Easy Tiger – France 2 Productions.

Brizé, Stéphane, dir. (2015) *La Loi du marché*. Nord-Ouest Productions.

Bruneau, Sophie and Marc-Antoine Roidil, dirs. (2006) *Ils ne mouraient pas tous mais tous étaient frappés*. Bodega Films.

Cantet, Laurent, dir. (1999) *Ressources humaines*. Les Films du losange.

——. (2001) *L'Emploi du temps*. Les Films du losange.

Carles, Pierre, Christophe Coello and Stéphane Goxe, dirs. (2003) *Attention Danger Travail*. CP Productions.

Carré, Jean-Michel, dir. (2007) *J'ai (très) mal au travail*. Les Films Grain de sable.

Chapiron, Kim, dir. (2014) *La Crème de la crème*. Moonshaker Productions.

Charef, Medhi, dir. (2000) *Marie-Line*. Canal+ Productions.

Chibane, Malik, dir. (1994) *Hexagone*. Alhambra Films.

Clouzot, Henri, dir. (1943) *Le Corbeau*. Continental Films.

Corneau, Alain, dir. (2010) *Crime d'amour*. SBS Films.

Cros, Didier, dir. (2011) *La Gueule de l'emploi*. Zadig Productions.

Delépine, Benoît and Gustave Kervern, dirs. (2010) *Mammuth*. No Money Productions.

——. (2014) *Near Death Experience*. No Money Productions.

Faucon, Philippe, dir. (2012) *La Désintégration*. Istiqlal Productions.

Gintzburger, Anne and Franck Vrignon, dirs. (2013) *La Promesse de Florange*. Chasseur d'étoiles.

Goupil, Romain, dir. (2010) *Les Mains en l'air*. Canal+, Les Films du Losange.

Guédiguian, Robert, dir. (2000) *La Ville est tranquille*. Agat Films & Cie.

——. (2011) *Les Neiges du Kilimandjaro*. Agat Films & Cie.

Kassovitz, Mathieu, dir. (1995) *La Haine*. Canal+ Productions.

Kaurismäki, Aki, dir. (2011) *Le Havre*. Sputnik Productions.

Kechiche, Abdellatif, dir. (2007) *La Graine et le mulet*. Pathé Renn Productions.

Lioret, Philippe, dir. (2009) *Welcome*. Nord Ouest Productions.

Mention-Schaar, Marie-Castille, dir. (2012) *Bowling*. Loma Nasha Films.

266   *Republican Citizens, Precarious Subjects*

Moutout, Jean-Marc, dir. (2003) *Violence des échanges en milieu tempéré,* Les Films du Losange.
——. (2010) *De Bon Matin.* Les Films du losange.
Nakache, Olivier and Éric Tolédano, dirs. (2014) *Samba.* Quad Productions.
Petit, Louis-Julien, dir. (2016) *Carole Matthieu.* Elemiah Productions.
Ruffin, François, dir. (2016) *Merci Patron!* Fakir and Jour de fête Productions.
Silhol, Nicholas, dir. (2017) *Corporate.* Kazak Productions.
Veber, Francis (2001) *Le Placard.* Studio Canal.
Viallet, Jean-Robert, dir. (2009) *La Mise à mort du travail.* France 3 Productions.

Index

Abdelnour, Sarah 204–06, 209
Aglietta, Michel and Antoine Rebérioux
Dérives du capitalisme financier 46
AI (Artificial Intelligence) *see* robotisation
Algan, Yann, Pierre Cahuc, and André Zylberberg
La Fabrique de la défiance 15, 92
Amable, Bruno 17
Anglo-Saxon model 16, 17, 18–21, 24, 176
Attali, Jacques 204
atypical employment 36, 242, 250–51
Aubenas, Florence
Le Quai de Ouistreham 3, 21–22, 54, 77, 142–43, 145, 158–72
Auchan 32

Balbastre, Gilles
Fortunes et infortunes des familles du Nord 31–32
Balibar, Étienne 21
Balzac, Honoré de
Illusions perdues 180–81
banlieue 26, 27, 38, 131, 142, 164, 177, 179–80, 193, 195–97, 247
banlieue film 132, 177, 195–202
Béart, Emmanuelle 211–12, 239 n.1
Beaud, Stéphane and Gérard Mauger
Une Génération sacrifiée 172–73, 196

Beaud, Stéphane and Michel Pialoux
Retour sur la condition ouvrière 177, 203
Violences urbaines, violence sociale 50–51, 164, 177, 202–03
Becker, Gary 68, 215, 239 n.4
Begag, Azouz 131–32, 196
Beinstingel, Thierry 2
Retour aux mots sauvages 105, 108–09, 121–28, 129, 133, 134, 136, 246
Benguigi, Yamina 131
Benjamin, Walter 229–30, 232
Benyamina, Houda
Divines 197–202
Bérégovoy, Pierre 12, 42
Bergeron, Marion 3
Besson, Éric 223
Beveridge Report 9
Blin, Thierry 214
Bokassa, Jean-Bedel 232
Boltanski, Luc and Eve Chiapello 2, 23
Bon, François
Daewoo 142, 158–72, 248
Boulogne-Billancourt 31–32
Bourdieu, Pierre
La Distinction 117–18, 191
La Noblesse d'état 187–88
Boyer, Robert 5, 21, 35
Bretton Woods system 35, 41

268   *Republican Citizens, Precarious Subjects*

Brizé, Stéphane
   La Loi du marché 83–85, 95,
     104–05
Bruneau, Sophie and Marc-Antoine
   Roidil
   *Ils ne mouraient pas tous mais tous
     étaient frappés* 3
Brunel, Valérie
   Les Managers de l'âme 68, 77,
     83–84, 115, 190–91
Burke, Edmund 110–11

Cabral, Amilcar 231
Cantet, Laurent
   L'Emploi du temps 3, 105, 108–09,
     113–21, 128, 129, 133, 134,
     135, 136, 191, 215, 246
   Ressources humaines 3, 142, 178,
     180–81, 191–93, 247
Carles, Pierre, Christophe Coello,
   and Stéhane Goxe
   Attention Danger Travail 14
Caroli, Eve and Jean-Luc Gautié 11,
   57
Carré, Jean-Michel
   J'ai (très) mal au travail 3
Castel, Robert 23, 106, 179
Castells, Manuel 137 n.2
Cette France-là collective 233, 237
CFDT (*Confédération française
   démocratique du travail*) 97
CGT (*Confédération générale du travail*)
   97, 142
Chapiron, Kim
   La Crème de la crème 178, 193–95,
     197, 201
Charef, Mehdi
   Marie-Line 142
Chibane, Malik
   Hexagone 196–97
Chirac, Jacques 43, 235
Cissé, Madiguène 211–13, 213–14
Citroën 32, 49
Clarke, Jackie 29 n.2, 172, 185
Clot, Yves 127–28

Clouzot, Henri
   Le Corbeau 223
CMU (*Couverture maladie universelle*)
   12, 13
CNPF (*Conseil national du patronat
   français*) 43
cognitive capitalism *see* Moulier
   Boutang, Yann
Collectif des cinéastes pour les sans papiers
   232–34
Combrexelle, Jean-Denis 92
Comte, Auguste 185
Conseil d'État 14, 57, 95, 207–08
contrat première embauche 1
Corneau, Alain
   Crime d'amour 19, 20, 141, 145,
     150–52, 157, 246
Cros, Didier
   La Gueule de l'emploi 76
Crozier, Michel 92
Curiel, Jonathan 178

Daewoo 159–63
Danone 77
Dardenne brothers 28 n.1
Dardot, Pierre 44–45
Darmon, Muriel 189–91, 198–99, 201
Debré Law 223–24
Decathlon 32
deindustrialisation 31–36
Dejours, Christophe 2, 4, 52, 75
   workplace suffering 4, 75, 80, 127,
     219, 220, 238
Délepine, Benoît and Gustave
   Kervern
   Mammuth 103–04
   Near Death Experience 3, 105
Deleuze, Gilles
   asservissement/servo-servitude
     70–71, 79, 94–95
   modulation 25, 66, 69, 72, 73–98,
     166
   mould 25, 69, 72–73, 93, 97
   societies of control 25, 68–69, 73,
     89, 93, 94, 124, 165

délit de solidarité 225
Delorme, Christian 131–32, 196
Deming, W. Edwards 51
Depardieu, Gérard 103–04
Diamond, Hannah 172
digital Taylorism 78
Diome, Fatou
   Le Ventre de l'Atlantique 239 n.3
Diop, Ababacar 213–14
Disneyland Paris 31
doomed youth, figure of 26, 175–210,
   238, 245
Duménil, Gérard and Dominique
   Lévy 58
Durkheim, Émile 112, 242
   corporatism 8–11, 13, 14, 24, 25,
      83, 86, 107, 242
   De la division du travail social 10,
      82–83, 173, 208
   intermediary bodies 10, 15,
      89–90, 112, 242–43, 245
   social solidarity 10, 15, 19, 24, 26,
      82–83, 153, 177, 208, 242
Duvoux, Nicolas 13, 83, 86

El Khomri Law 1, 14, 87, 88–90, 92,
   95
Eluard, Paul 224
EMS (European Monetary System)
   42
Esping-Andersen, Gosta 9, 11
Esson, James 226–27
Etcherelli, Claire
   Élise ou la vraie vie 22
EU (European Union) 44, 58, 160,
   161, 215, 235–36
Evrard, Audrey 3, 28 n.2
Ewald, François 92, 99 n.4

Fanon, Frantz 221
Fassin, Didier 213, 234
Faucon, Philippe 197
Feher, Michel 45, 95
femme forte, figure of 26, 139–74, 238,
   245

Fenwick 50–51
Filhol, Elisabeth 2
financialisation 41–45
Flaubert, Gustave 180–81
Fleming, Peter 28 n.3
flexicurity 86–91, 242, 251
Flocco, Gaëtan 46–47
Florange 40–41
Flottes, Anne 127–28
Flunch 32
Fordism 4, 8, 22, 24, 31–66, 93, 97,
   107, 126, 241, 244
Fordist nostalgia 21–22, 107, 109–13,
   126, 172
Foucault, Michel
   entrepreneur of the self 45, 62, 66,
      71, 74, 79, 93, 94, 133, 136,
      179, 180, 198–209, 227, 252
   governmentality 61, 67, 78, 124,
      125, 208
   Naissance de la biopolitique 62, 93,
      190
   Surveiller et punir 61, 66, 67–68,
      122, 165, 190
Françafrique 28 n.4
France Télécom 2, 77–79, 124, 126
French Communist Party 31, 33, 39
French education
   grandes écoles 26, 117, 119, 175,
      184–95
   republican elite 177, 184–88, 192,
      195, 209
   Republican School 27, 173, 179,
      195, 198–200, 201, 209–10,
      248–49
French model 8–11, 16–21, 24
Friedmann, Georges 22
Friot, Bernard 96, 97
Front National 39–40

Gaulejac, Vincent de 4, 68
Gauz, aka Armand Gabaka-Brédé
   227
   Debout-Payé 218, 227–33
gilets jaunes 1, 15, 241–45

270 *Republican Citizens, Precarious Subjects*

Gintzburger, Anne and Franck
  Vrignon
  La Promesse de Florange 66 n.1
globalisation 5, 37, 145, 148
Google 61, 63–64
Goupil, Romain
  Les Mains en l'air 224, 234
Grameen Bank 205
Gramsci, Antonio 58
Guattari, Félix 71
Guédiguian, Robert
  Les Neiges du Kilimandjaro 3, 104,
    107
  La Ville est tranquille 142
Guilluy, Christophe 40

Hancké, Bob 48
Harvey, David 161, 163
Hayes, Graeme 2
Hollande, François 25, 70, 85, 87, 93,
  206, 217, 225, 242
Houellebecq, Michel 2, 105, 126,
  135, 245
  La Carte et le territoire 107, 108,
    109–13, 117, 133, 136, 248
  Les Particules élémentaires 113
  Soumission 113
Hudson, Michael 63, 66 n.2
human capital 26, 62, 65, 67–69, 74,
  76, 80, 89, 93, 127, 133, 136, 165,
  179, 180, 200, 215, 236, 238
Hurel, François 205

IMF (International Monetary Fund)
  118–19, 160, 161, 212, 214
Iribarne, Philippe d' 92
Isnards, Alexandre des and Thomas
  Zuber 178
ISO9000 52, 58

JIT (Just in Time) 47–51, 55, 56, 63,
  64, 74, 79, 203, 244
Jospin, Lionel 43, 234
Juppé, Alain
  Juppé Plan 2

Kassovitz, Mathieu
  La Haine 177, 196–97
Kaurismäki, Aki
  Le Havre 224, 229
Kechiche, Abdellatif
  La Graine et le mulet 104, 108, 109,
    128–35, 136, 246
Keynesianism 35, 42, 44, 96
Kokoref, Michel and Jacques
  Rodriguez 71–72, 80, 137 n.1
Kuperman, Nathalie 2
  Nous étions des êtres vivants 19,
    139–40, 152–57, 170, 246,
    247

Labadie, Aurore 2
Laclos, Choderlos de
  Les Liaisons dangereuses 140
La Défense 27, 145, 147, 150, 151,
  175, 180, 182–83, 247
Lallement, Michel 71, 73, 75
La Poste 77
Laroque, Pierre 9
Larrouturou, Pierre 96
Laval, Christian 44–45, 199–200
Lavoine, Lucie 10–11
Le Bras, Hervé 158
Leclerc, Michel 32
Lefebvre, Frédéric 236
Lindon, Vincent 104, 221
Linhart, Danièle 4, 7, 23, 52, 65, 67,
  127, 133
Linhart, Robert
  L'Établi 22, 49–50
Lioret, Philippe
  Welcome 217–18, 221–27, 229,
    234
Lipietz, Alain 241–42
Lordon, Frédéric 4, 58–60, 64, 65

Maastricht Treaty 21, 44
Macron, Emmanuel 1, 15, 25, 70, 85,
  87, 90–91, 93, 204, 206, 217, 241,
  242, 243, 251–52
Madelin, Alain 206

Maier, Corinne
Bonjour Paresse 3, 54
Maris, Bernard 112
Marks, John 115
Marshall Aid 35
Marx, Karl 77
masculinity 24, 26, 103–27, 142,
147–48, 164–65, 168–73
Maurani, Margaret 143, 158
Maurras, Charles 112
May 1968 23, 31, 36, 244
Mazzucato, Mariana 64
Méda, Dominique 10–11, 96
MEDEF (*Mouvement des entreprises de
France*) 43, 74, 92
Mention-Schaar, Marie-Castille
Bowling 141, 157
Meron, Margaret 143, 158
Michelin 109–11
minima sociaux 13, 86
Mitterrand, François 42, 204
Mordillat, Gérard 2
Moretti, Franco 181–82
Morin, François 43, 64
Morini, Cristina 104, 123
Mother Courage figure 143,
164–68
Mouhoud, El Mouhoub and
Dominique Plihon
Le Savoir et la finance 18, 40,
64–65, 120, 136, 159, 162
Moulier Boutang, Yann 13, 14, 21,
44, 49, 55, 58, 95, 192
cognitive capitalism, theory of
60–64, 68
Moutout, Jean-Marc
De Bon Matin 3, 105–06
*Violence des échanges en milieu
tempéré* 3, 19, 20, 175–77,
180–88, 191–93, 246, 247
Mulliez, Gérard 32

Nakache, Olivier and Éric
Toledano
Samba 217–18, 218–21, 229

natalism 24
national champions 35, 47, 162
neo-liberalism 17, 18, 20, 23, 24, 34,
41–42, 44–45, 62, 65, 85, 99 n.4,
119, 145, 148, 161, 205, 213, 214,
217, 226, 252
New Deal 9
Nixon, Richard 41
Novelli, Henri 205–06
nuclear family 24, 103–37, 149, 144,
150–51, 155–56, 157–58, 171–72,
246, 248
Nuit debout 1, 3, 14, 244–45

off-shoring 23, 37
O'Shaugnessey, Martin 2, 115
outsourcing 37, 46, 219–20

Palheta, Ugo 197, 198
Palier, Bruno 9, 12, 24, 157
Paradeise, Catherine and Yves
Lichtenberger 71, 72–73
Parienty, Arnaud 188–89
Parodi decrees 72–73
Paugam, Serge 10
Petit, Louis-Julien
Carole Mathieu 3
Piketty, Thomas 20, 59
Pimot, Jérôme 95
Pôle Emploi 82
Pompidou, Georges 232
post-Fordism 6, 8, 13, 24, 25, 31–66,
93, 97
precarity 1, 4, 6, 7, 11, 13, 16, 18,
24, 27, 33, 57, 63, 85, 106, 145,
159, 165, 168, 169, 170, 172, 173,
192–93, 200, 210, 230, 244, 250,
253

Quintreau, Laurent
Marge brute 19, 140–41, 157

Ramaux, Christophe 96
*Rassemblement National see Front
National*

272   *Republican Citizens, Precarious Subjects*

Reagan, Ronald 17
Reinhardt, Éric 2
  Le Système Victoria 141, 145–49,
    157, 170, 247–48
Regulation School 5
Renault 2, 31, 32, 172
RESF (*Réseau d'éducation sans
  frontières*) 224, 233, 234,
  239 n.2
RMI (*Revenu minimum d'insertion*)
  99 n.3
robotisation 5, 57, 252
Ross, Andrew 28 n.3
Ross, Kristin
  Fast Cars, Clean Bodies 6, 186
Rousseau, Jean-Jacques 10
Roy, Ivan du 126
RSA (*Revenu de solidarité active*) 81–83,
  86
Ruffin, François
  Merci Patron! 3

Saada, Emmanuelle 216
Saint Bernard Church 211–14,
  228–29, 234
Saint Maclou 32
Saint Simon, Henri de 185
Sam, Anna 53–54, 77
sans papiers 15, 27, 210, 211–39, 245,
  249–50
Sarkozy, Nicolas 25, 70, 81–83, 85,
  87, 90, 93, 205, 215, 217, 226,
  233, 235, 236, 237, 242, 251
Sartre, Jean-Paul 31, 52–54
Sayad, Abdelmalek 130–31, 132
Seillière, Ernest-Antoine 43
shareholder value 45–47
Shin, Jang-Sup and Ha-Joon Chang
  160–61
Silhol, Nicolas
  Corporate 3, 19, 20
Silver, Beverly 51
Southwood, Ivor 28 n.3, 76
Standing, Guy 28 n.3, 51
Stiglitz, Joseph 119

Strauss-Kahn, Dominique 56
Streeck, Wolfgang 44
suicide 4, 105, 106, 122, 124,
  168

Taddei, Dominique and Benjamin
  Coriat
  Made in France 56–57
Talneau, Sophie 178
Tarnac 14
Tarr, Carrie 132, 196
Taylorism 35, 48–50, 110, 162–63
Terray, Emmanuel 219–20
terroir 109–13, 141, 151, 170, 245–46,
  248
tertiarisation 31–32, 36, 73, 244
Tévanian, Pierre 21
Thatcher, Margaret 17
35 hour week 56–57, 142, 178
Thomas, Dominic 215
Ticktin, Miriam 234–35
Toyotism 47–51
TQM (Total Quality Management)
  47–51, 55, 56, 58, 63, 64, 74, 79,
  203
trente glorieuses 17, 22, 107, 230
Triolet, Elsa 186
true value accounting 45–47

Uber 27, 94–95, 202–09, 252
uberisation 6, 57, 94–95, 202–09,
  241–42, 252
UMP (*Union pour un mouvement
  populaire*) 236
universal income 95–96, 251

Valls, Manuel 92
Vasset, Philippe
  Journal intime d'une prédatrice 141,
    159
Veber, Francis
  Le Placard 105
Viallet, Robert
  La Mise à mort du travail 3, 49–51,
    76, 246

Villepin de, Dominique 1
Vouteau, Sophie 207, 209

Waters, Sarah 2, 18
Weber, Florence 38
Windebank, Jan 158
Woo-Chong, Kim 161–62

World Bank 118–19, 160, 161, 212, 214

Zarifian, Philippe 68, 77–80, 123
Zimmer, Hélène
  Fairy Tale 77

Printed and bound by CPI Group (UK) Ltd, Croydon, CR0 4YY

10/03/2024

14467798-0004